TOWARDS A TRANSPARENT LABOUR MARKET FOR EDUCATIONAL DECISIONS

Towards a Transparent Labour Market for Educational Decisions

Edited by
HANS HEIJKE and LEX BORGHANS
Research Centre for Education and the Labour Market
Maastricht University

LONDON AND NEW YORK

First published 1998 by Ashgate Publishing

Reissued 2018 by Routledge
2 Park Square, Milton Park, Abingdon, Oxon, OX14 4RN
52 Vanderbilt Avenue, New York, NY 10017

Routledge is an imprint of the Taylor & Francis Group, an informa business

Copyright © Hans Heijke and Lex Borghans 1998

All rights reserved. No part of this book may be reprinted or reproduced or utilised in any form or by any electronic, mechanical, or other means, now known or hereafter invented, including photocopying and recording, or in any information storage or retrieval system, without permission in writing from the publishers.

Notice:
Product or corporate names may be trademarks or registered trademarks, and are used only for identification and explanation without intent to infringe.

Publisher's Note
The publisher has gone to great lengths to ensure the quality of this reprint but points out that some imperfections in the original copies may be apparent.

Disclaimer
The publisher has made every effort to trace copyright holders and welcomes correspondence from those they have been unable to contact.

A Library of Congress record exists under LC control number: 98070153

ISBN 13: 978-1-138-36495-0 (hbk)
ISBN 13: 978-1-138-36496-7 (pbk)
ISBN 13: 978-0-429-43100-5 (ebk)

Contents

Contributors   vii

Acknowledgements   xi

Foreword
The Need for Labour Market Transparency in a Changing Economy   xiii
Wil Albeda

Introduction
1   Investing in Education   1
    Hans Heijke and Lex Borghans

Part One: Prospects

2   Future Developments in the Job Level and Domain of   21
    High-skilled Workers
    Andries de Grip, Lex Borghans and Wendy Smits

3   The Return to Education   57
    Jaap de Koning

4   Labour Market Forecasts and Choice of Education   83
    Dinand Webbink

Part Two: Flexibility

5   A Job to Match your Education: Does it Matter?   99
    Joop Hartog and Nicole Jonker

vi   Contents

6   Flexibility and Structure of the Dutch Labour Market   119
    Lex Borghans and Hans Heijke

7   Asymmetric Skill Substitution, Labour Market Flexibility, and the   151
    Allocation of Qualifications
    Adriaan van Zon, Joan Muysken and Huub Meijers

Part Three: Curriculum

8   Curriculum Characteristics and Labour Market Perspectives   197
    Wim Nijhof

9   Does Curriculum Matter? A Theoretical Clue to an Empirical Puzzle   223
    Arie Glebbeek and Sietske Waslander

10 Education, Skills and Wages   253
    Hans Heijke, Mieke Koeslag and Rolf van der Velden

Appendix
The Dutch Education System   273

Contributors

Wil Albeda is an Emeritus Professor of Socio-Economic Policy. After a career in the Trade Union, he was Dutch Minister of Social Affairs and Chairman of the Dutch Scientific Council for Government Policy.

Lex Borghans is a Senior Researcher at the Research Centre for Education and the Labour Market (ROA) of Maastricht University. His main research interests are expectations and welfare economics, forecasting the employment structure by occupation and type of education, and adjustment processes on the labour market.

Arie Glebbeek is an Assistant Professor of Sociology at the Department of Sociology, University of Groningen. His speciality fields are the labour market and the transition from school to work.

Andries de Grip is a Chief Researcher at the Research Centre for Education and the Labour Market (ROA) of Maastricht University. His main research interests are in labour economics, in particular manpower analyses, human capital, skill mismatches, labour market mobility and continuing training.

Joop Hartog is a Professor of Economics at the Department of Economics and Econometrics at the University of Amsterdam. He is mainly doing research on various topics in microeconomics and with an emphasis on labour economics.

Hans Heijke is the Director of the Research Centre for Education and the Labour Market (ROA) and a Professor of Education and the Labour Market in the Department of Economics and Business Administration at Maastricht University. His main research interests are in labour economics, in particular manpower forecasting, training, school-leavers and graduates in the labour market, and international migration.

Nicole Jonker is a Ph.D. student at the Department of Economics and Econometrics of the University of Amsterdam. Her main research interests are in labour economics.

Mieke Koeslag is a Ph.D. student at the Research Centre for Education and the Labour Market (ROA) of Maastricht University. Her main research interests are in youth labour markets, especially the role played by initial education in the transition from school to work.

Jaap de Koning is the Director of the Department for Labour and Education Research of the Netherlands Economic Institute (NEI) and a member of the Management Board of NEI. His research interests include the evaluation of labour market policies, economic aspects of education and other topics of labour economics.

Huub Meijers is a Research Fellow of the Maastricht Economic Research Institute on Innovation and Technology (MERIT) of Maastricht University. His main research topics are the modelling of technological change, technology diffusion, vintage models, labour market issues, and the information society.

Joan Muysken is a Professor of Economics at the Department of Economics and Business Administration of Maastricht University. His research interests are (in general): skill formation and development and estimation of sectoral models, endogenous growth and analysis of unemployment.

Wim Nijhof is a Professor of Education at the Department of Educational Science and Technology of the University of Twente, Enschede. His research is mainly focused on the design, implementation and effects of (vocational) education and training systems.

Wendy Smits is a Researcher at the Research Centre for Education and the Labour Market (ROA) of Maastricht University. Her main research interests include labour economics, in particular labour demand and training.

Rolf van der Velden is a Chief Researcher at the Research Centre for Education and the Labour Market (ROA) of Maastricht University. His main research interests are: education and the labour market, in particular skills development, the transition from school to work and occupational careers.

Sietske Waslander is a Researcher at the Department of Sociology of the University of Groningen. She co-ordinates an international pilot study, the aim of which is to develop indicators for cross-curricular competencies for the OECD, she is also writing a Ph.D. thesis on the marketisation of education.

Dinand Webbink works at the secretariat of the Dutch Educational Council. He advises on the economic aspects of educational policies. His contribution to this book was written during the time when he was working at the Foundation for Economic Research (SEO) of the University of Amsterdam.

Adriaan van Zon is a Senior Research Fellow of the Maastricht Economic Research Institute on Innovation and Technology (MERIT), and an Assistant Professor in the Department of Economics and Business Administration of Maastricht University. His main research interests are technical change and the role of asymmetries with respect to substitution possibilities and technological capabilities as determinants of employment and growth perspectives.

Acknowledgements

The present book combines a number of papers presented during a symposium held on the occasion of the tenth anniversary of the Research Centre for Education and the Labour Market (ROA), a research institute of the Department of Economics and Business Administration of Maastricht University. The symposium was held on 6 and 7 June 1996 at Kasteel Vaeshartelt near Maastricht. The theme of the symposium concerns the central mission of ROA, which can be summarised making a scientific contribution to the process of increasing the transparency of the labour market for those with an interest in investing in education and training.

The participants of the symposium were individually invited from the circle of researchers and government and organisation officials who work at the crossroads of research and policy. The chairman was professor Wil Albeda, former Dutch Minister for Social Affairs and founder of both the Department of Economics en Business Administration of Maastricht University and of the ROA. In order to obtain as complete a picture as possible of the problems concerned, the topics to be dealt with were established first, after which the scientists were approached with the request to give a paper on one of these topics. Under the expert supervision of Wil Albeda, elaborate discussions were held in response to the papers that were presented. Ample time had been reserved for this in the programme. Judging by the enthusiastic reactions, the participants of the symposium greatly appreciated this setup. After the symposium the authors wrote the final versions of their contributions to the present book, partly on the basis of the discussions after the presentations and the comments by the editors. The chairman was glad to give his views of the problems, initially presented as a general introduction to the theme of the symposium, in the preface of this book.

Hence, not only the authors, but also the chairman and the participants of the symposium have made an important contribution to the creation of this book. The editors, also the initiators of the symposium, are greatly indebted to them for their efforts. They are also very grateful to Margo Romans who took it upon herself to organise the symposium in a very composed and professional manner. Converting the texts that were submitted into a uniform camera-ready layout was done by Miranda Boere. The editors would like to thank her for all she has done in this respect.

Hans Heijke & Lex Borghans
Research Centre for Education and the Labour Market
Maastricht University

Foreword

The Need for Labour Market Transparency in a Changing Economy

Wil Albeda

The objective of this book is to develop insights, ideas, and experiences concerning the possibilities for increasing the transparency of the labour market. Everybody has come to realise that the quality of labour has rapidly become the key factor in economic and social development. Investment in human capital, primary and secondary general and professional education, and of course academic learning must take a central place in any policy aiming at economic growth and social development. And transparency is what we need if we want this investment (both for individuals and for the community as whole) to be placed in the right direction.

There seems to be a glaring contradiction between the current mass unemployment in all European nations, both in urban and rural areas, affecting people of different levels of education (but mostly those with low skills levels or ethnic backgrounds), and the idea that labour is the most important source of wealth. In practice, the exclusion of so many people not only from the labour market but as a result also from other areas of society, is a catastrophe for individuals and a waste for society as a whole. Nobody doubts the vital importance of a well-educated, well-motivated and creative labour force but we fail miserably in preparing young people for the ever-changing labour market with unknown possibilities. The new demand for highly skilled workers seems to give us, on the one hand, increasing inequality of incomes while on the other hand it excludes a large minority from the labour market, and thus from active participation in a society with more potential for human activity than ever.

These considerations underline the importance of the topic of this book. More and more have I become convinced that our time is, to a certain extent and in a certain sense, comparable to that of the thirties. The possibilities, the potential of the new insights in technology and organisation, and of the new global economy seem to be almost unlimited. At the same time, we may speak of a 'silent depression' (Peterson, 1994) that keeps all of us in its grip.

Let me begin by saying that, in my opinion, better professional and general education, a transparent labour market, and well thought-out labour market policies will not suffice to deliver us from this silent depression. Both national and international macroeconomic policies play an important role. Like in the thirties, we need a new economic paradigm such as the one introduced by Keynes, to overcome the silent depression.

At the same time, we know that if and when the Western nations overcome this depression by means of concerted action, the demands on professional education and the labour market will become even greater and it is not unrealistic to expect that the crucial significance of labour, its quality, and its ability to adapt to a growing economy will become the single most important limiting factor for new economic growth.

In this book, several experts present their views on the relationship between education and the labour market. I shall restrict my contribution to a few more or less 'general' remarks.

We first need to take a fresh look at what exactly education does, can do and should do. The idea that young people acquire a certain amount of useful 'luggage' during their school days, which they can subsequently take with them into their professional careers is outdated and should be discarded. Knowledge and technology have developed in such a way as to render it impossible for this 'luggage' to be broad and complete enough for students to serve for the rest of their lives. In addition, part of this luggage is obsolete before it enters the classroom.

To develop a system of education that can function in tomorrow's society, we need a form of entrepreneurial thinking: on the basis of incomplete knowledge, we are forced to take decisions about investments that will only yield results in the medium or long term. The insecurities with which we are confronted seem dramatic, when we realise that a newly created system of education (such as the present system of basic education) or a new faculty will only deliver its first results after a number of years. During that period, the world of labour continues to change ever more rapidly (de Closets, 1996).

What do we know about these changes? This in itself could be the subject of many papers. Let me restrict myself to a few remarks. In the first place, I think that demographic changes will play an important role in the immediate future. Lower birth rates will lead to a relatively old workforce. Already the rapid changes of technology have made it impossible for changes to be implemented by a succession of different generations. The demographic changes will intensify this development: everybody will constantly have to adapt to new developments in technology and organisation.

At the same time, the Western world must meet the challenges of immigrants from the surrounding – not so developed – world. Although we may profit from the brain drain of the emigration nations, we also find that many first- and second-generation immigrants lack the necessary education for a modern society. In addition, they enter a society which is developing new attitudes and changing values, knowing only and partly preserving their own old values and traditions.

An evolving society, moreover, that already places high demands on the education of its native labour force.

The world has become a global marketplace, with a new technology that has introduced the concepts of customised products and the automated workplace. Fundamental changes in the mission, content and methods of all types of teaching and learning are essential (Dede, 1992). No longer is learning the privilege of the young or the monopoly of specialised institutions. Life-long learning and permanent education, both in the workplace and elsewhere, are necessary because technological changes are taking place more rapidly than ever before. There is a high rate of innovation. We constantly see new applications of information technology. We need people who are able to use their knowledge and skills working with others in interdisciplinary teams. The market changes from day to day. We are leaving 'producer capitalism' to enter new forms of 'consumer capitalism'. Production systems are forced to adapt more to the wishes of the consumer. The time when mass production could impose its products on the public is long gone.

It is clear that these few observations already show how many factors play a role, and how difficult it is to draw conclusions for the development of a system of education and professional qualification.

Today, we are witnessing developments, both in Europe and in the rest of the world, which will have a similar impact as the developments in the manufacturing industry of 150 years ago. There is a revolutionary innovation of manufacturing and an expanding service industry. There is a parallel with the beginning of the 19th century, when workers had to prepare for their role in this new form of production. The new industrial society was unthinkable without a literate population, followed by a well-developed school system, and universities with educational and research tasks. Today, literacy (including computer literacy) is also essential. The school system must undergo important changes to adapt to the information society. But I spoke of a change, not an intensification of existing trends. Everywhere, people will be confronted with the results of scientific work: in agriculture, in manufacturing, and in the service industry. There was a time when the term 'learned professions' was limited to law, medicine and theology. Nowadays, this term would apply to a large and increasing number of jobs. But that is not all. We must also face the fact that science and technology are developing faster than ever. The time when the changing structure of the jobs pyramid could be accommodated by the natural process of older people withdrawing from the labour market and younger people entering, lies far behind us. Modern man faces the need to permanently acquire new knowledge and new skills. This has a number of important consequences:

1. In modern society, no job is complete if it does not include (as part of regular practice) continued, permanent education both on and off the job.

2 The idea that professional education can adequately prepare young people for the labour market cannot be maintained. Professional education is rarely be complete and up to date enough to allow immediate entry in a job. In most cases, an introductory period will be necessary.
3 The most important role of general and professional education may well be that it prepares young people for a life of permanent learning. We now know that it is a fallacy (or a prejudice) to think that people cannot learn after a certain age. The ability to learn need never end, provided that the practice of learning is there all the time.

In this context, I think not only of the ability to absorb new information and to acquire new skills, but also of the need for young people to learn to regard every new situation as a possibility to learn (self-learning).

This brings me to the role of education in modern society. I am becoming more and more convinced that we have become victims of a dangerous misconception. Education systems as we know them are based upon the idea that there is a time in our lives when we acquire a certain package of knowledge. That time is of course the time of childhood and adolescence. Already, this time has been extended from 12 to 16 or 18 years of age, or even later. But nevertheless education is (a) limited to this period and (b) to certain institutions (Danzin, 1993). This is a comfortable and clearly defined state of affairs. We know what should happen, where it should happen, and when.

Education is the subject matter of a specialised institution during a specific period. More and more, this view is showing its obsolescence. *The real school is life itself*. Education as it takes place in specialised institutions can do no more than prepare young people for the real school. Useful knowledge is acquired during work and in free time, leisure. As Danzin said in a recent book:

> Education begins at birth and stops only with death, there is no longer a time specialised for study, and hardly a privileged time. We are all autodidacts!

This view has, of course, consequences for the specialised educational institutions, for institutions of adult education, and for all institutions where non-intentional education takes place which should be changed into intentional education.

Perhaps the most difficult tasks concern the schools for general and professional education. Learning to learn should be high on the agenda everywhere. Educational obsolescence threatens for those who have taken professional training aiming at complete preparation for a job or a professional career. I remember discussions I had in the 1970s with workers of the Dutch shipbuilding industry who lost their jobs because of changing technology and capacity reductions in this industry. I will never forget hearing people of 40 years of age complain that they had no future, because they believed that learning a new job at their age was impossible. They had never had the preparation for, nor the experience of permanent learning and self-learning.

The challenge of this new reality for the school system is an huge one. Schools must engage in a permanent process of gradual adaptation to the new realities of culture and the labour market. All the time, they must keep in mind that preparation for life-long learning is the primary goal.

This gives me the opportunity to refer to the work of the Research Centre for Education and the Labour Market (ROA) in Maastricht, who organised the conference on which this book is based. We cannot restrict ourselves to general remarks about labour market trends. We need concrete information on what is happening and what we can expect in the different sectors of industry and the increasingly diverse service industry. Here ROA plays the important role of providing the different actors of the educational system, labour market authorities, firms, and other organisations, with an information system that supports them in taking decisions.

As early as the sixties, the idea was launched that education, including professional training, should be broad enough to enable people to not only participate in the world of science and technology, but also in the world of cultural, social, and economic development.

At the same time, young people must decide (preferably as late in life as possible) when to take their professional training (or to proceed to tertiary or university education). Although professional training can never be general, it should not be too narrowly concentrated on one particular job. It should always provide opportunities for wider, more general skills, and further development.

This presents us with the last paradox. We need a system of professional education that can function in the European market. This implies that the structure of education in the European Union is harmonised, so that credentials are recognised everywhere. At the same time, in order to remain up to date and provide relevant training, schools must work closely together with local industry and be in touch with local activities in general. This requires partnerships to be set up with local firms and institutions.

References

Closets, F. de, (1996), *Le bonheur d'apprendre, et comme on l'assassine*, Seuil: Paris.

Danzin, A. (1993), *La croissance? Autrement,* Editions Européennes Thermique et Industrie (E.E.T.I): Paris.

Dede, Ch. (1992), 'Education in the Twenty-first Century', *Annals of the American Academy of Political Science*, 522, pp. 104-116.

Peterson, W.C. (1994), *Silent Depression: the Fate of the American Dream*, Norton: New York.

Introduction

1 Investing in Education

Hans Heijke and Lex Borghans

In highly developed societies, education is given a very prominent role in the process of maintaining and increasing the level of development. This has not only a cultural, but also a social and an economic dimension. Education is considered to be important for the creation and transfer of norms and values in society, the utilisation of the talents present in the population, the creation of equal opportunities and the promotion of economic development. Although education as a 'product' has indeed a number of consumptive aspects – it can be very challenging and entertaining – the investment character prevails. This means that the economic resources for education must be created today, whereas the returns can only be expected in the longer term. Countries with a high development level are prepared to invest a great deal in education. Youths in OECD countries spend between twelve and twenty years in regular education, without the need to provide any substantial contribution to production during that period, the government spending 4 to 7 per cent of GDP on maintaining an extensive and highly accessible system of educational facilities (OECD, 1992, p. 41). All these sacrifices are made on the basis of the fundamental conviction that they are worth being made, in spite of the fact that the larger part of the returns of these sacrifices will only be achieved in the far future, spread out across many decades.

The fact that decisions with regard to education, both at the level of individuals and of society, mainly have the nature of investments, does not mean that they are the result of simple return-on-investment calculations, as was stated in neo-classical investment theories. In particular the future returns of education prove very difficult to measure. These measuring problems already manifest themselves when it comes to the traditional economic returns, such as productivity and wages. With regard to returns in terms of culture and society, such as 'transfer of norms and values', 'utilisation of talents' and 'equal opportunities', however, it is even more difficult to estimate the future returns. It has proved difficult enough to determine the relationship between education and wages or productivity, or the social and cultural returns of education, for the past. Even if we had found a relationship between the various possible returns and the investments in education made in the past, then the question would be justified to what extent such relationships can be expected to be valid in the future. After all, we may safely assume that society will change in such a way during the next few decades that the returns of certain types of education and the contents of this education will change too. Hence we cannot simply apply the returns on education found in the past to the period that lies ahead of us.

At a time when government expenses are clearly weighed against the ensuing tax burden and additional government expenses are only possible if they are presented with a means of funding, there seems to be a danger of the social debate on investments in education being dominated by the expenses to be made and who should pay the bill. The basic notion that such investments also yield future returns, then runs the risk of being pushed into the background. To be able to adequately weigh such investment decisions, it seems crucial to have insight in the returns of educational investments. Such information could support policy-making when it comes to taking decisions about the size of educational investments, but also with regard to the direction in which these means can best be utilised and the best way to implement such education.

Government, however, is not the only party interested in adequate information to support investments in education. Employers, educational institutions and employment organisations also invest in education. Here too, an effective deployment of resources requires adequate information regarding the expected returns. Lastly, those who take part in education are also important investors in education. This applies both to pupils and students in initial education, and to those who continue their training during their working lives. Even if these consumers of education do not pay (part of) the direct costs of education, they nevertheless make considerable investments in the form of time – and hence loss of income – and energy. Also, the returns of education will be felt in particular by this category. For many different parties involved in education, the existence of adequate information concerning the returns of education – both at the level of the individual and at the level of society – seems of great importance.

To enhance rational decision-making in education, we shall have to take a route *towards a transparent labour market for educational decisions*, as indicated by the title of the present book. The aim of this book is to provide a scientific contribution to the process of making the labour market more transparent. It has an economic perspective. This means, firstly, that the returns on investments in education largely concern the returns of an economic nature, such as the chances of finding a job, career opportunities, the wages received, and mobility in the labour market, given the nature of the education concerned. This does not mean, however, that the above-mentioned social and cultural returns are considered unimportant. After all, the returns of education consist of both economic and social/cultural elements. This book does not deal with the quantification of such social and cultural returns, although they play an implicit role in the educational selection process discussed. The second implication of this economic perspective is that all contributions consider investments in education – whether aimed at increasing productivity or cultural development – against the background of a framework in which the costs – in terms of required funds, time, et cetera – are weighed against the benefits.

This publication deals with three different aspects. To obtain an overview of the returns of education, we must first gain insight in the *prospects* of various educational programmes. In practice, individuals with a particular educational background appear to a certain extent to be employable in a range of jobs. Hence, investments in education do not fix future possibilities entirely by excluding others. The existence of such *flexibility* determines in a way the meaning of education as an investment. To gain adequate insight in the effects of investments in education, it is not only important to know which programmes yield high returns, but also why a particular *curriculum* leads to such returns.

Although the main objective of this book is to collect a number of views regarding the way in which the labour market can be made transparent, all chapters contain empirical data to support the train of thoughts. All empirical data relate to the Netherlands, which optimises the mutual coherence. The Appendix of this book gives a description of the Dutch education system.

Prospects

In the past, two approaches were developed to indicate the effects of investments in education on the labour market. The first approach concerns the rate of return (see e.g. Psacharopoulos, 1981). This is done by comparing for a graduate from a particular course the range of future benefits on education, in terms of additional wages to be earned, with the investments that must be made to complete the course, in terms of direct costs of education and loss of income. The outcome of this comparison is often expressed in an internal rate of return, i.e. the discount rate which makes the range of possible future benefits equal to the costs of the investment in education. The higher this rate of return is above the market interest rate, the more profitable the investment in the course concerned is – if we consider the issue purely from the point of view of financial considerations.

The second approach that was developed, concerns the manpower requirement approach (see e.g. Ahamad and Blaug, 1973; Heijke, 1994). This first deduces from the expected growth in the different economic sectors and different occupations the number of graduates of each course that will be necessary in the future in order to fill the existing vacancies. This is set off against the expected number of workers with the proper educational background already present in the labour market. From this, it is deduced how many additional young people will have to be trained, or change the study of their choice, in order to eliminate the shortages and surpluses.

The two approaches appear to be completely different from one another, and cannot be reconciled. Blaug (1969) stressed that calculations of the returns of education assume a labour market in which the market mechanism, with free wage formation, operates, whereas the manpower requirement approach in his views supposes that markets are inflexible and different categories of skilled workers cannot substitute one another. To be able to asses the value of both views, three different aspects are important. Firstly, it is important to determine which (implicit) assumptions are made regarding the way in which the labour market functions. Empirical data on the labour market can only be used properly from an adequate theoretical framework of the labour market. Secondly, one may ask how the information provided can be utilised to support investment decisions by those involved. Thirdly, it is important to determine to what extent these data can be used to anticipate future developments. An essential difference between the two approaches is that the rate-of-return approach expresses the labour market prospects of educational courses in the level of wages, whereas the manpower requirement approach presents the prospects in terms of the amount of work demanded and supplied. The economic mechanisms that determine the wages and the amount of labour, however, could nevertheless be interconnected. For example, the effects of the price mechanism in the labour market will simultaneously influence both the wages and the amounts demanded and supplied. This can be illustrated as follows. Assume the following labour market model for a particular course:

$$S = c + aW \tag{1}$$
$$D = d - bW \tag{2}$$

where: S = supply
D = demand
W = wages

When this market in balanced, and hence $S = D$, then it follows that:

$$W = \frac{d-c}{a+b} \tag{3}$$

and:

$$S = D = \frac{cb+da}{a+b} \tag{4}$$

Exogenous shifts of supply and demand – i.e. shifts of the parameters a, b, c or d – lead to both a change of W and a change of S and D. From the point of view of investments, however, it is interesting in particular to know the wage level. This figure represents the individual returns – or at least the pecuniary component – and a comparison with the investment costs and the non-pecuniary returns could assist in the decision-making with respect to investments. Information regarding the total amounts of labour demanded and supplied at this balanced price seems to be irrelevant for individual investment decisions.

It is probably this observation that constitutes the basis for Blaug's (1969) conclusion that in a labour market with free wage negotiation the rate-of-return approach should be used. In an inflexible labour market with fixed wages, however, wages would no longer be a relevant decision criterion. Instead, a discrepancy emerges between supply and demand:

$$S - D = c - d + (a+b)W \qquad (5)$$

The excess supply $(S-D)$ gives an indication of the rate of employment that can be expected for the course concerned. As the wages are fixed, the discrepancy between supply and demand will change with shifts of the parameters a, b, c and d. In this situation, it would therefore be the unemployment indicator that provides the most relevant information, rather than the fixed (i.e. known) wages.

Borghans and Heijke (1996) and Borghans and Willems (1996) show, however, that the discrepancy between supply and demand, as calculated in a manpower requirement approach, is also relevant in a situation of free wage formation. Let us assume the hypothetical situation that in a situation of free wage formation, wages in the future would no longer change, and remain the same as the present wages ($\hat{W}$). This is shown in Figure 1 for the course concerned. If shifts of supply and demand are expected in the years to come, the demand will start to deviate from the supply at this wage rate. A discrepancy between supply and demand emerges. As:

$$\hat{W} = \frac{(S-D) + (d-c)}{a+b} \qquad (6)$$

we may conclude that:

$$W - \hat{W} = \frac{D-S}{a+b} \qquad (7)$$

This means that there is a direct relationship between the discrepancy between supply and demand resulting from the absence of wage adjustments $(D-S)$, and the wage adjustments that would be required in order to create an equilibrium between supply and demand $(W-\hat{W})$. The hypothetical discrepancy between supply and demand is therefore an indicator of the tension in the labour market for the course concerned. In the case of free wage formation, this tension manifests itself in a wage change, whereas such tension would also manifest itself in unemployment and unfilled vacancies if the adjustment processes in the market were non-existent or only partially effective.

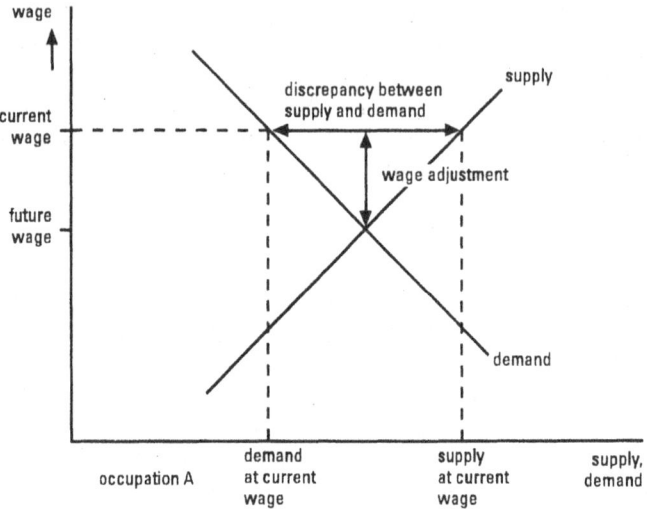

Figure 1   Relationship between wage changes and the discrepancy between supply and demand from the manpower requirement approach

The concept of a market in which wages constitute the entire allocation mechanism, is a highly simplifying one. In practice, the employment relationship between employers and employees has more aspects. A shift of the relationship between supply and demand may also affect the distribution of power between employers and employees, and hence affect the nature of the work that can be found by individuals with a particular educational background, the nature of their contracts (permanent of temporary), et cetera. This means that the discrepancy between supply and demand can be regarded as an indicator of the labour market position of the group concerned, without making explicit how this labour market position will in fact manifest itself.

The most important difference between the rate-of-return approach and the manpower requirement approach therefore does not concern the theoretical assumptions that constitute the basis of the way in which the labour market functions. The two aspects, in which the rate-of-return approach differs from the manpower requirement approach, to be discussed now are the information that these two methods provide with regard to the investment decision and the extent to which the approach can be used to forecast future market developments.

For the investors, it is important to obtain insight in the benefits of investments in education. By relating these benefits to the costs and personal preferences, education investment decisions can in principle be taken. One of the strengths of the rate-of-return approach is that it shows a crucial element of the returns – the wages across the entire professional career. In case the allocation mechanism fails, or other elements than wages also play a role, such aspects should be made visible too. In addition to the monetary rate of return, we should also analyse the expected duration of unemployment, the degree of certainty of finding a job, et cetera. The manpower requirement approach leads to an indicator that only indirectly provides the information necessary to take an investment decision. It is not the tension indicator itself, but the expected effects reflected by this indicator, which are important. An advantage of this is that the indicator, in principle, incorporates all possible adjustment processes and hence renders superfluous the need to make explicit all the different aspects relevant for the labour market. A weak point, however, is the very fact that these aspects cannot be specified, and also that the indicator only shows shifts of the labour market position. Naturally, the absolute level of returns is also relevant to be able to take the right investment decision.

The third important aspect to be discussed if we wish to make the labour market more transparent for educational investment decisions, concerns the degree to which the method concerned is capable of forecasting the *future* returns in the labour market. In addition to trend-related shifts of the labour market position of a particular course, sudden shifts of this labour market position are caused in particular by shifts of supply and demand. The wages – or the rate of return – constitute the result of developments in supply and demand. Wage shifts cannot therefore be attributed directly to shifts of either supply or demand. As a result, it is difficult for the rate-of-return approach to arrive at forecasts of future developments by means of extrapolation, even if shifts of the rate of return are analysed.[1] As the manpower requirement approach is based on such developments of supply and demand, this method is much more suitable to forecast future developments. To this should be added that, if the labour market position is determined not only by wages, but also by other aspects such as unemployment, underutilisation, having a permanent contract, et cetera, the rate-of-return approach should explicitly chart all these aspects. The assumptions to be made regarding the way in which the labour market functions, will therefore affect the rate-of-return approach to a greater extent than the manpower requirement approach. The fact that the manpower requirement approach forecasts the labour market tension as such, makes this method less sensitive to the exact nature of these labour market mechanisms and renders the character of the forecasts more robust.

Table 1
A comparison between the rate-of-return approach and the manpower requirement approach regarding the usefulness of these analyses to support educational investment decisions

	rate-of-return	manpower requirement
assumptions regarding the way in which the labour market functions	no specific assumption required forecasts, however, require adequate suppositions of the mechanisms	no specific assumption required approach is also very robust with respect to the actual mechanisms, because the tension indicator is based on a hypothetical development without adjustments
informative power for investment decision	direct insight in the core variable in the investment decision in a market in which not only wages are important, however, all other aspects must be made visible	only an indirect tension indicator, which indicates labour market shifts without showing the exact nature; also, this tension indicator is only a relative one, which does not present a picture of the level of the 'returns' of the educational investment
forecasting capabilities	very difficult to use for forecasts	eminently suitable for forecasts

Although the two variables, wages and labour market tension, are interrelated, it proves very difficult in practice to integrate the wage-based rate-of-return approach and the employment-based manpower requirement approach. The comparison between the two approaches, presented in summary in Table 1, shows that both give only a restricted picture of the returns to be expected for investment decisions. As long as integration remains impossible and the wage rates and job opportunities each have their own informative values for investors in education, it remains useful to apply both methods simultaneously. In highly simplified terms, we could say that the rate-of-return approach provides information on the wages in the labour market as they are or were in the recent past: $\hat{W}$. In itself, this is important information for investors, but in fact one should know the future wages (W) rather than the present ones. The manpower requirement approach provides the tension indicator $S-D$. The latter contains no information on the absolute level of wages, but does provide the relationship between $\hat{W}$ and W, as is shown in equation (8). Combining the two methods should therefore lead to the ideal set of data for educational investment decisions. However, this requires an explicit specification of equation (8). It must be determined explicitly how discrepancies between supply and demand affect wage levels in all different aspects. Borghans and Wieling (1995) have explored this relationship, but there is as yet insufficient insight in such mechanisms to be able to fully integrate the existing approaches.

Flexibility

So far, this discussion of the way in which the labour market functions has not dealt explicitly with the consequences of the simultaneous existence of the various educational submarkets. The idea has long been abandoned that an education provides preparation that can only be used within a specific occupational field. It is true that in practice vocational courses often focus on a specific occupational domain, but this concerns primarily the subject-specific knowledge and skills. During the course, students also acquire general skills, which are usually more widely applicable, in particular in occupational domains in which subject-specialisation is less important. In addition, certain subject fields may be so closely related that the exact nature of the subspecialisation is not very relevant for proper performance. See, for example, the occupational domain of information engineers, which recruits candidates from specific information science courses as well as from completely different subject areas with a considerable information science component. In general, courses have comparative advantages for certain occupational domains, but they may also offer acceptable returns outside these domains. This adaptive capability can be enhanced if employers are prepared to make the necessary adjustment costs in the form of on-the-job or off-the-job training. Some courses offer distinct advantages in this area, because they generate powerful learning and adaptation capabilities in students.

School-leavers from different courses are therefore interchangeable to a certain extent when it comes to filling vacancies in a certain occupational domain. In the labour market model for an educational submarket outlined above, account should be taken of such possibilities of substitution between courses. This creates more or less strong interdependencies between submarkets. If the wage level in a particular submarket decreases in relation to other submarkets, the demand for labour offering the knowledge and skills required in this submarket will increase as a result of the cost-savings that can be achieved if more of this type of labour can be productively employed. Because of the existence of the possibility of substitution by other courses, the demand will also partly shift from the course which was originally regarded as the most suitable one to related courses, the productive disadvantages of which are now regarded as less of a problem by employers. If the range of courses from which employees can be recruited is wide, the demand for labour will increase more rapidly in the case of wage decreases than would be the case if employers had no alternatives. Also in the case of wage increases, adjustment will take place more rapidly, albeit in the opposite direction. The existence of relationships between courses therefore increases the wage flexibility of demand, i.e. parameter b in the labour market model.

The relative wage decrease also affects the supply side. The lower wage level renders the submarket concerned less attractive for both suppliers of labour who have the required educational qualifications, but who now see the wages in submarkets in which they would be less productive increase in relative terms, and for those who have related qualifications and are more productive elsewhere and see their wages increase in relative terms. The existence of such alternative job opportunities will therefore cause the supply of labour to decrease more rapidly in case of wage decreases. Wage flexibility of supply, i.e. parameter a in the labour market model, will also be greater.

From equation (7), one can easily deduce that if the values of b and a are greater, any discrepancy between supply and demand will have less effect on wage shifts. In the case of strong relationships with other courses, the equilibrium in a submarket will therefore be restored relatively easily, although this may involve majors shifts of workers between submarkets. Hence it is not surprising that Klaassen and Heijke (1975) have developed a method to determine this relationship between courses by means of an analysis of mobility behaviour. Another way of determining this relationship was developed several years ago by Borghans (1992), who used a more statistic approach by investigating to what extent the occupational domain of the different courses overlap. A third method was recently developed by van Eijs and Heijke (1996), who deduce the relationship between courses from the wage function, on the basis of the differences the latter reflect of the efforts made for additional training between the various combinations of occupation and education.

As stated above, if parameters a and b are large, and hence the flexibility of the deployment of human capital is great, any discrepancy between supply and demand will create a smaller shift of wages. Future wages will then deviate changes less from the present levels. A flexible labour market therefore decreases the need for adequate forecasts of the shifts of the labour market. Instead of manpower requirement forecasts, a strategy aimed at a wider employability of individuals with a particular educational background may decrease many of the investment risks. If such a strategy required adaptation of the curriculum of a particular course, this would have certain implications requiring further investigation. This will be discussed below.

Curriculum

The parameters of the supply and demand curve affect the match between education and the labour market, and hence the returns of education. Changes of the supply and demand parameters can be achieved by shifting the emphasis in education itself. This relationship between curriculum and the way in which the labour market functions has far-reaching implications for the way investment decisions in education are regarded. Traditionally, decisions on investments in education are represented as choosing between different educational courses. This means that students choose whether to take a course in electronic engineering or in mechanical engineering. Government must also take such decisions, for example to provide more funds for certain courses in order to increase their capacity. If the issue is presented in this way, one assumes that each occupation has its own course and that the objectives set by this course are clear. The economic problem is then to take the best possible choice between the different courses, while, given this choice, the educational problem consists of achieving the learning objectives as efficiently as possible.

If we assume, however, that the labour market position is not merely determined on the one hand by supply and demand in a particular submarket and on the other hand by the degree to which one has the required skills for the occupation concerned, but if we accept that due to uncertainties in the labour market, the existence of flexibility and transition skills also plays a role, then we create an interrelationship between the content of the course and considerations regarding the labour market prospects. Optimal curriculum development cannot then be regarded as being unrelated to the labour market characteristics of the course concerned.

Considerations regarding the width of the occupational domain for a course are examples. The need to provide students with a wide education, in order to render them less dependent on a specific submarket of the labour market will vary from one subject field to another. The labour market for both technical and commercial occupations is quite sensitive to economic fluctuations. This means that the uncertainty relating to investments in education in these fields is fairly great. Areas such as theology and jobs in the civil service or the military are hardly subject to economic fluctuations. Hence the risks of specialising in these areas are small. One could therefore consider to make the technical and commercial courses mentioned above wider in order to limit the risks in the labour market. To be able to take investment decisions regarding courses on the basis of such labour market information, however, requires insight in the educational possibilities. Figure 2 provides an imaginary example. In this figure, the horizontal axis lists the number of occupations for which the course provides training. This in fact constitutes the width of the course. The vertical axis indicates the productivity reached within these occupations. As wider courses must deal with more topics, the depth of the course (at an equal educational effort) will decrease, causing productivity to drop.

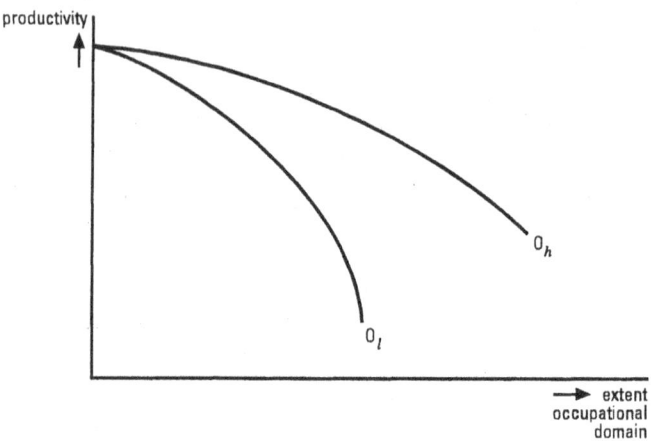

Figure 2   Productivity in relation to the size of the occupational domain

If the different occupations for which one can be trained are completely unrelated to one another from an educational point of view, then training for two different subject fields would require double the amount of time. Inversely, if the effort remained the same, productivity would be halved. In practice, however, such extreme situations will not exist. In many cases, it will be possible to train for two or more subject fields which are closely related. Without losing too much depth, training can then be given for a wider range of occupations because the required contents of the course to some extent overlaps with others, and subjects can be learnt more quickly if others have already been mastered. This is indicated by curve O_h. For certain subject fields, however, it will be difficult to find a suitable combination. The relationship between width and productivity in this case is represented in curve O_l.

In the second case, productivity declines rapidly if the curriculum is made wider. A marginal widening of the curriculum in such courses therefore involves greater expenses than in a course in which relevant aspects of other subject fields or occupations can be integrated relatively easily. The costs of widening by one unit (access to one more occupation) are given in Figure 3 for both the course in which combinations of subjects are easy to achieve (O_h') and for courses in which integration is more difficult (O_l').

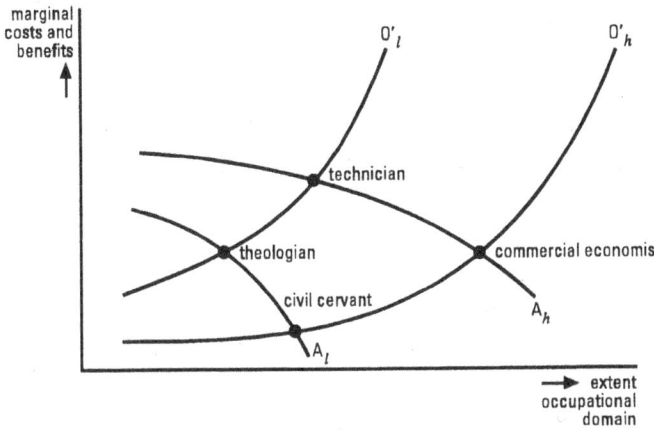

Figure 3 Marginal returns and costs in relation to the size of the occupational domain

Allowing a course to provide access to more than one subject field, however, also decreases the employment risks in the labour market. Students who take a wide course, postpone their labour market choices to some extent. They need not weigh the possibilities offered by the labour market for the various jobs until after they have completed their courses. Such students can choose between the alternatives left when they actually enter the labour market. If they had taken a specialist education, the choices would have been made at the start of the course, with the ensuing uncertainty regarding the developments in the specific submarket. A wide education therefore has an option value which is dependent on the degree to which the specific market development can be accommodated (Dothan and Williams, 1981). This return is also represented in the figure. In a greatly fluctuating market, this option value will be high (A_h), whereas a predictable labour market has a low option value (A_l). The wider the occupational domain of a course, the less relevant any further widening of this domain will be as an increasingly greater part of the risks will be covered. Both curves are therefore downward.

Figure 3 shows that the combination of curriculum possibilities (O'_h versus O'_l) and the degree of labour market security (A_h versus A_l) is decisive for the optimisation of the contents of education. Table 2 summarises the results. For a job as a theologist, a highly specialised education is obvious. The course is difficult to expand into other subject fields, but the labour market position provides no need for such an extension, because the risks are limited as a result of the small sensitivity to economic fluctuations of the jobs. Commercial economics, on the other hand, should focus on a wide occupational domain. From the point of view of education, this is very well possible, whereas the labour market advantages are great. For jobs in the civil service, an average width of the educational course seems obvious. Technically, widening is very well possible, but the returns in terms of decreased risks are small. In such a situation, one may expect high returns of the investment in education. On the basis of Figure 3, we may expect courses training for technical occupations to have an average width of the occupational domain. The cause is the reverse here. The need for widening is great from a labour market point of view, but in terms of education, the possibilities are limited. As a result, an investment in a technical education and the ensuing risks, and the difficulty of compensating for this by widening the curriculum, is expensive. The returns of technical education will then be lower.

Table 2
Ideal structure of the curriculum balancing productivity
in case of widening and labour market risk

	predictable market	unpredictable market
curriculum easy to widen	civil servant average occupational domain, high returns	commercial staff wide occupational domain
curriculum difficult to widen	theologist narrow occupational domain	engineer average occupational domain low returns

This example shows that in addition to insight in the mechanisms of the labour market, we must also have insight in the way in which the structure of the curriculum affects the position in the labour market if we want to arrive at an adequate decision regarding educational investments.

Plan of the book

In the discussion above on the way in which the labour market functions in relation to education, three aspects were dealt with. The first aspect concerned the labour market prospects of courses. It was indicated that these can be expressed in terms of wages or returns, or in the degree of difficulty of finding employment. It appeared useful to apply the two points of view side by side. The second aspect discussed concerned the possibilities of substitution between courses. This focused on the shifts in the relationships in which courses are used for the jobs within a particular occupational domain if the degrees of shortages between the courses change. The degree of relationship between the courses concerned played a major role here. The third aspect discussed was the explanation of the possibilities of substitution between courses on the basis of the characteristics of the underlying curriculums. We outlined the possible implications of a general versus a job-specific curriculum for the accessibility of certain occupational domains. These three aspects of the relationship between education and the labour market have been taken as the starting point for the structure of this publication. The three Parts are therefore called *Prospects*, *Flexibility* and *Curriculum* respectively. Each of these Parts contains three contributions, making a total of nine.

This introductory chapter and the contributions divided into three Parts are preceded by an elaborate foreword by Albeda, who placed the theme of this book within the framework of his views on the changes that the education system should undergo in order to fulfil its future role in society in the best possible way. Albeda expects that far-reaching, increasingly rapid changes in technology and organisation of the labour process will make it necessary for young people to prepare for life of permanent learning. Rather than merely training for a specific occupation, education will have to focus on creating the possibilities of acquiring general skills and further development. Education should do no more than prepare for the real school which is life itself. In such a changing and increasingly complex interrelationship between education and the labour market, adequate information that may help students take their investment decisions, will be of great importance.

The first contribution in the Part *Prospects* is by de Grip, Borghans and Smits. They present an explorative study for the medium-term developments in the occupational levels and occupational domains of the higher educated. Their approach is in line with the manpower requirement approach. Their contribution, however, focuses on the adjustment processes in the labour market that result from the discrepancies between supply and demand. Thus, they show how the manpower requirement approach can be used to illustrate such market mechanisms. The second contribution in this Part is by de Koning, who discusses the labour market prospects of courses in terms of returns. This concerns a rate-of-return approach. He pays attention not only to the educational level attained but also to the route taken through the educational system. His analyses show that the returns of education may vary greatly from one type of education to the next, and that patterns may emerge that would not at first have been expected. General education, for example, appears to provide better returns than intermediate vocational education, and the returns of detours in education are considerable. The third contribution is by Webbink, who investigated the role of labour market forecasts for study choices made by students in higher education. If labour market prospects provide important information to support decisions regarding the choice of studies, then it can be expected that such decisions are influenced by this information. Webbink has found, however, that this relationship is at least not a direct one. It seems therefore that the available labour market information is hardly used by young people choosing their studies.

In the Part *Flexibility* the first contribution is by Hartog and Jonker. They have investigated the rates of return of education if the level of education does not match the level of the job accepted and hence there is undereducation of overeducation. They have also investigated the developments of the return of education in *over- and underinvestment* over time. Their contribution therefore discusses the consequences of a certain (mis)allocation of workers across occupational levels. In accordance with earlier research in this field, they also found that a mismatch has a negative effect on wages, but that the returns remain positive. Hence the loss of productivity resulting from a different allocation appears to develop gradually, which means that in the case of shifts of supply and demand, the available human capital can still be utilised with acceptable productivity. In the following contribution, by Borghans and Heijke, the existing allocation of courses across occupations is analysed, as well as the resulting relationships between courses. The authors show how shifts of demand affect the position of different types of education. In general, there seems to have been a concentration of occupational domains, both between the education levels and the education types. The demand of the labour market is apparently becoming less focused on a certain educational background. The third contribution in this Part is by van Zon, Muysken and Meijers. They have developed a labour market model in which certain educational categories are distinguished and which simultaneously describes both wage developments and supply and demand. This model therefore integrates elements of the manpower requirement approach and the rate-of-return approach. The authors assume an asymmetric substitutability between higher and lower educated. The higher educated may do the work of the lower educated, but not vice versa. They have investigated in particular how the bumping-down process works, in which the higher educated force the lower educated from the labour market and on the other hand, an increase of the number of jobs available for the higher educated may serve as a chimney for the position of the lower educated.

The Part *Curriculum* starts with a contribution by Nijhof, showing which elements of the curriculum constitute in particular vocational education and what the consequences may be of each of these elements of the curriculum for the way in which graduates perform in the labour market in terms of job opportunities and careers. Nijhof has developed a research model for this, which he tries to validate on the basis of a number of empirical studies. Although these studies show the importance of subject-specific skills for career development, they provide insufficient evidence to create a link between the various characteristics of the curriculum. The subsequent contribution by Glebbeek and Waslander is focused more on the labour market. After a discussion of the aspects of the curriculum that may be of importance for labour market performance, they present an empirical study which investigates whether the different university courses also lead to clearly recognisable positions in the labour market. Their research results are then set off against those of a number of other studies. On the basis of this, they qualify the importance of the curriculum for the labour market position. The educational level appears to dominate the degree of labour market success. In the contribution by Heijke, Koeslag and van der Velden, attention is shifted to the labour market even more. They have investigated for recent graduates of higher vocational education which types of knowledge and skills of a general or occupation-specific nature are required both within and outside their education-specific occupational domains, and whether the education taken (and the knowledge and skills acquired in this way) have a specific influence on the level of wages. The results of their research show that there is a relatively large effect on wages for occupations which match the education taken both as to level and as to subject, as well as of the occupation-specific knowledge and skills acquired in it.

References

Ahamad, B., and Blaug M. (eds.) (1973), *The Practice of Manpower Forecasting*, Elsevier: Amsterdam.

Blaug, M. (1967), 'Approaches to Educational Planning'. *Economic Journal*, pp. 262-287.

Borghans, L. (1992), *A Histo-Topographic Map of the Dutch University Studies*, ROA-W-1992/5E, Research Centre for Education and the Labour Market: Maastricht.

Borghans, L., and Heijke, H. (1996), 'Forecasting the Educational Structure of Occupations: a Manpower Requirement Approach with Substitution', *Labour*, 10 (1), pp. 151-192.

Borghans, L., and Willems, E. (1996), *Interpreting Gaps in Manpower Forecasting Models*, Research Centre for Education and the Labour Market: Maastricht.

Dothan, U., and Williams, J. (1981), 'Education as an Option', *Journal of Business*, 54, pp. 117-139.

Eijs, P. van, and Heijke, H. (1996), *The Relation between the Wage, Job-related Training and the Quality of the Match between Occupation and Types of Education*, ROA-RM-1996/6E, Research Centre for Education and the Labour Market: Maastricht.

Heijke, H. (ed.) (1994), *Forecasting the Labour Market by Occupation and Education*, Kluwer Academic Publishers: Boston/Dordrecht/London.

Klaassen, L.H., and Heijke, H. (1975), 'Some Indicators of Regional Labour Market Equilibrium', *Économie Appliquée*, 28 (2/3), pp. 497-509.

OECD (1992), *Education at a Glance, OECD Indicators*, OECD: Paris.

Psacharopoulos, G. (1981), 'Returns to education: An updated international comparison'. *Comp. Educ.*, 17, pp. 321-341.

Wieling, M., Borghans, L. (1995), *Discrepancies between Demand and Supply and Adjustment Processes on the Labour Market*, ROA-RM-1995/4E, Research Centre for Education and the Labour Market: Maastricht.

Note

1   To this should be added that if the rate-of-return approach actually wishes to present the discounted value of the entire professional career, it will only have sufficient data to make an estimate at the end of the careers of a cohort, which means that the data in principle lag behind the current developments by about forty years. To be able to also estimate the rate of return of later cohorts, suppositions must be made regarding the part of their careers which still lies ahead of them.

Part One
PROSPECTS

2 Future Developments in the Job Level and Domain of High-skilled Workers

Andries de Grip, Lex Borghans and Wendy Smits

Introduction

Since Freeman's (1976) *Overeducated American*, various studies on the relationship between education and job levels have been published (see e.g. Duncan and Hoffman, 1981; Tsang and Levin, 1985; Verdugo and Verdugo, 1989; Groot, 1993; Cohn and Kahn, 1995). In particular the studies of Huijgen (see e.g. Huijgen, 1989) initiated a debate on the overeducation of the labour force in the Netherlands. However, it has proved very difficult to give an appropriate definition of overeducation. The concept of overeducation is very sensitive to the point of reference chosen, so that measurements of overeducation are highly dependent on the measurement approach. Huijgen's approach is based on the classification of occupational categories by experts and generates a much higher percentage of overeducated workers than when the workers themselves are asked about the level of the job they fill (see de Grip et al., 1993). Despite the measurement difficulties, there is a widespread consensus that during the seventies and eighties people with higher education tended to find employment in jobs at lower levels. The supply of highly-educated workers (those with a tertiary qualification) seemed to be increasing more rapidly than the increase in demand for a highly-educated workforce.

One remarkable feature of the most recent forecasts of the Research Centre for Education and the Labour Market (ROA, 1995) with respect to labour market developments in the Netherlands in the period 1995-2000 is the favourable forecasts of the future labour market situation in the year 2000 for graduates from most types of tertiary education (see Borghans, de Grip and Smits, 1996). The demand for highly-educated newcomers on the labour market will increase due to the continued upgrading of the labour force and a rapid increase of replacement demand due to the ageing of the workforce, while the supply of graduates will decrease slightly due to a fall in the number of students at universities and in tertiary-level vocational education.[1] However, in the light of the experiences of the last two decades, there is some reason to suspect that an improvement in the labour market prospects of various fields of study in higher education may actually relate, to some extent, to employment below the tertiary level or outside the specific occupational domain of these types of education. In other words, it may reflect the continuation of 'crowding-out' processes in the labour market (see e.g. Spee and Coppens, 1996).

This Chapter investigates the expected consequences of the changing ratio between supply and demand for those with higher education. A broad approach to this question is adopted by analyzing the relation between the expected developments in supply and demand on the one hand and, on the other hand, the shifts in both the job *level* and the occupational *domain* of high-skilled workers in the next few years in the Netherlands. With respect to the occupational domain, the analysis focuses particularly on the extent to which employment growth relates to the *specific* occupational field of the type of education, the *shared* domain in which workers with the type of education concerned compete to a large extent with workers with another educational background and the *alternative* domains, which refer to occupations that do not recruit workers with a particular educational background and occupations which are more or less specific domains of other types of education. The various components of the expected shifts are also analyzed. These components relate to shifts in the industry structure of employment (the industry effect), shifts in the occupational structure of employment within economic sectors (the occupational effect), shifts in the skill structure of the workers in the various occupational segments (the educational effect) or to substitution processes on the labour market due to ex ante supply-demand mismatches for particular types of education (the substitution effect). This analysis makes it possible to gain a better understanding of the substitution processes which can result from ex ante discrepancies between demand and supply in the labour market.

The Chapter is organised as follows. Next Section sketches the structure of the labour market forecasting model used. The modular structure of the model makes it possible to distinguish the various components of the employment growth at the different job levels and occupational domains. The third Section discusses the conceptual framework that makes it possible to distinguish the job level and domain effects due to demand-side developments from those developments that occur as a result of the interaction between supply and demand in the various labour market segments. The fourth Section describes the procedure used to classify the job level and domain of the 48 occupational segments distinguished in ROA's forecasting model. The fifth Section presents an overview of the current labour market structure for the various types of education within higher education, distinguishing 20 types of education at the higher vocational level and 16 types of education at the university level. The sixth Section presents the results of the breakdown of the employment forecasts for the various types of education, in three steps. The first step is an analysis of the extent to which the forecast change in employment levels for the various types of education are due to industry, occupational, educational or substitution effects. The second is to ascertain the extent to which the changes in employment levels for the various types of education relate to high-level jobs and to the specific occupational domain of the type of education, to the shared domain, or to the alternative domains. Third, some illustrations are given of the relative importance of the sectoral, occupational and skill structure effects, and of the substitution effects, for the changes in employment at the job levels and occupational domains distinguished. The last Section presents some conclusions.

ROA's labour market forecasting model

ROA's Information System on Education and the Labour Market seeks to increase the transparency of the match between education and the labour market by providing a differentiated, representative view of the educational and occupational structure of the labour market and the expected changes in labour demand and supply in the various segments of the labour market that can be distinguished. The forecasts are compiled for a total of 93 occupational classes and 79 types of education, over the full width of the labour market.

Figure 1 gives a schematic overview of the modules of the forecasting model which generate the forecasts of the future labour market prospects of newcomers to the labour market.[2] One flow volume which is important for the demand side of the labour market is the *expansion demand,* which reflects the change in employment levels in a particular occupational class or for a particular type of education. The forecasts of expansion demand are based on the employment level forecasts for economic sectors which are produced by the Dutch Central Planning Bureau. Because particular occupational segments within an economic sector grow more rapidly than others, ROA translates these changes in the economic sectors into the expansion demand for 48 different occupational segments.[3] Then the implications of the predicted growth in the various occupational classes for the expansion demand for each type of education are determined. An allowance is made at this point for any shifts which may be occurring in the educational structure of occupational classes. The expansion demand per type of education relates to the number of people with a particular educational background that employers would like to be able to employ. The actual change in employment levels per type of education will generally differ from this because changes on the supply side affect relative scarcities and lead to substitution processes.

Demand for newcomers on the labour market consists not only of expansion demand, but also of *replacement demand,* which arises when workers retire, leave the labour force under the early retirement scheme or due to work disability or withdraw from the labour market temporarily. However, replacement demand only arises if the departure of an employee actually leads directly or indirectly to a vacancy for a new entrant. If the departure of a worker is taken as an opportunity

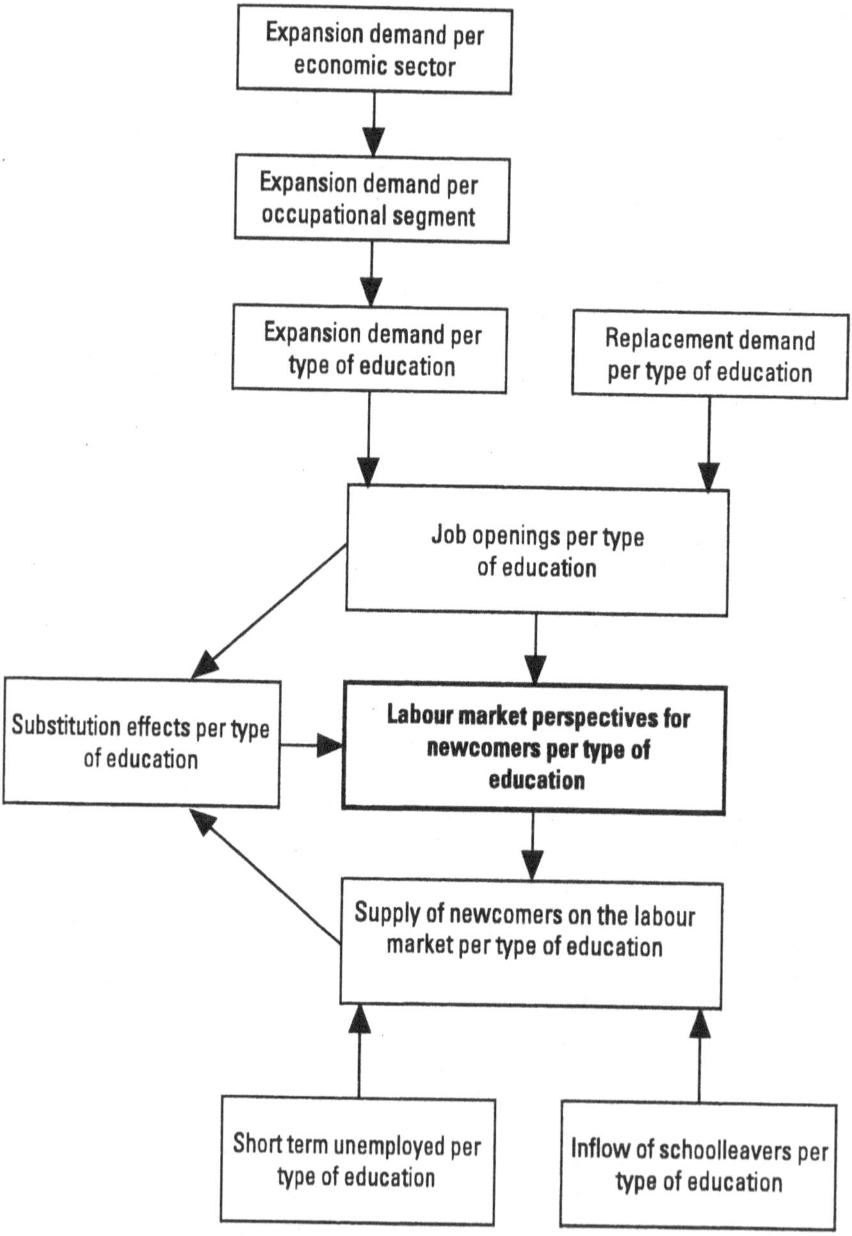

Figure 1 Modules of the forecasting model of the labour market prospects for newcomers to the labour market

to cut employment levels, no replacement demand results. These flows out of the labour market are in fact irrelevant for newcomers. Thus only part of the flows leaving the market generate replacement demand. Moreover, there is an important difference between the replacement demand per occupational class and per type of education, because occupational mobility has an influence on the replacement demand per occupational class, but not on the replacement demand per type of education. When a worker with a certain educational background changes occupational classes, this does not, on balance, create a new job for a newcomer with the same educational background. The replacement demand for a certain occupational class that is created by this occupational mobility is balanced by an equal flow of labour into another occupational class (see Willems and de Grip, 1993).

If employment levels are rising, the expansion demand and replacement demand together comprise the *job openings* for newcomers to the labour market. If employment levels are declining, job openings can only arise due to replacement demand.

In the labour market, the total demand for newcomers confronts the expected supply of newcomers, which consists of the future flow of *school-leavers* entering the market during the forecast period and the supply of short-term *unemployed* people waiting to enter the market at the start of this period. It is assumed that the long-term unemployed, who have been looking for work for longer than a year, no longer constitute serious competition for school-leavers.

The forecasts of the flows of school-leavers entering the labour market correspond to the *Referentieramingen 1995* (Reference forecasts) which are compiled by the Ministry of Education, Culture and Science for courses in the 'regular' (i.e., full-time initial) education system. ROA disaggregates these forecasts, and supplementary data is used to estimate the effects of the flows from non-regular education on the educational makeup of the flows entering the labour market.

An indication of the labour market *prospects* for newcomers to the labour market is derived, for each type of education, by confronting the expected flows of demand and supply with each other. This indicator shows what discrepancy may be expected between the demand and supply for each type of education. But excess supply does not imply that the group in question will as a matter of course become unemployed, and a supply shortfall does not automatically mean that there will be unfilled vacancies. In practice, it appears that school-leavers with a type of education for which the supply exceeds demand do suffer from a deterioration of their position, for example because they are more likely to have to accept work below their level, get less favourable contracts, are less well paid or more likely to work part-time involuntarily (Wieling and Borghans, 1995). In such a situation, it will become easier (and cheaper) for employers who normally recruit workers with a lower educational background to recruit school-leavers from this type of education. These employers will therefore modify their demand and recruit more workers with a higher educational background than was originally contemplated, but for these workers at less favourable conditions than they were used to. On the other hand, if there is a supply shortage the position of school-leavers will improve, and they will then not have to accept a job at a lower level, for lower wages, etc. These adjustments in response to labour market discrepancies are indicated as *active* substitution. Employment opportunities due to active substitution, e.g. due to the need to accept jobs at a lower educational level, do not influence the labour market prospects for that particular type of education, but rather are the result of certain labour market prospects.

However, substitution processes will mean that there are fewer job openings for those with the types of education which suffer from 'crowding-out' processes by types of education with an excess supply (Borghans and Heijke, 1996). On the other hand, there will be extra job openings for those with educational backgrounds which are closely related to types of education which are in short supply. These *passive* substitution effects are therefore important determinants of the labour market prospects of types of education.

Occupational domain and interaction between supply and demand

Although the various types of education, particularly those in vocational education, focus on specific labour market segments, in practice there are almost no exclusive relationships between particular types of education and occupations or economic sectors. People with the same education find work in various occupations and economic sectors, and many occupations can be practised by personnel with a variety of educational backgrounds. And even where a particular occupation can only be practised by those with a specific qualification, this does not mean that those who have this type of education can only find work in that occupation.

Although it is therefore not possible to identify a separate occupational domain for each type of education, the labour market does seem to have a reasonably clear structure when differentiated by types of education. Nevertheless, the overlap between the occupational domains makes it possible for both those seeking labour and those offering their labour to adjust their requirements according to changes in the relationship between demand and supply in the labour market.

The choice of a particular type of education always entails a certain risk. Every course is intended to some extent to impart specific skills, which are required for particular occupations but not for other occupations. Thus a type of education which offers graduates the chance to switch to many occupations and economic sectors will be attractive. Wide opportunities to switch to other sectors of the labour market will, prima facie, improve the market position of workers. The drawback is that types of education which are intended to be relevant to a broad segment of the labour market will be less able to concentrate on the specific skills which each of the occupations demands (see Borghans, 1992).

Because workers with a particular educational background can switch to several occupations, and employers can recruit personnel with diverse educational backgrounds for a particular occupation, there may be an overlap in the labour market between the occupational domains of types of education. In ROA (1995) this overlap has been represented in the form of a *competition index* for each pair of educational types, based on Borghans (1992). The results of this analysis indicate that there are a number of types of education, especially in higher education, which serve a very distinctive occupational domain. In the occupation which forms their major domain, they are not competing with other types of education, while in case they are not working in this specific job they are spread over a large range of alternative occupations.

Naturally there are distinct occupational domains for University Education (UE) in Veterinary and medical sciences and dentistry and UE Pharmacy. The same holds for UE Arts and UE Fine Arts, for which the main occupational domains are teaching in secondary and higher education within the relevant fields[4] and also UE Theology which has its own clear domain as training for the pastoral vocations. At the level of Higher Vocational Education (HVE), three types of education have reasonably clearly demarcated occupational domains: HVE Teacher training, which has a clearly demarcated occupational field in the educational professions, HVE Interpreter and translator, whose graduates largely work as linguists, interpreters and translators, and HVE Transport and harbour, with its own clear occupational domain among pilots and transport and freight supervisors.

On the other hand there are occupations which offer employers many opportunities to substitute workers with alternative educational backgrounds. Clear examples are the typical management occupations and the civil servants. For these occupations, the specific educational background of the workers is apparently not so important. Some other occupations are the shared domain for people from particular types of education, e.g. the administrative occupations of book-keepers and bank employees and the occupation of programmers and system analysts. In the latter occupation one finds people with the following educational backgrounds: HVE Commercial information science; UE Information science; HVE Electronic and information technology; UE Electrical engineering and information technology; HVE Business administration technology and UE Mathematics and natural sciences. This example clearly illustrates the flexibility which the labour market can exhibit where there are large discrepancies between demand and supply. To meet the enormous growth in the demand for computer and information science specialists, graduates from various types of education have been recruited in past years. Because a large part of the demand in computer-related occupations has been satisfied in this manner, this discrepancy has also improved the prospects of those with these types of education. Employers have been required to make their jobs sufficiently attractive to be able to recruit graduates from other types of education. Additional training might have played a major role in this proces.

For employers it may become necessary to change the educational structure of an occupation because of changes in the nature of the occupation, so that the type of education which is most suitable for that occupation gradually changes. This can be caused both by influences on the demand and the supply side of the labour market. On the demand side, these changes can, for example, arise due to the arrival of new technologies, which can lead to an upgrading process if the complexity of the technologies being adopted makes a higher educational level necessary. On the other hand, there can also be downgrading, if automation means that there is less need for trade skills in the production process (See e.g. Spenner, 1985).

On the other hand also influence on the supply side or discrepancies between demand and supply can result in shifts in the educational structure of occupations. An oversupply of people with a particular type of education will result in school-leavers switching to the labour market segments previously occupied by those with somewhat related types of education. For example, excess supply of those with higher education can lead to the crowding-out of those with lower levels of education and, vice versa, if there are recruitment problems with a particular educational category employers can substitute school-leavers from other types of education.[5]

It is evident that the substitution processes that occur due to ex ante gaps between demand and supply for a particular type of education affect both the occupational structure of employment of the workers of that particular type of education and the occupational structure of employment of related types of education. These effects can be qualified as the active and passive substitution effects, respectively. Figure 2 illustrates active substitution, i.e. the way in which an ex ante supply and demand mismatch for a particular type of education may affect the occupational structure of employment for that type of education. At $t=0$, labour supply (S_0) and demand (D_{A+B}) are in equilibrium, with wage level w_0. At that moment A_0 of the workers with this particular educational background are employed in occupation A, in which these workers are assumed to be most productive, and B_0-A_0 work in occupation B. If in the forecasting period labour supply decreases from S_0 to S_1,[6] ex ante forecasts will indicate a demand-supply mismatch at wage level w_0. However this gap, which is interpreted as 'good labour market prospects' for the graduates of this type of education, will increase the wage level from w_0 to w_1. Moreover, most employers who recruited workers with this educational background for occupation B will no longer recruit these workers. Their wage costs exceed the benefits for the employer, who will perhaps start recruiting people with another educational background. This means that at the new equilibrium the majority of the workers are employed in the occupation in which workers with this particular educational background are most productive: occupation A. Only a minority ($B_1 - A_0$) will still be employed in occupation B.

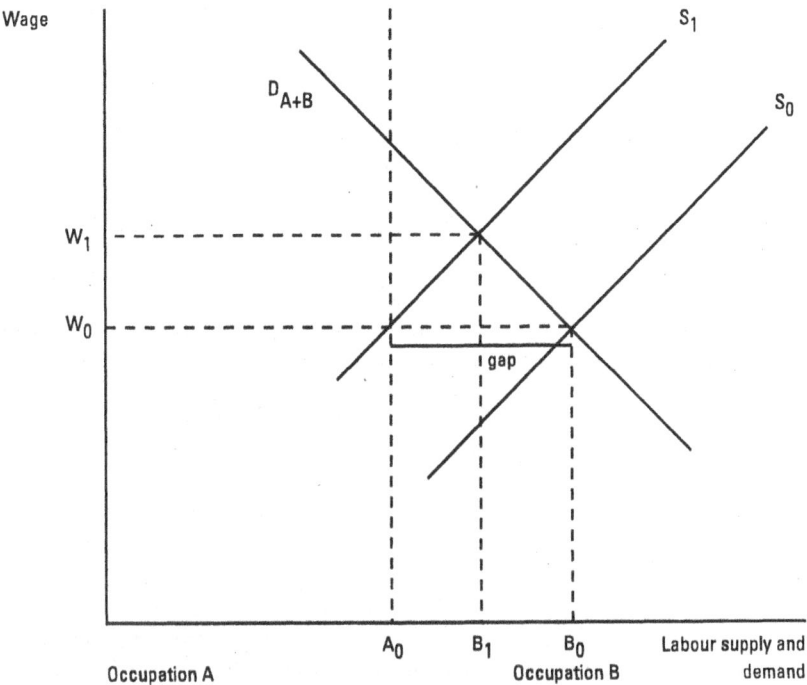

Figure 2 The effects of an ex ante supply shortage on the occupational structure of employment for a particular type of education (active substitution)

Figure 3 illustrates the possible effects of passive substitution processes on the occupational structure of employment for a particular type of education. The left part of the figure relates to type of education i, for which supply and demand are in ex ante equilibrium at wage level w_{ea}. In this case the majority of the workers (A_0) are employed in occupation A. The right part of the figure relates to type of education j. Ex ante forecasts of supply and demand for this type of education indicate excess demand at wage level w_j, which is interpreted as 'good labour market prospects' for the graduates of this type of education. However, this gap will attract more workers with education i to occupation B jobs, which effects the

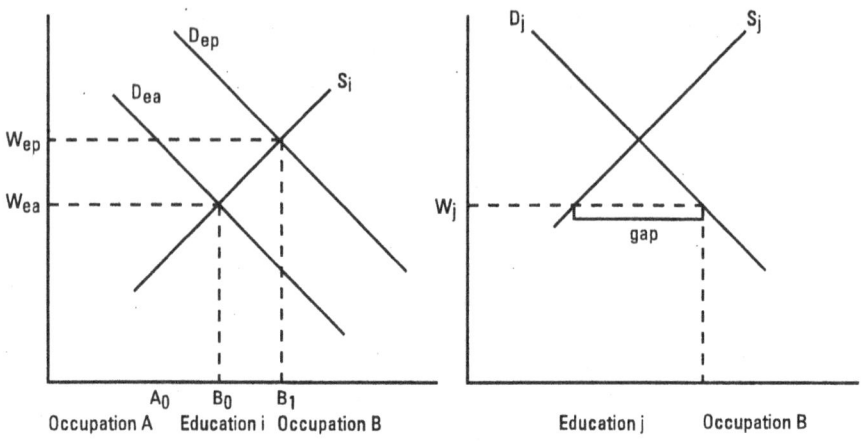

Figure 3 The effects of excess demand for education *j* on the occupational structure of employment for education *i* (passive substitution)

occupational structure of employment for the latter type of education. The demand curve D_{ea} will shift to the right to D_{ep}. Due to this passive substitution effect in occupation *B*, graduates from type of education *i* will also have good labour market prospects.

Figure 4 gives an overview of the four possible substitution effects due to ex ante labour supply mismatches. Both active and passive substitution can be possitive or negative. For a particular type of education different substitution processes may occur on the various labour market segments which are relevant for that particular type of education: e.g. a positive passive substitution due to the supply shortage of a related type of education could be combined with a negative active substitution process due to the supply shortage of workers with the education background concerned. However, it should be noticed that strictly speaking the latter just means that the excess demand for this type of education will be rationed.

Classification of the job level and domain of occupational segments

To be able to analyze the developments of the job level and domain of studies in higher education, the various occupational segments have to be classified with respect to both the level and the field of education which is required. In general two different approaches can be distinguished. The first is that occupational

Substitution	Character of substitution process	Effect on labour market prospects
Active substitution	Demand adjustment due to ex ante supply-demand mismatch	No effect on prospects, but implication of bad or good prospects
Positive	Additional demand due to ex ante excess supply	
Negative	Rationed demand due to ex ante excess demand	
Passive substitution	Demand adjustments due to ex ante supply-demand mismatches for another related type of education	
Positive	Additional demand due to ex ante excess demand for another type of education	Positive effect
Negative	Demand decrease due to ex ante excess supply of another type of education	Negative effect

Figure 4 Overview of the possible substitution effects

experts determine the job level and domain by means of more or less objective criteria. The second approach is to classify the occupations by means of the actual educational background of the workers employed in jobs concerned. In the Chapter we will apply the second approach. Although this approach may leave the disadvantage that actual discrepancies between the job level and the educational level of the workers are not taken into account, it avoids the major disadvantages of the available job level classification based on experts' judgements, which is based on a very limited number of job observations and has become severely obsolete.

The job level classification we here develop is based on the educational background of the working population employed in the occupational segment, as measured in the 1994 Dutch Labour Force Survey of Statistics Netherlands. We differentiated between 5 skill levels and 9 fields of education. Each occupation is assigned to the level and field of the dominant educational level(s) and field(s) among the workers in that particular occupation.

Occupational level

To classify the job level of each occupational segment, the types of education distinguished have to be grouped by educational levels.[7] The skill level of a type of education is defined institutionally. Five educational levels are distinguished: primary education only, lower education (junior general secondary education and pre-vocational education), intermediate education (senior general secondary education and intermediate vocational education), higher vocational education and university education. Each occupation is classified on the basis of the fractions of people working in that occupation who have a certain educational level. If more than 50 per cent of all people working in an occupation have been trained at a certain level, and the percentage of workers at every other skill level is much lower, that occupation is assigned to that level. If none of the educational levels meet this limit, but two or more educational levels together have more than 50 per cent of all persons in that occupation, the occupation is assigned to both levels (see Appendix A).

Appendix B (table B1) shows the resulting classification of the job level of each occupation. Workers with a particular educational background are said to work on their own occupational level if they are employed in any occupation with that level. Since this Chapter focuses on high-skilled workers only, the occupations will be grouped for the analysis of changes in employment patterns into occupations at the (1) 'university level' (UE), (2) 'higher vocational education level' (HVE), (3) 'high level', which is a combination of higher vocational education and university education or of either of these with intermediate educational levels (HVE/UE), and (4) 'intermediate and lower level' (IVE). So occupations at the UE and HVE levels comprise the occupational domains for people with university or higher vocational educational level, respectively, and the HVE/UE level occupations comprise their shared domain. University graduates working in an occupation at HVE or IVE level are considered to be working below their occupational level. The same holds for HVE graduates employed in IVE-level occupations.

Occupational domain

In a similar way, the occupational domain of each occupational segment is determined according to the dominant field of study of the workers employed in the occupation concerned. Table B2 in Appendix B gives the 9 fields of study which are the basis of this classification and the types of education that fall under each field. The grouping of the various types of education by fields is independent of the educational level of a type of education. However, there are some fields that correspond only to particular levels of education, e.g. the fields 'teaching' and 'general education'.

Appendix B (table B3) shows the resulting classification of the occupational domain of each occupation. Several occupational segments can be classified as specific occupational domains for a particular field of study. Other segments could be considered as the combined domain of two fields of study. Only a few occupations are classified as general: intermediate sports occupations, lower administrative occupations and the intermediate socio-cultural occupations. In these occupations the educational background of the workers is very diverse. In presenting the results of the analyses of employment shifts we will distinguish between workers who are employed in their own occupational domain, those in a domain that is shared with graduates of another field of education (the *shared domain*), and those employed in alternative domains, which refer to occupations that do no recruit workers with a particular educational background and occupations which are the more or less specific domains of other types of education.

The actual labour market position of high-skilled workers

This Section presents an overview of the actual job level and domain structure of employment for the various types of education within higher education, based on the classification procedure described in the previous Section. Table 1 shows the employment structure, by job level, for each type of education. As mentioned in the previous Section, we have regrouped the job levels into 4 categories:
- intermediate and less than intermediate level occupations: IVE;
- higher vocational education level occupations: HVE;
- university level occupations: UE;
- high level occupations: HVE/UE.[8]

The table shows that almost a third of the graduates of higher vocational education are employed in IVE-level jobs, whereas almost 30% of the graduates of university education work in jobs below university level.

The table also shows that many high-skilled workers are employed in the combined HVE/UE level jobs. This holds for both Higher Vocational Education (43%) and University Education (54%). These high percentages are partly due to the relatively high level of aggregation at which we had to classify the job level of occupations.

Table 2 gives a similar overview with respect to the occupational domain structure of employment for each type of education. The table shows that almost half of the graduates of both Higher Vocational Education and University Education are employed in the specific domain of their educational background, whereas 37% and 48%, respectively, work in alternative domains which do not recruit workers with a particular educational background or are the specific domain of another type of education.

Table 1
Employment structure by job level per type of education, 1994

	IVE %	HVE %	UE %	HVE/UE %
Higher Vocational Education	*31*	*23*	*3*	*43*
HVE Teacher training	16	71	1	12
HVE Interpreter and translator	39	18	1	42
HVE Agriculture and environmental science	43	3	13	41
HVE Non-medical laboratory	18	4	8	70
HVE Civil engineering	27	2	5	66
HVE Mechanical engineering	26	2	6	66
HVE Electronic and information technology	21	3	3	72
HVE Transport and harbour	40	2	4	55
HVE Medical laboratory	19	1	1	79
HVE Nursing and paramedical services	54	2	0	44
HVE Business administration	51	5	1	43
HVE Accounting	41	1	1	58
HVE Commercial information science	13	1	1	85
HVE Tourism and recreation	81	1	1	17
HVE Commerce	66	1	1	32
HVE Business administration technology	32	0	3	65
HVE Administrative, legal and fiscal	47	2	23	28
HVE Social and cultural	26	5	3	66
HVE Fine Arts	12	47	0	42
HVE Police, fire and defense forces	54	4	17	26
University Education	*13*	*16*	*17*	*54*
UE Arts	17	40	2	41
UE Theology	4	16	62	18
UE Agriculture and environmental science	11	14	23	52
UE Mathematics and natural sciences	5	26	29	40
UE Civil engineering	7	6	14	73
UE Mechanical engineering	8	13	22	57
UE Electrical engineering and information technology	8	9	9	73
UE Veterinary and medical sciences and dentistry	3	3	3	90
UE Pharmacy	0	9	12	79
UE Economics, econometrics and business administration	21	9	6	64
UE Management	19	4	4	73
UE Information science	26	5	4	65
UE Law	22	6	54	18
UE Public administration	17	3	30	49
UE Social sciences	16	21	6	57
UE Fine Arts	4	77	1	18

Source: ROA

Table 2
Employment structure by occupational domain per type of education, 1994

	specific domain %	shared domain %	alternative domains %	main competitor
Higher Vocational Education				
HVE Teacher training	49	14	37	Commerce & administration/General Education
HVE Interpreter and translator	70	-	30	Commerce & administration/General Education
HVE Agriculture and environmental science	27	-	73	Technical
HVE Non-medical laboratory	24	-	76	Medical
HVE Civil engineering	46	6	48	Commerce & administration/General Education
HVE Mechanical engineering	75	4	21	Commerce & administration/General Education
HVE Electronic and information technology	62	6	32	Commerce & administration
HVE Transport and harbour	46	5	48	Commerce & administration
HVE Medical laboratory	51	19	30	Commerce & administration/General Education
HVE Nursing and paramedical services	68	-	32	Technical
HVE Business administration	80	-	20	Technical/General Education
HVE Accounting	16	53	31	Technical
HVE Commercial information science	31	50	19	Technical
HVE Tourism and recreation	69	12	19	Technical
HVE Commerce	1	79	21	Technical
HVE Business administration technology	9	74	17	Technical
HVE Administrative, legal and fiscal	23	31	46	Technical
HVE Social and cultural	35	48	17	Technical
HVE Fine Arts	43	-	57	Commerce & administration/General Education
HVE Police, fire and defense forces	39	21	40	Technical
	50	-	50	Technical

Table 2 (continued)
Employment structure by occupational domain per type of education, 1994

	specific domain %	shared domain %	alternative domains %	main competitor
University Education				
UE Arts	44	8	48	Teaching
UE Theology	15	-	85	Teaching
UE Agriculture and environmental science	66	-	34	Technical
UE Mathematics and natural sciences	17	-	83	Teaching
UE Civil engineering	36	3	61	Commerce & administration
UE Mechanical engineering	65	3	31	Teaching
UE Electrical engineering and information technology	61	4	35	Commerce & administration
UE Veterinary and medical sciences and dentistry	45	4	51	Social, Cultural and Arts
UE Pharmacy	81	-	19	Technical
UE Economics, econometrics and business administration	56	-	44	Technical
UE Management	37	28	35	Technical
UE Information science	15	36	49	Technical
UE Law	51	31	18	Technical
UE Public administration	56	26	19	Technical
UE Social sciences	62	18	21	Teaching
UE Fine Arts	30	-	70	Teaching
	29	-	71	Teaching

It can be seen that HVE Tourism and recreation, HVE Commerce and HVE Business administration have particularly many graduates employed in the shared domain. Only a few types of education at the academic level have a substantial group of graduates employed in this segment. However, several types of education have large groups of graduates working in an alternative domain. This holds in particular for graduates from the agricultural and environmental sciences at both HVE and university level, who are employed mainly in the occupational domain of technical studies.

Future changes in the occupational level and domain of high-skilled workers 1995-2000

Components of the change in employment levels

As mentioned in the second Section, on ROA's forecasting model, the employment available for particular types of education is determined by several processes. First, changes in the labour demand in an economic sector affect employment for the skill categories employed in that sector. In addition to this *industry effect*, there will also be different changes in the employment levels for the various occupational classes within a single economic sector. This *occupational effect* is due to some extent to the heterogeneity of the economic sectors as these are defined, but also to changes in the activities within an economic sector. Moreover, the skills which are demanded in these occupations also change. Because of these changes, some types of education which are better adapted to the developments in the demand for qualifications will show a positive *education effect*. These three effects combined represent the total expansion demand for a particular type of education. As a result of discrepancies between labour demand[9] and supply there are, inevitably, additional shifts in demand as employers adjust their needs in accordance with the availability of workers. The latter effect is designated the *substitution effect*. As described in the fourth Section, on the classification of occupational segments, we can differentiate here between *active* substitution, resulting from supply-demand mismatches for the type of education concerned, and *passive* substitution due to spill-over effects from supply-demand mismatches for other types of education.

In recent years demand has lagged behind supply for a number of specific disciplines at University and Intermediate Vocational Education levels, for the Higher Vocational Education level, and especially at the Preparatory Vocational Education level (Borghans, 1997). This has meant that school-leavers from these types of education have been forced to switch to other occupations. However, because of the expected decline in the supply of school-leavers and the increasing demand for newcomers, the macro-relations between demand and supply for school-leavers are expected to become more favourable in coming years. This means that the crowding-out processes on the labour market will be much reduced and opposite tendencies may occur as labour market discrepancies are expected to move in the direction of excess demand in the coming years. Obviously these discrepancies will also result in shifts in the occupational domains of particular types of education.

Table 3 gives an overview of the relevance of the various components of the expected development of employment in the period 1995-2000 for each type of higher education. The table shows that Higher Vocational Education and University Education have similar industry effects. However, the increase in employment for graduates of university education is higher than the employment increase for HVE graduates due to somewhat higher occupational, educational and passive substitution effects. The negative active substitution effects indicate that, due to labour shortages, a substantial part of the increase in labour demand for both HVE and university education will probably not be filled by people from the skill categories at which demand was initially directed.

In general the differences between the industry effects for the various types of education are not large. Types of education which are dependent on employment levels in the public sector show the smallest industry effects. On the other hand, the types of education which are concentrated in non-commercial services (in particular the health sector) show the highest industry effects.

The variance in the occupational effect is much larger. The information technology studies, at both HVE and University level, are expected to have very high occupational effects, whereas for UE Law and UE Theology the occupational effects are even expected to be negative. For the latter type of education this negative effect indicates that the employment for pastoral vocations does not follow the relatively high employment growth in non-commercial services.

The technical, economic, management and social sciences studies at university level show particularly high educational effects. This means that for various occupations employers will upgrade demands for these types of education from lower to higher levels of education. Due to the gradual differences, in economic/-administrative occupations, between jobs at different levels, upgrading is in practice rather easy for these types of education. These studies also have the highest passive substitution effects due to the severe supply shortages expected in the labour market segments where the graduates from these fields are employed. This can be explained by the fact that shortages are predicted for the economic/administrative types of education at the higher levels, and there are also many other types of education which are rather similar to these types of education.

The negative active substitution effects for these studies indicate that a substantial part of the increase in labour demand for these types of education will not be met, due to shortages in labour supply. The same holds for the medical and laboratory studies at both HVE and academic level and for HVE Teacher training

Table 3
Components of the change in employment levels per type of education, 1995-2000

	industry effect %	occupational effect %	educational effect %	substitution effect passive %	substitution effect active %
Higher Vocational Education					
HVE Teacher training	-1	6	5	4	-14
HVE Interpreter and translator	3	6	2	1	-9
HVE Agriculture and environmental science	2	6	4	4	-2
HVE Non-medical laboratory	6	10	6	7	-37
HVE Civil engineering	5	5	5	7	-28
HVE Mechanical engineering	5	6	6	6	-9
HVE Electronic and information technology	5	16	6	9	-24
HVE Transport and harbour	4	2	9	1	-21
HVE Medical laboratory	8	5	3	1	-17
HVE Nursing and paramedical services	9	3	6	1	-11
HVE Business administration	4	6	7	5	-3
HVE Accounting	5	13	7	8	-45
HVE Commercial information science	5	26	5	11	-40
HVE Tourism and recreation	3	-3	7	1	26
HVE Commerce	5	5	8	5	5
HVE Business administration technology	5	11	6	7	4
HVE Administrative, legal and fiscal	3	3	2	5	-6
HVE Social and cultural	5	3	4	5	-9
HVE Fine Arts	6	4	6	3	-8
HVE Police, fire and defense forces	0	-5	8	6	9

Table 3 (continued)
Components of the change in employment levels per type of education, 1995-2000

	industry effect %	occupational effect %	educational effect %	substitution effect	
				passive %	active %
University Education					
UE Arts	4	7	9	7	-14
UE Theology	1	7	9	4	1
UE Agriculture and environmental science	8	-2	9	4	-38
UE Mathematics and natural sciences	2	7	8	9	9
UE Civil engineering	3	11	8	10	-22
UE Mechanical engineering	4	5	11	12	-32
UE Electrical engineering and information technology	3	8	11	11	-4
UE Veterinary and medical sciences and dentistry	4	15	12	12	-19
UE Pharmacy	9	5	3	2	-22
UE Economics, econometrics and business administration	6	5	4	5	5
UE Management	4	16	14	9	-27
UE Information science	5	11	16	9	-15
UE Law	4	17	13	11	-15
UE Public administration	2	-2	9	6	3
UE Social sciences	3	10	11	9	-18
UE Fine Arts	3	5	10	6	-13
	0	5	5	4	22

and UE Theology.

Changes in occupational levels

Table 4 offers more insight into the relevance of the various components of the change in employment levels at each of the job levels distinguished. The table shows that the rationing effects of supply shortages for studies at the HVE and University levels are not heavily concentrated at a particular job level. For both HVE and University studies, the negative active substitution effects are strongest in jobs at the shared HVE/UE level. However it should be remembered that the increase in labour demand for both HVE and university graduates is by far the highest at this job level. This indicates that employers in the growth segments of the labour market for high-skilled workers will find it particularly difficult to recruit the number of high-skilled people they need.

Table 4
Components of the change in employment levels at each occupational level, 1995-2000

	IVE %	HVE %	UE %	HVE/UE %	All segments %
Higher vocational education					
Industry effect	5	-2	3	6	4
Occupational effect	-3	6	2	12	6
Educational effect	9	0	-4	5	5
Substitution effect: passive	-1	0	14	8	4
Substitution effect: active	-16	-1	-14	-20	-14
Total	-5	4	3	12	4
University education					
Industry effect	4	-3	3	6	4
Occupational effect	-4	6	1	12	7
Educational effect	16	0	6	12	9
Substitution effect: passive	0	0	13	10	7
Substitution effect: active	-12	1	-16	-19	-14
Total	4	4	7	21	13

The table also shows that active substitution effects are relatively strong in the IVE-level jobs. This means that the excess demand in the market segments for several studies in higher education does decrease the number of high-skilled workers employed at relatively low job levels, as might be expected. As mentioned above this relates particularly to laboratory studies, accounting and the information science studies at HVE level and to mathematics and natural sciences at university level. Moreover, the positive passive substitution effects are concentrated at the high level jobs (UE and HVE/UE), which indicates that the pull-effects which result from the excess demand for related types of education are strongest at these job levels.

The high positive educational effects for both HVE and university graduates in jobs at the IVE level are remarkable. This indicates that there are substantial autonomous upgrading processes which cause an increasing demand for high-skilled workers in these jobs. The different signs of the educational effect in UE-level jobs for the HVE and UE graduates indicate that in these jobs upgrading processes are shifting labour demand in favour of workers with a university background. But for HVE Tourism and recreation, in particular, the increase in employment at the IVE level results to a much larger extent from the HVE graduates crowding less skilled workers out due to the excess supply for this type of education.

Table 4 gives an overview of the expected change in employment levels for high-skilled workers at the various job levels distinguished. The table shows that employment growth for graduates of both HVE and University Education is expected to be highest at the shared HVE/UE level. University Education will also have a relatively high employment growth in university-level jobs.

The employment decrease for HVE graduates in IVE-level jobs is a particular indicator that the overeducation of high-skilled workers can be expected to diminish. However there are large differences between the various types of education in this respect.[10] Laboratory studies, accounting and the commercial information science studies at HVE level show particularly large decreases in employment in occupations at IVE level. On the other hand, HVE Tourism and recreation, HVE Commerce, UE Fine Arts and UE Law show relatively high increases in employment in IVE-level jobs.

The table also shows that several types of education will have different employment changes at the various job-levels. For instance, HVE Commercial information science is expected to face a large fall in employment decrease in IVE-level jobs, but a substantial increase in employment in HVE/UE-level jobs. Moreover, the table clearly indicates that for some studies supply shortages will be manifest at a particular job level, for instance for HVE Medical laboratory, HVE Accounting, HVE Commercial information science, UE Theology and UE Veterinary and medical sciences and dentistry.

Table 5
Future employment growth at each occupational level per type of education, 1995-2000

	IVE %	HVE %	UE %	HVE/UE %
Higher Vocational Education	-5	4	3	12
HVE Teacher training	-19	3	-1	-2
HVE Interpreter and translator	17	3	0	26
HVE Agriculture and environmental science	-1	3	35	28
HVE Non-medical laboratory	-34	3	-9	-3
HVE Civil engineering	-21	2	2	-3
HVE Mechanical engineering	0	1	22	21
HVE Electronic and information technology	-11	4	2	17
HVE Transport and harbour	-15	2	9	2
HVE Medical laboratory	-27	1	-30	7
HVE Nursing and paramedical services	11	-1	0	2
HVE Business administration	5	5	25	41
HVE Accounting	-38	17	32	4
HVE Commercial information science	-32	1	-14	13
HVE Tourism and recreation	43	0	56	72
HVE Commerce	20	2	38	48
HVE Business administration technology	13	0	23	44
HVE Administrative, legal and fiscal	-3	1	-13	35
HVE Social and cultural	2	4	-17	12
HVE Fine Arts	-1	12	-1	14
HVE Police, fire and defense forces	14	1	7	34
University Education	4	4	7	21
UE Arts	16	3	6	44
UE Theology	-89	-5	2	-122
UE Agriculture and environmental science	18	3	55	41
UE Mathematics and natural sciences	-18	3	11	20
UE Civil engineering	-3	3	-8	1
UE Mechanical engineering	4	3	47	41
UE Electrical engineering and information technology	-1	3	26	33
UE Veterinary and medical sciences and dentistry	-14	3	-104	-1
UE Pharmacy	0	1	40	26
UE Economics, econometrics & business administration	-12	3	-1	28
UE Management	2	2	94	33
UE Information science	1	0	78	54
UE Law	21	4	8	49
UE Public administration	-5	1	-19	50
UE Social sciences	2	3	-2	18
UE Fine Arts	52	22	45	72

Table 6
Future changes in employment in each occupational domain per type of education, 1995-2000

	specific domain %	shared domain %	alternative domains %
Higher Vocational Education	*8*	*-3*	*2*
HVE Teacher training	3	0	-11
HVE Interpreter and translator	19	0	19
HVE Agriculture and environmental science	-7	0	24
HVE Non-medical laboratory	-17	138	-2
HVE Civil engineering	-9	4	1
HVE Mechanical engineering	14	18	15
HVE Electronic and information technology	-1	4	23
HVE Transport and harbour	-6	-5	-2
HVE Medical laboratory	15	0	-30
HVE Nursing and paramedical services	18	0	-31
HVE Business administration	60	8	18
HVE Accounting	16	-31	-11
HVE Commercial information science	17	-27	-9
HVE Tourism and recreation	29	43	20
HVE Commerce	67	23	27
HVE Business administration technology	68	15	28
HVE Administrative, legal and fiscal	12	6	-2
HVE Social and cultural	7	0	9
HVE Fine Arts	14	10	9
HVE Police, fire and defense forces	14	0	20
University Education	*16*	*12*	*11*
UE Arts	27	0	21
UE Theology	-6	0	-3
UE Agriculture and environmental science	29	0	37
UE Mathematics and natural sciences	12	10	9
UE Civil engineering	-5	9	9
UE Mechanical engineering	35	38	20
UE Electrical engineering and information technology	19	19	27
UE Veterinary and medical sciences and dentistry	15	0	-83
UE Pharmacy	14	0	32
UE Economics, econometrics & business administration	39	-4	7
UE Management	61	17	21
UE Information science	58	12	8
UE Law	10	26	26
UE Public administration	21	-2	13
UE Social sciences	11	0	11
UE Fine Arts	80	0	19

Shifts in the occupational domain

Table 6 shows that the increase in employment for both HVE and university education is concentrated to some extent in the specific occupational domains of the various types of education. For HVE graduates the employment increase in this specific domain is 8%, for university graduates 16%. Employment for HVE graduates in the shared domain is even expected to decrease, whereas employment in the alternative domains shows only a slight increase. Employment for UE graduates in the shared and alternative domains will also increase substantially, although less than in the specific domain. The commercial and business administration studies at HVE level and the management, information sciences and Fine Arts studies at university level are expected to enjoy large increases in employment in their specific occupational domains. There are several fields of study for which the change in employment will be different in the three occupational domains distinguished here. Once again, this indicates that supply shortages are probably concentrated in particular domains, particularly in the shared domain and the alternative domains. This holds, for example, for HVE Accounting, HVE Medical laboratory, HVE Nursing and paramedical services, HVE Commercial information science, UE Theology and UE Veterinary and medical sciences and dentistry.

Table 7 gives an overview of the relevance of the various components of the change in employment levels for the three occupational domains distinguished. The table clearly shows that, particularly for the studies at HVE level, the rationing of employment due to the expected excess demand for several types of education is concentrated in the shared and alternative occupational domains. This indicates that the specific occupational domain suffers less from these active substitution effects. However, for several types of education, such as HVE Non-medical laboratory, HVE Accounting, HVE Commercial information sciences and UE Civil engineering, the rationing of labour demand in the specific occupational segment is also high. The specific occupational domain also appears to have the largest positive passive substitution processes. This means that supply shortages for related types of education that occur in the specific domain of a particular type of education are resolved partly by recruiting more graduates from the latter type of education. This in particular relates to the commerce and administration studies at HVE and university level. It can be concluded that both passive and active substitution processes lead to a shift in the occupational structure of employment of these types of education in the direction of the specific occupational domains.

On the other hand, the educational effects show that upgrading processes in favour of high-skilled workers are strongest in the shared or general domain. These effects are strongest for studies in the information science, technical, law and public administration fields at university level. However the relatively low occupational effects in this shared domain show that the employment shares of these occupations are expected to decrease. Although the differences are relatively small, the table shows that for university graduates the industry effect is strongest in their specific domains, whereas for the HVE graduates the industry effect is strongest in the shared and alternative domains.

Table 7
Components of the change in employment levels in each occupational domain, 1995-2000

	Specific domain %	Shared domain %	Alternative domains %	All segments %
Higher vocational education				
Industry effect	3	5	5	4
Occupational effect	8	-1	6	6
Educational effect	3	9	6	5
Substitution effect: passive	4	1	4	4
Substitution effect: active	-9	-18	-18	-14
Total	8	-3	2	4
University education				
Industry effect	6	5	2	4
Occupational effect	7	1	8	7
Educational effect	8	18	9	9
Substitution effect: passive	9	4	6	7
Substitution effect: active	-13	-16	-14	-14
Total	16	12	11	13

Conclusions

This Chapter has analyzed the implications of the expected changes in supply and demand for high-skilled workers in the Netherlands in the period 1995-2000 for shifts in both the job level and the occupational domain of high-skilled workers. It has also examined the various components of the expected changes, i.e. the industry effect, occupational effect, educational effect and the substitution effects due to ex ante supply-demand mismatches. Since the ex ante gap between supply and demand for a particular type of education affects both the occupational structure of employment for that particular type of education and the employment structure for related types of education, we distinguished between active and passive substitution effects, respectively.

The analyses show that expansion demand for university graduates is expected to be higher than expansion demand for the graduates of Higher Vocational Education. This is due particularly to higher occupational, educational and passive (pull) substitution effects. However, there is a large variance in these three effects for the various types of education at HVE and university level. Due to the expected excess demand, employment growth for both HVE and university graduates will be rationed considerably, as indicated by the relatively large active substitution effects.

Employment growth for graduates of both HVE and University Education is expected to be highest in jobs at the shared HVE/UE level, and university studies will also have a relatively high employment growth in jobs at the university level. The decline in employment for HVE graduates in IVE-level jobs indicates that the job level of high-skilled workers can be expected to increase, although there are substantial differences between the various types of education in this respect. More detailed analyses showed that the decrease in employment in IVE-level jobs is indeed to a large extent due to excess demand for graduates from the types of higher education concerned. However, for several types of education the educational upgrading effect reveals a substantial increase in labour demand for high-skilled workers in occupational segments which are classified at a lower job level. The expansion demand for high-skilled workers due to these demand-led upgrading processes can be expected to be substantially rationed in the coming years for several types of education.

The analyses of expected developments in the occupational domains of high-skilled workers showed that, for both HVE and University Education, the increase in employment will be concentrated largely in the specific occupational domains of the various types of education. Particularly for studies at the HVE level, the rationing of employment due to the expected excess demand for several of these studies is concentrated in the shared and alternative occupational domains, while the specific occupational domains will suffer less from these substitution processes. Altogether, this means that both active and passive (pull) substitution processes will lead to a shift in the occupational structure of employment for various studies in higher education in the direction of the specific occupational domains. In a pattern similar to that which emerged from the analysis of expected shifts in job levels, the expansion demand due to demand-led upgrading processes will also suffer most from rationing, due to the expected excess demand for several studies, in the shared occupational domains.

Notes

1. i.e., in *hogescholen*, approximately equivalent to technical institutes.
2. A comprehensive explanation can be found in Borghans et al. (1995). See also de Grip, Borghans and Willems (1995).
3. For the occupational forecasts, an additional module separates these forecasts into forecasts for 93 occupational classes.
4. Because of the heterogeneity of teaching as a profession, the degree of overlap in this occupation has not been included when calculating the competition index.
5. In that case employers will probably have to compensate for the lower productivity of these workers by giving them additional training.
6. For convenience sake we assume that demand does not change.
7. For this analysis we used the 54 types of education distinguished in the earlier versions of ROA's information system instead of the 79 types of education distinguished in the most recent version, because the more aggregated data leads to less empty cells in the education x occupation matrix.
8. Strictly speaking the HVE/UE level also refers to occupational segments which are dominated by a combination of higher vocational education or university education and intermediate educational levels.
9. This demand refers to both expansion and replacement demand (see Figure 1).
10. It should be mentioned here that the figures only indicate the employment growth percentages for the various job-level segments, and in several cases the absolute numbers of graduates employed in these segments are small (cf. Table 1).

References

Borghans, L. (1992), *A histo-topographic map of the Dutch university studies*, ROA-W-1992/5E, Research Centre for Education and the Labour Market: Maastricht.

Borghans, L., Grip, A. de, Dekker, R., Matheeuwsen, A., Smits, W., Willems, E. (1995), *Methodiek van het informatiesysteem onderwijs-arbeidsmarkt 1995*, ROA-W-1995/3, Research Centre for Education and the Labour Market: Maastricht.

Borghans, L., Grip, A. de, and Smits, W. (1996), 'De arbeidsmarkt voor hoger opgeleiden tot 2000', *Tijdschrift voor Hoger Onderwijs*, 14 (1), pp. 3-21.

Borghans, L. (1997), *Effects of Supply and Demand on the Employment Structure*, (forthcoming), Research Centre for Education and the Labour Market: Maastricht.

Borghans, L., Heijke, H. (1996), 'Forecasting the Educational Structure of Occupations: A Manpower Requirement Approach with Substitution', *Labour*, 10 (1), pp. 151-192.

Cohn, E., and Kahn, S.P. (1995), 'The Wage Effects of Overschooling Revisited', *Labour Economics*, 2 (1), pp. 67-77.

Duncan, G.J., Hoffman, S.D. (1981), 'The Incidence and Wage Effects of Overeducation', *Economics of Education Review*, 1 (1), pp. 57-83.

Freeman, R.B. (1976), *The Overeducated American*, Academic Press: New York.

Grip, A. de, Borghans, L., Willems, E. (1995), *Methodology of the ROA information system on occupational groups and types of education*, ROA-W-1995/1E, Research Centre for Education and the Labour Market: Maastricht.

Grip, A. de, Velden, R.K.W. van der, Wieling, M.H. (1993), *De inpassing van schoolverlatersinformatie in het ROA-informatiesysteem onderwijs-arbeidsmarkt*, ROA-R-1993/9, Research Centre for Education and the Labour Market: Maastricht.

Groot, W. (1993), 'Overeducation and the Returns to Enterprise-related Schooling', *Economics of Education Review*, 12 (4), pp. 299-309.

Huijgen, F. (1989), *De kwalitatieve structuur van de werkgelegenheid in Nederland, deel I*, OSA-Voorstudie V33, OSA: Den Haag.

ROA (1995), *The Labour Market by Education and Occupation to 2000*, ROA-R-1995/3E, Research Centre for Education and the Labour Market: Maastricht.

Spee, A.A.J., Coppens, I.M.T. (1996), 'Tussen hoop en hopeloos: Parallellen van belangen in het Hoger Onderwijs', *Tijdschrift voor Hoger Onderwijs*, 14 (1), pp. 22-36.

Spenner, K.I. (1985), 'The Upgrading and Downgrading of Occupations: Issues, Evidence, and Implications for Education', *Review of Educational Research*, 55 (2), pp. 125-154.

Tsang, M., Levin, H. (1985), The Economics of Overeducation, *Economics of Education Review*, 4 (2) , pp. 93-104.

Verdugo, R., Verdugo, N. (1989), 'The impact of surplus schooling on earnings: some additional findings', *Journal of Human Resources*, 24 (4), pp. 629-643.

Wieling, M.H., Borghans, L. (1995), *Discrepancies between Demand and Supply and Adjustment Processes on the Labour Market*, ROA-RM-1995/5E, Research Centre for Education and the Labour Market: Maastricht.

Willems, E.J.T.A, Grip, A. de (1993), 'Forecasting Replacement Demand by Occupation and Education', *International Journal of Forecasting*, 9 (3), pp. 173-185.

Appendix A: Classification criteria

Job level

To classify the job level of each occupational segment we used the following criteria:

If $x_{ij} > 0.5$ and $x_{i-1j} < 0.4$ and $x_{i+1j} < 0.4$ then level$_j = i$
If $x_{ij} > 0.5$ and $x_{i-1j} > 0.4$ then level$_j = i-1/i$
If $x_{ij} > 0.5$ and $x_{i+1j} > 0.4$ then level$_j = i/i+1$
If $x_{ij} < 0.5$ $\forall i$ and $x_{ij}+x_{i-1j} > 0.5$ and $x_{ij}+x_{i+1j} < 0.5$ then level$_j = i-1/i$
If $x_{ij} < 0.5$ $\forall i$ and $x_{ij}+x_{i+1j} > 0.5$ and $x_{ij}+x_{i-1j} < 0.5$ then level$_j = i/i+1$
If $x_{ij} < 0.5$ $\forall i$ and $x_{ij}+x_{i-1j} > 0.5$ and $x_{ij}+x_{i+1j} > 0.5$ then level$_j = i-1/i/i+1$

Where:
x_{ij} is the proportion of people working in occupation j who have an educational level i, j = 1,...,49

Job domain

To classify the job domain of each occupational segment we used criteria similar to those used with respect to the job level:

If $y_{kj} > 0.5$ and $y_{kj}-y_{lj} > 0.1$ $\forall$ l then field$_j = k$
If $y_{kj} > 0.5$ and $\exists$ l $y_{kj}-y_{lj} < 0.1$ then field$_j = k/l$
If $y_{kj} < 0.5$ and $\exists$ l $y_{kj}+y_{lj} > 0.5$ and $y_{kj}+y_{mj} < 0.5$ $\forall$ m ≠ l then field$_j = k/l$
If $0.4 < y_{kj} < 0.5$ and $\exists$ l $y_{kj}+y_{lj} > 0.5$ and $\exists$ m $y_{kj}+y_{mj} > 0.5$ and $y_{lj} > 0.2$ and $y_{lm} < 0.2$ then field$_j = k/l$
If $0.4 < y_{kj} < 0.5$ and $\exists$ l $y_{kj}+y_{lj} > 0.5$ and $\exists$ m $y_{kj}+y_{mj} > 0.5$ and $y_{lj} < 0.2$ $\forall$ l then field$_j = k$/general
Otherwise field$_j$ = general

Where:
y_{kj} is the proportion of people working in occupation j who have an education in field k, j = 1,...,49

Appendix B:

Table B1
Classification of the job level of the occupational segments

Occupational segment	Job level
Higher teaching professions	HVE
Intermediate sports occupations	IVE
Higher literary professions	HVE/UE
Higher theological vocations	UE
Intermediate art & design trades	IVE/HVE
Higher professions in the arts and design	HVE
Lower agricultural occupations	PVE/IVE
Higher agricultural professions	HVE/UE
Lower technical and industrial occupations	Primary/PVE/IVE
Intermediate technical and industrial trades	IVE/HVE
Higher technical and industrial professions	UE
Lower food and beverage occupations	PVE/IVE
Lower textile occupations	Primary/PVE/IVE
Lower wood and paper occupations	PVE/IVE
Lower printing industry occupations	IVE
Lower chemical industry occupations	IVE
Lower metals industry occupations	PVE/IVE
Intermediate mechanical trades	IVE
Higher mechanical and metals industry professions	IVE/HVE
Lower electrical occupations	Primary/PVE/IVE
Intermediate electrical trades	IVE
Higher electrical professions	IVE/HVE
Lower building materials industry occupations	Primary/PVE/IVE
Lower construction and installation occupations	Primary/PVE/IVE
Intermediate construction and installation trades	IVE
Higher construction and installation professions	IVE/HVE/UE
Lower transport occupations	Primary/PVE/IVE
Lower marine and inland waterway occupations	PVE/IVE
Intermediate marine and inland waterways occupations	IVE/HVE
Lower road and rail occupations	Primary/PVE/IVE
Intermediate air transport and miscellaneous transport occupations	PVE/IVE/HVE
Intermediate medical and paramedical occupations	IVE
Higher medical and paramedical professions	HVE/UE
Higher commercial and administrative professions	IVE/HVE
Lower administrative occupations	PVE/IVE
Intermediate administrative occupations	IVE
Higher administrative professions	IVE/HVE
Lower sales and purchasing occupations	PVE/IVE

Table B1 (continued)
Classification of the job level of the occupational segments

Occupational segment	Job level
Intermediate sales and purchasing occupations	IVE
Higher legal and government professions	UE
Intermediate social-cultural occupations	IVE/HVE/UE
Higher social-cultural professions	IVE/HVE/UE
Lower hotel and catering occupations	PVE/IVE
Intermediate hotel and catering occupations	IVE
Lower service occupations	PVE/IVE
Intermediate service occupations	IVE
Intermediate police, fire, and security occupations	IVE
Intermediate military occupations	IVE
Occupations not classified above	PVE/IVE/HVE

PVE = Preparatory Vocational Education
IVE = Intermediate Vocational Education
HVE = Higher Vocational Education
UE = University Education

Table B2
Fields of study and related types of education

Technical
Preparatory Vocational Education, Technical
Preparatory Vocational Education, Transport & harbour
Intermediate Vocational Education, Non-Medical laboratory
Intermediate Vocational Education, Engineering
Intermediate Vocational Education, Transport & harbour
Higher Vocational Education, non-medical laboratory
Higher Vocational Education, Engineering
Higher Transport & harbour
Academic Education, Mathematics & natural sciences
Academic Education, Engineering

Agriculture
Preparatory Vocational Education, Agriculture
Intermediate Vocational Education, Agriculture
Higher Vocational Education, Agriculture
Academic Education, Agriculture

Community services
Preparatory Vocational Education, Community care, hotel & catering
Intermediate Vocational Education, Community care
Intermediate Vocational Education, Hotel, catering & hairdressing
Higher Vocational Education, Hotel & catering industry

Medical
Intermediate Vocational Education, Medical laboratory
Intermediate Vocational Education, Nursing & para-medical services
Higher Vocational Education, Medical laboratory
Higher Vocational Education, Nursing & physiotherapy etc.
Academic Education, Veterinary & medical sciences & dentistry
Academic Education, Pharmacy

Commerce & administration
Preparatory Vocational Education, Commerce & administration
Intermediate Vocational Education, Commerce & administration
Intermediate Vocational Education, administrative, legal & fiscal
Higher Vocational Education, Commerce & administration
Higher Vocational Education, Business administration technology
Higher Vocational Education, Administrative, legal & fiscal
Academic Education, Economics, Econometrics & business administration
Academic Education, Law & public administration

Table B2 (continued)
Fields of study and related types of education

Socio-cultural /Arts
Intermediate Vocational Education, Social & cultural
Higher Vocational Education, Interpreter & translator
Higher Vocational Education, Theology
Higher Vocational Education, Social & cultural
Higher Vocational Education, Fine Arts
Academic Education, Arts
Academic Education, Theology
Academic Education, Social sciences
Academic Education, Fine Arts

Teaching
Higher Vocational Education, Teacher training
Academic Education, Teacher training

Security
Preparatory Vocational Education, Security
Intermediate Vocational Education, Police, fire & defense forces
Higher Vocational Education, Police, fire & defense forces

General Education
Primary Education
Preparatory General Secondary Education
Higher General Secondary Education

Table B3
Occupational domains of the various occupational segments

Occupational segment	Domain
Higher teaching professions	Teaching
Intermediate sports occupations	General
Higher literary professions	Socio-cultural and arts
Higher theological vocations	Socio-cultural and arts
Intermediate art & design trades	Technical/Socio-cultural & arts
Higher professions in the arts and design	Socio-cultural and arts
Lower agricultural occupations	Agriculture
Higher agricultural professions	Agriculture
Lower technical and industrial occupations	Technical
Intermediate technical and industrial trades	Technical
Higher technical and industrial professions	Technical
Lower food and beverage occupations	Technical
Lower textile occupations	Technical/General Education
Lower wood and paper occupations	Technical
Lower printing industry occupations	Technical
Lower chemical industry occupations	Technical
Lower metals industry occupations	Technical
Intermediate mechanical trades	Technical
Higher mechanical and metals industry professions	Technical
Lower electrical occupations	Technical/General Education
Intermediate electrical trades	Technical
Higher electrical professions	Technical
Lower building materials industry occupations	Technical/General Education
Lower construction and installation occupations	Technical
Intermediate construction and installation trades	Technical
Higher construction and installation professions	Technical
Lower transport occupations	Technical/General Education
Lower marine and inland waterway occupations	Technical
Intermediate marine and inland waterways occupations	Technical
Lower road and rail occupations	Technical/General Education
Intermediate air transport and miscellaneous transport occupations	Technical/General Education
Intermediate medical and paramedical occupations	Medical
Higher medical and paramedical professions	Medical
Higher commercial and administrative professions	Commerce & administration/General
Lower administrative occupations	General
Intermediate administrative occupations	Commerce & administration/ General Education

Table B3 (continued)
Occupational domains of the various occupational segments

Occupational segment	Domain
Higher administrative professions	Commerce & administration
Lower sales and purchasing occupations	Commerce & administration/ General Education
Intermediate sales and purchasing occupations	Commerce & administration/ General Education
Higher legal and government professions	Commerce & administration
Intermediate social-cultural occupations	General
Higher social-cultural professions	Socio-cultural and arts
Lower hotel and catering occupations	Community care/General Education
Intermediate hotel and catering occupations	Community care/General Education
Lower service occupations	Community care/General Education
Intermediate service occupations	Community care
Intermediate police, fire, and security occupations	Security
Intermediate military occupations	Security
Occupations n.e.c.	Technical/General Education

3 The Return to Education

Jaap de Koning

Introduction

People use education to acquire knowledge in order to increase their productive capacity in the labour process. Utilising such knowledge leads to higher production per unit of time compared to a situation in which no education was received. Taking part in education, however, shortens the productive period. In addition, educational production requires other means, such as teachers, buildings, etc. The loss of production resulting from people taking education and the production costs of education can be regarded as investments, which will be recovered with a return if the production increase attributable to education is large enough. This is entirely analogous to investments in machinery and other capital goods. The analogy can be extended if we consider that knowledge is also subject to ageing and wear. We may therefore regard productive knowledge as a production factor – 'human capital' – which is created by education. Schultz (1960) introduced this way of looking at education during the fifties. Further development of the human capital theory, in particular its microeconomic foundation, must be attributed to Becker (1964).

Education can therefore be regarded as an investment (capable of) producing a return. The next question concerns the volume of this return. The answer to this question is important both for the authorities spending public funds on education and for families/individuals and enterprises spending their money on it. Their investments are made with the expectation that these will create an adequate return.[1] As the rate of return may differ from one type of education to another, it is also important to calculate the rate of return for each type of education. This information could help governments, individuals/families, and enterprises to make better choices with respect to education, creating greater prosperity both for society and for its individual members.

A common method of determining the rate of return to education is the so-called individual rate of return approximation on the basis of individual incomes. In this Chapter, we shall make extensive use of this method. As far as possible, the presentation of rate of return figures will differentiate between the various types of education. Important aspects here are the level and type of school, but also the study route taken.

The most important reason for the popularity of the individual rate of return method is that it is relatively easy to apply.[2] This method, however, does not necessarily produce a reliable picture of the economic significance of education. Only if the costs of education were paid for entirely by individuals, and higher production only benefited the same individuals, could the financial return to education become clearly visible in individual incomes. The income effects and productivity effects, however, need not be the same.[3] As is indicated by the screening hypothesis (Spence, 1973), it is even possible that education merely makes visible the inherent talents, without adding anything to the productive capacity of the individual concerned. Education could then still have a positive return for individuals, but in social terms the only return would be that talents were made visible. Although the latter is important, the question would soon arise whether there this is the cheapest way of obtaining information on talents. If such an option exists, this implies in terms of the suppositions of the screening hypothesis that the social rate of return to education is lower than the individual rate of return.

It is equally possible, however, that the individual income returns underestimate the productivity effect of education. Institutions such as minimum wages may cause the actual wage differences to be smaller than would have been the case in a situation in which wages move freely. The wage level difference between individuals with higher and lower education could then be smaller than the productivity difference. We may also consider the role of education in the development and diffusion of knowledge, which will manifest itself primarily in a general productivity and income growth[4] rather than in individual income returns represented by larger income differences between individuals with higher and those with lower education. As a result of these factors, the social rate of return to education may actually be higher than the individual rate of return.

We also refer to the possible effects of short-term market conditions on individual rates of return.[5] Although short-term fluctuations affect most segments of the labour market, their intensity may differ. Some sectors are more sensitive to cyclical fluctuations than others. This may have consequences for the relative labour market positions of education categories and therefore also for their relative remunerations. A counter-argument would be that individual rates of return are calculated on a life-time basis, and hence market trends are levelled out. It is possible, however, that this levelling is not complete and that market fluctuations affect the calculated returns.[6] This would decrease the value of this information, because new investors in some courses would get too positive a prospect with regard to their future (relative) incomes, whereas the picture for others would be too negative.

Hence, microeconomic and macroeconomic rates of return do not automatically correspond to one another, which may create serious co-ordination problems. It is then possible that high individual returns encourage a high rate of participation in education, resulting in an increase of the total available resources in terms of human capital, whereas total prosperity does not increase and may even decrease. On the other hand, the individual rates of return may be low, constituting little incentive to take part in education, whereas a better educated labour force would lead to a higher domestic product. The government has various options to achieve a proper balance between microeconomic and macroeconomic returns, including its contribution to the funding of education, implementing a numerus clausus, and income policies.

The possible divergence between the microeconomic and macroeconomic rate of return to education is the reason why this Chapter also looks at research approaches that consider the effect of education on productivity. Most of these approaches study this relationship at a higher aggregation level. This is because productivity is difficult to measure at the individual level. Productivity data are available for the company level, sector level, and macroeconomic level. We will make an inventory of information available with respect to the effect of the education structure of employment on productivity. In principle, this type of research provides a better basis for the determination of the economic value of education, but in practice there are many restrictions. An important one concerns the fact that the available data at company, sector and macroeconomic level only allow a very general classification as to types of education.

We will concentrate on the rate of return to initial education. To a limited extent, we will also look at other types of education and training. Some of these other types of education and training can also be regarded as substitutes for initial education. General initial education followed by in-service training courses during the active period constitutes an alternative to initial vocational education. This Chapter only refers to the situation in the Netherlands.

The main questions to which we attempt to find answers are the following:

1 What is the individual income return to education?
2 What gives a greater return: general education or vocational education? What differences can we observe for the two types?
3 What is the return to detours in education?
4 What is the effect of education on productivity?
5 What is the relationship between education and the development and diffusion of knowledge?

The Chapter has the following structure. The next Section discusses the most important results of the individual income return approach. Refinements and methodological aspects are dealt with in the third Section. In the fourth Section we look at the productivity effects at various aggregation levels, and at the relationship between education and the development and diffusion of knowledge. The final Section summarises the conclusions.

Measurements of individual returns

Introduction

Individuals who have passed the age of compulsory education have the choice between taking a job and taking further education. Taking further education involves incurring expenses. There is the loss of wages which one would have earned if one had taken a job, but there are also directly related costs. This is offset by the fact that the higher educated usually earn more. As a result of extending the period of education, the period in which one can earn wages is shorter, but the annual income during this period is higher. The extensive international studies of the individual return to education show that in general the benefits greatly outweigh the costs.

A commonly used concept to compare the costs and benefits of education is the internal rate of return (e.g. Oosterbeek and Odink, 1990). This is the discount rate where, during one's entire lifetime, the calculated benefits of education equal the calculated costs. This internal rate of return is then compared to the interest rate in the capital market (e.g. on government bonds) in order to determine whether the investment in education can be regarded as financially profitable.

Below, we will give an overview of the rate of return calculations carried out for the Netherlands. In doing so, we will attempt to present the results at as disaggregated a level as possible, i.e. with the highest possible subdivision into levels and types of education. This is done on the basis of a study carried out by the Netherlands Economic Institute (NEI) a few years ago for the Organisation for Strategic Labour Market Research (OSA).[7] This study includes not only rate of return calculations for different levels and types of education, but also looks at the return to different study paths in education. A university degree, for example, can be obtained in different ways. After primary school, pupils may go directly to pre-university education (PUE) and then immediately to university (UE). They may also take one or more intermediate steps, however, such as higher general secondary education (HGSE) followed by pre-university education. In this example, each subsequent step leads to a higher education level, but there are also study paths with 'side-steps'. An example would be the path higher general secondary education – intermediate vocational education (IVE) – higher vocational education (HVE). The level of higher general secondary education is comparable to that of intermediate vocational education.

For a technical explanation of the rate of return calculations, we refer to Gelderblom and de Koning (1994) and Gelderblom et al. (1994). We will discuss a few main points. Firstly, it is important that the returns have a relative nature. We always deal with the costs and benefits of an education path in relation to the costs and benefits of another path. For example: the rate of return to the path lower general secondary education (LGSE) – intermediate vocational education is determined by the costs and benefits compared to those of the lower general secondary education 'path'.

Another important point is that the benefits are based on age-income profiles estimated on the basis of data from the OSA supply panel. This was done to allow a fairly detailed subclassification into study paths, given the relatively small sample population. The third point concerns our use of cross-sectional data relating to one point in time. This means that we assume that, apart from inflation, the relationship between age and income does not change with time. These points could affect the results. For this reason, a comparison will be made with other rate of return studies carried out in the Netherlands, which used different data and methods.

Results of the NEI study

Table 1 shows an overview of the results of the NEI study for study paths, where one subsequent step was taken after the first stage in secondary education. The calculations were based on individuals who had completed their studies. The calculations also assumed that individuals worked full time from the moment they left initial education until they reached the age of 65. The results have been split out for men and women.

The table contains two columns of results. The first column is based on the assumption that the estimated income differences between individuals with different education can be attributed entirely to education, whereas in the second column this is only the case for 60 per cent. The reason for attributing income differences only partly to education is that a selection effect may have occurred. This effect may occur because we have no data on such characteristics as intelligence. It is very well possible that in particular the naturally intelligent children will take a higher education. The higher incomes they earn later in life can be partially attributed to their higher natural intelligence. If we fail to take this factor into account, we overestimate the effect of education. With respect to social background, a similar argument can be used. The percentage of 60 must be regarded as purely indicative; it is not based on solid research data.[8]

Table 1 shows that most study paths can be regarded as cost-effective. The real long-term capital market interest rate averages between 0 and 2.5 per cent. Most rates of return in the table are higher, even if only 60 per cent of the income

Table 1
Rates of return corresponding to one additional step

Education path		Total study time	Education 100% responsible for income differences		Education 60% responsible for income differences	
Pre-traject	Traject		Men %	Women %	Men %	Women %
LGSE	HGSE	starting at age 17, duration 2 years	5	10	4	7
LGSE	IVE	starting at age 17, duration 4 years	-1	3	-2	1
LVE(t)	IVE(t)	starting at age 17, duration 4 years	4	8	2	5
LVE(e)	IVE(e)		5	9	3	6
LVE(c)	IVE(c)		6	10	4	7
HGSE	HVE(t)	starting at age 18, duration 4 years	8	6	5	3
HGSE	HVE(e)		12	10	8	6
HGSE	HVE(c)		5	1	2	-1
HGSE	HVE(h)		5	2	3	0
IVE(t)	HVE(t)	starting at age 21, duration 4 years	9	7	6	4
IVE(e)	HVE(e)		11	10	7	6
IVE(c)	HVE(c)		5	3	3	1
HGSE	UE	starting at age 18, duration 5 years	6	4	4	2
HVE	UE	starting at age 22, duration 3 years	7	7	5	5

The addition '(t)' refers to technical studies, '(e)' to economic studies, '(c)' to community care, hotel and catering studies, and '(h)' to teaching and the humanities
Source: Gelderblom and de Koning, 1994

differences are attributed to education. Below we list a number of remarkable results:

1 The LGSE-HGSE path has a relatively high rate of return.
2 The rate of return to the LGSE-IVE path is very low, or even negative for men.
3 The PVE-IVE path has an average rate of return, where we should note that the community care, hotel and catering study has the highest rate of return to the three options.

4 The IVE-HVE and HGSE-HVE paths have a relatively high score for the technical en economic studies, but – in particular for women – a low score for the community care, hotel and catering studies and teaching and the humanities.
5 Paths which end in UE, on average, have a slightly lower than average rate of return.[9]

The most striking result is the low – for men even negative – rate of return to the LGSE-IVE path. The reference group consisted only of individuals who had completed a LGSE study. The age income profile of these persons is relatively favourable. This is partly due to the fact that they take more part in in-service training during their productive life than any other employees, even more than IVE graduates. The effect of this on the return to the LGSE-IVE path, however, is not very great. If the incomes were corrected for the effect of in-service training, the return to the last path increases slightly, but not much. We add here that the LGSE-HGSE path does have a relatively high return. General studies such as LGSE and HGSE therefore score quite well in terms of income effects.

The study paths from Table 1 represent the short routes in education. Many pupils, however, take longer study paths. For example, instead of taking the route primary education-PUE-UE, they first do HGSE after primary education (or even LGSE first) to end up at UE via PUE. This is also called stacking. Government policies aim to prevent such study paths as much as possible. The argument is clear: longer study paths are more expensive. To be able to make an accurate assessment, however, we must set the costs off against the benefits.

Table 2 contains estimates of the returns of a number of routes which include more than one subsequent stage and which must be regarded to a greater or lesser extent as detours. It is striking that most returns here are positive too. Of the LVE-IVE-HVE path, the rate of return is even 7 per cent, whereas for the very long route LGSE-HGSE-PUE-UE it is still 4 per cent. The table also shows that longer paths which have IVE as an intermediate stage, often have a higher return than shorter paths ending with IVE. An exception is the HGSE-IVE-HVE path, which has a low return. This is not surprising, however, if we consider that the intermediate step HGSE-IVE constitutes no increase of level.

We must add here that the returns apply to the subsequent steps in the path given the first-mentioned study. In the LGSE-HGSE-PUE-UE path, for example, LGSE is the reference education. Anyone taking this route, may have been able to take PUE immediately after primary education. The wrong advice given by school, or social restrictions, may cause pupils to first choose an education at a lower level. In such cases, it is useful to promote that pupils make the right choice immediately so as to avoid their taking detours. It is difficult to say, however, whether incorrect choices can always be avoided. It is also possible that pupils who successfully take a longer route would have had a greater chance of failure if they had taken a shorter one. This could be true in particular for children from lower social classes. This has not been studied, however.

Table 2
Rates of return corresponding to more than one subsequent step

Education path		Total study time	Education 60% responsible for income differences	
Pre-Traject	Traject		Men %	Women %
LGSE	HGSE-HVE(t)	starting at age 17, duration 6 years	4	4
LGSE	HGSE-HVE(e)		5	6
LGSE	HGSE-HVE(c)		2	3
LGSE	IVE-HVE(t)	starting at age 17, duration 7 years	3	3
LGSE	IVE-HVE(e)		3	4
LGSE	IVE-HVE(c)		2	2
LGSE	HGSE-PUE-UE	starting at age 17, duration 9 years	4	4
LVE(t)	IVE-HVE(t)	starting at age 17, duration 7 years	6	7
LVE(e)	IVE-HVE(e)		7	8
LVE(v)	IVE-HVE(c)		5	6
HGSE	IVE-HVE(t)	starting at age 18, duration 7 years	1	-1
HGSE	IVE-HVE(e)		3	2
HGSE	IVE-HVE(c)		-1	-4
HGSE	PUE-UE	starting at age 18, duration 7 years	5	3
PUE	HVE-UE	starting at age 18, duration 7 years	4	3

Source: Gelderblom and de Koning, 1994

Comparison with other studies and development in time

Several conclusions presented here are very remarkable. In general, the calculated returns are quite high, albeit that they are lower than the figures often found abroad (10 per cent). Also, the return to IVE is generally quite low, whereas the returns of LGSE and HGSE are quite high. The return to the LGSE-IVE path is even negative.

These results could be related to the method used. Not long after the NEI study, van Ingen (1996) carried out a study where similar rates of return were calculated, this time on the basis of different data and using a different method of calculation. He made use of CBS data on wages and age, gender and education. The number of observations was such that the rates of return could be calculated immediately;

it was not necessary to estimate the age-income profiles on the basis of regression analysis.

In spite of the fact that completely different data was used, the results largely correspond with the NEI results. The calculated rates of return are of the same order of magnitude and follow a similar pattern. Van Ingen also arrived at a negative return for the LGSE-IVE path. Where deviations in relation to the NEI study occurred, van Ingen's results were by no means always more likely. The negative return to the LGSE-IVE path found by van Ingen was very low indeed. It must be added here that the data used by van Ingen had a considerable number of disadvantages, relating both to the measurement of the education variable and the income variable.

Table 3
Some rate of return calculations in the Netherlands

Study	de Boer and van Ingen (1980)	Odink and van Breemen (1983)	Koss-Fiszer (1989)	NEI (1994)	
Year of analysis	1972	1979	1985	1990	1990
Income differences fully attributed to education	yes	no	yes	yes	no
Return to sec.ed.-HVE path	7-9%	3-4%	9%	5%	2%
Return to sec.ed.-UE path	11-13%	6-7%	13%	5%	3%
LVE-IVE			8%	7%	4%
LGSE-IVE			8%	1%	0%

Source: Gelderblom and de Koning, 1994

Table 3 displays some of the results of rate of return studies in the Netherlands during the eighties. In addition, the results of the rate of return calculations from the present Chapter have been included for comparison. A detailed overview of these and other results can be found in Oosterbeek and Odink (1990), and Groot (1991).

It is striking that the calculated rates of return in the present study are lower than those of previous studies. This may indicate decreasing returns in more recent years. In Psacharopoulos (1981), a decrease from 11 per cent to 5 per cent for higher education was described for the USA between 1940 and 1976. In more recent research in the USA, however, this decrease seems to have stopped. This decrease is perhaps attributable to the relative size of the populations and may therefore not be a structural trend. The causes for the relatively low results of our study, however, could also be a matter of methodology. The analysis of the present study concentrates on primary incomes, whereas secondary incomes may also differ between education categories, which may lead to an underestimation of the rates of return. It is also important for the comparison that similar suppositions are used with respect to the role of education in the explanation of income differences. The study carried out by Odink and van Breemen (1983), for example, arrived at fairly low results because not all of the income differences were attributed to education.

The results of our study indicate differences in the rates of return of different types of education. The study carried out by Koss-Fiszer (1989) also distinguishes various types in HVE. Both studies arrive at relatively high rates of return for economic/administrative studies.

An international comparison of return calculations can be found in Psacharopoulos (1981 and 1985). For developed countries, the return in different studies is around 12 per cent for both secondary and higher education. In most cases, it was assumed that the income differences could be attributed entirely to education.

Refinements and methodological issues

Correction for inactivity

The above-mentioned rate of return calculations were based on data referring to people in full-time employment. However, it is likely that the education which one has had not only influences the height of one's income if one has a job, but also affect the chances of getting a job. In general, it is true that inactivity among the higher educated is lower than among the lower educated. One would expect that a correction for inactivity would in general lead to higher returns.

This is confirmed by calculations made by Gelderblom and de Koning (1994) and van Ingen (1996).[10] In both cases – also in accordance with expectations – the effect is greatest among women. In van Ingen, the result of this correction is that the return to the LGSE-IVE path becomes positive. In the NEI study, such is not the case, but in the latter study, inactivity data from the OSA panel was used, which deviates from the national inactivity data. It is clear that the available data only allow a rough correction for inactivity, even though no benefit data is available per education category.

Part-time jobs are also to be regarded as (partial) inactivity. Working part time means that the return to education is less. Moreover, there are indications that people who work part time have fewer career possibilities than full-timers.

Non-financial gains

So far, we have only looked at the financial gains resulting from particular education routes. But there may also be non-financial gains involved. Some of these are nevertheless related to paid employment. We mention the following:

- possibilities for personal growth;
- favourable labour conditions;
- possibilities for making contact; and
- giving meaning to life.

Low-skilled labour will provide relatively little opportunity for personal growth. Also, unfavourable labour conditions (stench, noise, health hazards, etc.) are primarily related to low-skilled jobs. By definition, the lower educated have a greater chance of getting low-skilled jobs and therefore the non-financial gains for the lower educated seem less than for the higher educated. Non-financial benefits may also differ per type of education, at least insofar as there is a direct relationship between type of education and occupation: given the same reward, one job will be considered more attractive than another. If the non-financial benefits related to one type of education are higher than those of another, then in the case of the same reward people will opt for the education which is considered more attractive. This will have a negative effect on the financial return to the education concerned. The relatively high financial return to some types of education can therefore be related to the fact that the jobs to which these types of education give access are attractive from a non-financial point of view.[11]

On the basis of data from the OSA supply panel, Gelderblom et al. (1994) conclude that the higher educated generally work in more favourable circumstances than the lower educated. The type of education, however, also plays an important role. Technical studies do relatively badly in this respect. As far as job satisfaction and the link between education and work are concerned, the differences between the various types of education are limited.

Haveman and Wolfe (1984) also list a number of benefits from education which are not directly related to paid employment. They mention the following effects:

- a higher productivity in the household;
- a better health and a higher life expectancy; and
- more successful family planning.

Social returns

When we calculated the individual rates of return, we based ourselves on the net incomes and the costs directly experienced by individuals. The costs financed from public funds, however, have not been included here. Suppose that we attribute the total costs of education to the individual and assume that the individual is personally responsible for study financing. Would we then still record positive returns? From a social point of view, we would then underestimate the returns; we should take the gross incomes as a starting point. Social rates of return are then defined as returns based on gross incomes and where the total costs of education are included.

Table 4
Individual and social rates of return of various education paths [a]

Education path		Individual %	Individual rates of return if the individual is also responsible for the public expenses related to education and study financing %	Social rates of return %
Pre-traject	Traject			
LGSE	HGSE	5	3	5
LGSE	IVE	0	-2	0
LGSE	HGSE-HVE(t)	4	1	3
LGSE	HGSE-HVE(e)	6	2	5
LGSE	HGSE-HVE(c)	3	0	1
LVE	IVE	4	1	4
LVE(t)	IVE-HVE(t)	6	2	5
LVE(e)	IVE-HVE(e)	8	4	6
LVE(c)	IVE-HVE(c)	6	2	4
HGSE	HVE(e)	7	3	5
HGSE	HVE(t)	4	0	2
HGSE	HVE(c)	1	-2	-1
HGSE	IVE-HVE(t)	0	-2	-1
HGSE	IVE-HVE(e)	2	-1	-1
HGSE	IVE-HVE(c)	-3	-5	-4
HGSE	PUE-UE	4	1	3
PUE	UE	3	0	2
IVE(t)	HVE(t)	5	1	3
IVE(c)	HVE(c)	2	-1	1
HVE	UE	5	1	3

a) This concerns a selection and sometimes an aggregation of education paths
Source: Gelderblom and de Koning, 1994

Table 4 provides an overview of the results. The table includes the following:

- the individual rate of return;
- the individual rate of return if the individual were fully responsible for all costs; and
- the social rate of return. We have assumed again that education is responsible for 60 per cent of the income differences. The results indicate that the social rates of return are in general positive, except for paths where a 'side-step' occurs (HGSE-IVE-HVE) and for HGSE-HVE (community care, etc.). General education (LGSE-HGSE) scores well again; the LGSE-IVE path scores badly again. On average, the calculated rates of return are 1 to 2 per cent points lower than the individual rates of return.

Although the calculated social rates of return are somewhat lower than the individual returns, they are usually at a comparable level to the average real capital interest rate or slightly above. If individuals were to be responsible for all costs of education, the individual rates of return would in many cases be negative or only just positive. There would be little incentive to take an education.[12] This illustrates the importance of a financing system which allocates only part of the costs of education to the individual.

It is, however, the question whether the social rates of return listed above provide an accurate indication of the macroeconomic significance of education. There are many reasons why gross wages may deviate from marginal productivity (see Gelderblom and de Koning, 1994, p. 5 ff.).

Training

So far, we have only discussed initial education. We shall now turn to adult education, and more in particular to:

- training of the employed; and
- training of the unemployed.

The most extensive research of the return to in-service training in the Netherlands was carried out by Groot (1994). His study confirms a result shown before in foreign studies, i.e. that training the employed gives a high return, higher than that of initial education. The effects on income are also higher for courses in the economic/administrative area than for technical courses. 't Hoen et al. (1994) also found a clear effect of participation in in-service training on individual wage levels.

People who have completed a general education such as LGSE or HGSE take part in in-service training more often than people with a different previous education. This provides some of the explanation for the high returns of this general initial education: these can be attributed in part to the higher participation rates of in-service training during the active period. The higher participation rate of in-service training only explains the higher returns of LGSE and HGSE to a limited extent.

There are indications that training not only increases income but also individual productivity of employees. Groot (1994) finds clear productivity effects, both in the comparison before and after training, and between training and no training (effects in the order of magnitude of 10 to 15 per cent). The productivity measurement is here based on the opinion of supervisors. Gelderblom and de Koning (1996) have done similar research, where the judgement of employees constituted the basis for productivity measurements. Employees were asked the following:

- how their current productivity relates to their productivity five years before; and
- which bottlenecks they experience in their current functioning.

The study concerned civil servants; both participants and non-participants of courses were involved in the study. The study showed that participating in courses has a positive effect on productivity, and that employees who took courses in the past experience fewer bottlenecks in their functioning. The study was directed primarily at the importance of training for older employees, whose training decreased their chances of premature unemployment.

Training is one of the most important instruments used by the Employment Services and other institutions to promote the reintegration of the unemployed in the labour process. Re-entry being the main objective, almost all research in the Netherlands in this field is directed at the measurement of the effect of training on the possibility of finding suitable employment. An overview of this study is given in de Koning et al. (1995). In a limited number of studies, use is made of a control group of untrained unemployed job-seekers, (de Koning and van Nes, 1990; de Koning et al., 1991; de Koning et al., 1993; Bavink and van der Burgh, 1994). The study shows that training does in fact increase one's chances.

Methodological aspects

Rate of return calculations are counter-factual analyses. This means that an estimate is made of the income developments in a hypothetical situation, i.e. where someone did not take any, or a different, education. Others who have not had any, or a different, education in fact serve as a control group, as an approximation of what might have happened with the person mentioned first. This demands, however, that one can correct for all other factors affecting one's income in addition to education. We must therefore know both which factors have any effect and what these factors entail. In practice, this is generally not achieved.[13]

Various researchers have referred to the phenomenon of self-selection (Rosen, 1977). This means that people tend to choose the education which provides the highest return for them, for example because they have a special talent in this area or they are more highly motivated. In combination with the absence of important explanatory factors such as IQ, this may lead to highly distorted results. Rate of return calculations made on the basis of a straight-forward approach, then no longer provide a foundation for hard conclusions regarding the desired pattern of investments in education. If the calculated rate of return for a particular education path is higher than for another, this may not automatically lead to the conclusion that it would have been profitable for individuals in the latter path to have taken the first path. These individuals may still have made the best choice for themselves.

The question is how important self-selection is. Oosterbeek (1992) found indications to support this when he studied foreign data, but could not do the same on the basis of a Dutch data set. We must add, however, that he had data on the IQs of the persons in the sample, as well as their social backgrounds. In the OSA data, no information was available on these variables, and a fairly arbitrary 60 per cent of the income differences was attributed to education. This is not very different from Oosterbeek's findings, however.

Another issue requiring attention concerns the fact that most rate of return calculations are based on data relating to one point in time.[14] It is then assumed, for example, that someone who is now 30 years old can be compared to someone who will be 30 in ten years time. In other words: it is assumed that the pattern of incomes does not change with time. This is a debatable assumption. It is very well possible that someone who leaves school at a time of high unemployment has a higher chance of unemployment and is forced to accept lower wages in order to get a job. It is also thinkable that this has a lasting effect on wages later in life. Several other problems are also related to the dependence on time, such as changes in the structure of education and the quality/appreciation of studies, and changes in the relative costs of education.

But supposing that the calculated rates of return do in fact give a fair indication of the financial gain that individuals have as a result of education, what does this say about the importance of education for the economy? Strictly speaking, very little. As indicated above, there is even a theory which says that education only makes the productivity level of individuals visible, but adds nothing to it. It is also possible that wages are institutionally determined and that there is no direct connection between wages and productivity. In the next Section, we will discuss the relationship between education and productivity in greater detail.

Effects at company, sector, and macroeconomic level

Labour productivity and education

Measuring productivity at the level of the individual employee is difficult, not only in practical terms, but also conceptually. In most professional situations there is a division of labour, with groups of employees creating a product. We shall therefore not look at the relationship between education and productivity at the level of the individual employee, but at the company level and higher aggregation levels. We distinguish the following:

- studies at microeconomic level on the basis of data on individual enterprises;
- studies at mesoeconomic level on the basis of statistical data at sector level; and
- studies at macroeconomic level on the basis of macroeconomic data in a time sequence.

With respect to the last approach, use is made of a number of studies covering a large number of countries. The analytical instrument used consists of explicit or implicit production functions, where the factor labour is divided in types of education. We shall briefly discuss the results.

Gelderblom and de Koning (1994) carried out analyses on the basis of data from the OSA company panel, where productivity and wages at company level were explained against the background of the composition of employment for different types of education. The analyses show that the average wage level in a company is proportionally higher if the share of the higher educated in the employment as a whole is higher. With regard to productivity, the influence of education is less apparent: the results are very sensitive to the specification of the regression comparison used. It is remarkable that the effect of in-service training on productivity is greatest, whereas it affects the wage level much less.

Gelderblom et al. (1994) investigated the relationship between productivity and education at sector level. Their data set consists of sector data for different years. They use a regression equation which explains the production per hour of labour from the capital intensity and composition of employment for different types of education. They distinguish three categories of education: basic level, intermediate level, and higher level. The results confirm the expectation that the higher educated are more productive than the intermediately educated, who in turn are more productive than those with only basic education. Figure 1 gives an idea of the production differences. On the basis of the regression results, the effects of an increase of 1 per cent point on productivity were calculated for employees with a basic, intermediate, and higher education. The figure shows that an extension of the category of higher educated has the greatest effect: 2 to 2.5 per cent. It is remarkable that the effect of an extension of the category of intermediately

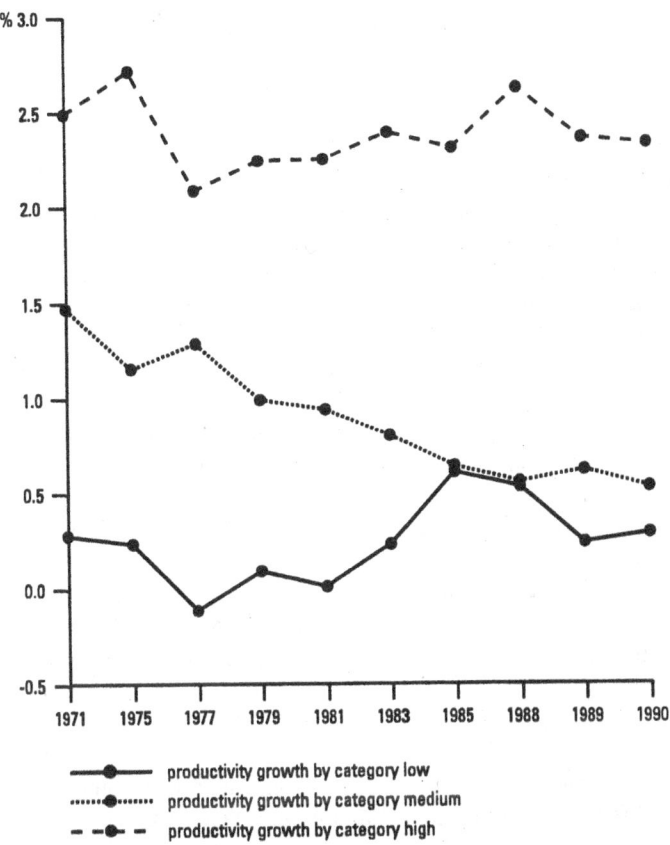

Figure 1 **Effect on production of a one per cent point increase of education categories**
Source: Gelderblom and de Koning, 1994

educated employees between 1971 and 1991 drops from 1.5 per cent to circa 0.5 per cent.[15] The share of the intermediately educated increased strongly during this period.

In addition, the influence of higher educated labour decreases in the regressions if participation in in-service training is also included as an explanatory variable: apparently, the effect of higher educated labour on productivity is partly attributable to the fact that the higher educated also take more part in in-service training. At this aggregation level we therefore also find an effect of in-service training on productivity.

A recent study by Gelderblom et al. (1996) distinguishes seven education categories: basic level, LVE, LGSE, IVE, HGSE/PUE, HVE and UE. The analysis is comparable to the one made in 1994. On the production scale, basic-level education scores lowest, and UE highest. The results show that in terms of productivity, the score of LVE in not higher than that of the basic level, IVE gains an average score and LGSE scores higher than IVE. The latter is surprising, but corresponds to the pattern of individual income returns. HGSE/PUE has a low score (lower than IVE), as is the case with HVE (the same score as IVE). These results are therefore not always easy to interpret.

There is no sufficiently long time series available in the Netherlands to estimate a macroeconomic production function with types of education. The problem here is also the almost total absence of data on wage costs per education category. As far as the macroeconomic level is concerned, we shall therefore look at international comparative studies.

The summarising article by Englander and Gurney (1994) provides an inventory of international comparative research of the effects of education on economic growth. Prompted by the new economic growth theory, which regards education as a major growth factor, a series of empirical studies appeared, which took the time series data of a number of countries to investigate to what extent education is a factor determining growth. According to Englander and Gurney, most studies are open to methodological criticism. Nevertheless, they also find a connection between productivity and education at the macroeconomic level.

Innovation and education

In the note 'Knowledge on the move' ('Kennis in beweging', Ministries of Economic Affairs, of Education, Culture and Sciences, and of Agriculture, Conservation and Fisheries, 1995), the government adopts the following views:

- knowledge is the single most important success factor in international competition and innovation is therefore a 'must'; and
- a well-educated labour force is a necessary precondition for innovation.

The note considers the level of R&D expenses as the major indicator for innovation. The fact that the Netherlands lags behind in this respect, and is surpassed by NICs such as South Korea, is regarded as an indication that all is not well with innovation in the Netherlands and that there is a risk of this nation lagging behind with respect to the level of knowledge. The emphasis on R&D expenses is perhaps too one-sided here, at the expense of other indicators of

Table 5
Relationship between the presence of education categories and the score of indicators of innovation

Innovation indicator	Correlation between score of said innovation indicator and share of:			
	UE/HVE	IVE/PUE/HGSE	LGSE/LVE	PE
Share of innovative products in turnover	+	+	–	0
Share of PC-users/terminals	+	+	–	–
Advantage/disadvantage in sector	+	+	0	–
Importance of advancedness for market position	+	0	–	0

	UE	HVE	IVE	PUE/HGSE	LGSE	LVE	PE
Share of R&D personnel	0	+	0	–	–	0	–
Share of enterprises with product innovations	+	+	0	0	0	0	–
Participation in in-service training	+	+	0	+	0	–	–
Patents	0	0	0	–	–	0	0
Total	+	+	0/+	0	–	0/–	–

+ = positively significant at 90% level
– = negatively significant at 90% level
0 = not significant
Source: Gelderblom et al., 1996

innovation. Another factor may be that the globalisation of the economy makes it easier to buy new knowledge abroad.

The question is then what the implications are for education policies. Which types of education are particularly important for the development and diffusion of knowledge? A recent study by Gelderblom et al. (1996) looked more closely at the relationship between innovation and education. The following were done:

1 A number of indicators of innovation was selected, including R&D efforts, and a sector average was produced of these indicators.

2 The statistic relationship was determined between the degree of innovation according to the various indicators and the educational structure of employment.

The study is therefore a descriptive analysis, and cannot be used to show causal relationships. Table 5 summarises the results.

From the analyses we may draw two important conclusions:

1 In general, there is a positive relationship between the education level in a company or sector and the innovation score of the same company/sector. For almost all indicators we can say that the correlation coefficient has the greatest positive score for the share of UE and HVE.
2 In the analyses where IVE can be separated from PUE/HGSE and LGSE from LVE, the score of the coefficient for vocational education is in most cases higher than for general education.[16] This applies to the innovation indicators in the area of R&D, product innovation, and patents. This is an indication for the importance of vocational education in this respect. Only in the case of participation in in-service training, the share of general education courses scores higher than vocational education. In a way, this is logical because in-service training often provides an opportunity to (partially) compensate for any lack of vocational education. The supposed relationship between education and innovation is therefore confirmed in these analyses. This also applies to the role of large companies; large companies score considerably higher in the various innovation indicators.

Conclusions

Looking at existing studies of the effects of education on wages and productivity, we must conclude that almost without exception the studies find a positive and significant influence of education. Whether we take the individual level, company level, sector level or – by means of international comparative studies – the macroeconomic level, the same conclusion must be drawn each time.

It is also probable that education is an explanatory factor for rewards and productivity, as is indicated by the human capital theory, and not merely makes the existing qualities visible, as the screening hypothesis says. This is shown both by microeconomic studies concentrating on the effect of talent and social environment, and by the studies at meso- and macroeconomic levels where a time-sequence element and/or an international comparative element was included.

Insofar as anything can be said on the basis of research, education appears to produce not only financial but also non-financial gains. The higher educated usually work in better labour conditions than the lower educated, for example.

If we wish to make statements with regard to the level and type of education, we must base ourselves almost entirely on analyses based on individual incomes. This provides only a limited insight in the economic importance of education. We must also add that most studies have methodological flaws. If we nevertheless take these studies into consideration, we can draw a number of remarkable conclusions:

1. General types of education such as LGSE and HGSE receive a good score on the income rate of return scale, whereas IVE and (in particular) LVE obtain a low score. With respect to the low score of IVE we must add that: a) education paths using IVE as an intermediate step often show a satisfactory rate of return; b) unemployment among IVE graduates is low; c) IVE graduates appear to play an important role in innovation.
2. Paths which end at the level of HVE or UE usually show a satisfactory rate of return, with the exception of paths with an illogical intermediate step and courses in the fields of community care, hotel and catering.
3. Detours in education often produce a positive rate of return. It is questionable whether it is wise to make detours impossible. This is only the case if we could always prevent the wrong choice from being made in the type of education taken after primary education.
4. If we look at the effects of education on gross incomes and take the total costs of education into consideration, the resulting 'social' rates of return often prove very positive. If individuals taking education were responsible for all costs involved, private rates of return would often be barely on the positive side, and there would be little incentive to take a long education. From this we may conclude that a major shift from collective to private financing is undesirable.
5. Recently, we seem to have been able to witness a trend towards lower rates of return, which could indicate a growing underutilisation of qualifications.

In this Chapter, the focus was on initial education. To a limited extent, attention was also paid to in-service training of employees and training the unemployed. The effects of training employees have been the subject of a fairly large number of studies. These consistently show that in-service training has a major effect on productivity and wages. The effects of initial education paths measured in other studies are in fact partly attributable to in-service training. In-service training can also have the function of improving the position of certain groups of employees, such as older employees, because in general the effects of such training on productivity greatly exceeds the effects on wages. The high return to in-service training indicates underinvestment, whereas the relatively low return to some initial education paths could indicate saturation. A great deal of research has also been done with respect to training employees, but in the Netherlands such research primarily focuses on the effect on re-entry in the labour market. This justifies the conclusion that training has a stimulating effect on placement.

Notes

1. To which we add that education also has a non-financial return. This implies that even in the case of a relatively low financial return, the government and individuals/families will invest in education. But then there will also be a lower limit, a minimum value which the returns must attain in order for the investment to be made.
2. Which doesn't do away with the fact that this method also has many disadvantages, as will be shown elsewhere in this Chapter. The major problem concerns the fact that in calculating the return, one compares the incomes of people with different education paths, which may differ for reasons unknown to the researcher.
3. Differences between micro- and macroeconomic returns will also occur because the different costs at these levels. This is because the government funds part of the costs. This can be solved, however, by attributing all costs of education to individuals. In that case, we must also use gross incomes. We then speak of social returns.
4. The fact that education has external effects, such as a well-educated labour force facilitating the diffusion of knowledge, is a major factor behind economic growth according to the new (endogenous) growth theory (Romer, 1986).
5. But the calculation of the macroeconomic return can also be affected by short-term trends. In a period of recession, unemployment among the higher educated will also increase and/or the higher educated will be employed in simpler jobs on a larger scale than would have been the case in more favourable economic circumstances (the so-called displacement effect, see also Teulings, 1990). The utilisation of human capital will then decrease.
6. For example, if the calculation were carried out when the economy had been in a state of recession for some time.
7. See Gelderblom et al. (1994).
8. See van Ingen (1996). Oosterbeek (1992) estimates the contribution of education to income differences to be circa 50 per cent.
9. Because of the small number of observations, a subdivision into types of education was not possible here.
10. In these calculations, voluntary inactivity was not taken into account.

11 This would mean that there were compensating income differences. Jobs with unfavourable labour conditions could then be compensated for by higher wages. Empirical research, however, has provided little to support this hypothesis, which assumes that there are no thresholds in education and career choices (de Koning and Zandvliet, 1996).
12 Apart from the intangible gains.
13 In experiment using a random selection of the experimental group and the control group, this problem does not occur, because the random allocation causes the experimental group and the control group to be composed similarly.
14 A technical problem in such a cross-section approach is the high degree of interdependence between a number of time-dependent variables. Age and work experience, for example, will be highly correlated.
15 This may be related to the low IVE return found before.
16 In Table 5, these differences do not become entirely clear, because only the significance and the sign are relevant here. In those cases, the 'score' in Table 5 is the same, the value of the correlation coefficient for IVE is higher than for HGSE/PUE and the one for LVE is higher than for LGSE.

References

Bavinck, S., and Burgh, Y. van der (1994), *Effectiviteit van het scholingsinstrumentarium*, Onderzoek naar Centrum Vakopleiding, KRA, KRA-WER en Sollicitatieclub in de regio Noord- en Midden-Limburg, Research voor Beleid: Leiden.

Becker, G.S. (1964), *Human Capital: A Theoretical and Empirical Analysis*, National Bureau of Economic Research, Columbia University Press: New York.

Boer, J. de, and Ingen, D.C. van (1981), *Een prijs voor onderwijs*, deel 2, Instituut voor Onderzoek van Overheidsuitgaven: Den Haag.

Englander, S., and Gurney, A. (1994), 'Productivity Growth: Medium-term Trends', OECD, *Economic Studies*, 22, pp. 111-130.

Gelderblom, A., and Koning, J. de, 'Evaluating Effects of Training within a Company: Methods, Problems, and one Application', to appear shortly in *Labour*.

Gelderblom, A., Koning, J. de, and Weijde, I. van de (1994), *Onderwijs en economische groei: een sectoranalyse*, OSA working document W118, Organisatie voor Strategisch Arbeidsmarktonderzoek: The Hague.

Gelderblom, A., Hoen, N.B.J.G. 't, and Koning, J. de (1994), *Wat wordt men wijzer van onderwijs?*, OSA working document W119, Organisatie voor Strategisch Arbeidsmarktonderzoek: The Hague.
Gelderblom, A., and Koning, J. de (1994), *Leren: batig investeren?*, OSA report V41, Organisatie voor Strategisch Arbeidsmarktonderzoek: The Hague.
Groot, W. (1994), *Het rendement van bedrijfsopleidingen*, Ministry of Social Affairs and Employment: The Hague.
Groot, W. (1991), *Scholing, arbeidsmarkt en economische ontwikkeling*, Ministry of Social Affairs and Employment: The Hague.
Haveman, R.H., Wolfe, B.L. (1984), 'Schooling and Economic Well-being: the Role of Non-market Effects', *Journal of Human Resources*, pp. 377-407.
Ingen, D.C. van (1996), *Rendement van beroepsonderwijs*, IOO, Max Goote/Facto.
Koning, J. de, and Zandvliet, C.Th. (1996), 'Economie van de arbeidsomstandigheden', *Economisch Statistische Berichten*, 81 (4045), pp. 132-137.
Koning, J. de, Donker van Heel, P.A., Gelderblom, A., Nes, P.J. van, and C.Th. Zandvliet (1995), *Arbeidsvoorziening in perspectief. Evaluatie Arbeidsvoorzieningswet 1991-1994, Deelonderzoek B: resultaten en kosten*, Ministry of Social Affairs and Employment: The Hague.
Koning, J. de, Zandvliet, C.Th., Bokhoven, E.F. van, and Olieman, R. (1993), *Effectiviteit scholing in de RBA-regio West-Utrecht*, OAV working document 94-03, Centraal Bureau voor de Arbeidsvoorziening: Rijswijk.
Koning, J. de, Koss, M., and Verkaik, A. (1991), 'A Quasi-Experimental Evaluation of the Vocational Training Centre for Adults', *Environment and Planning C: Government and Policy*, 9, pp. 143-153.
Koning, J. de, and Nes, P.J. van (1990), *Evaluatie van het CBB: Bereik en plaatsingseffecten*, OAV report 90-11, Centraal Bureau voor de Arbeidsvoorziening: Rijswijk.
Koss-Fiszer, A.J. (1988), 'Het economisch rendement van onderwijs', *Supplement bij de sociaal-economische maandstatistiek*, 6, pp. 4-11.
Ministries of Economic Affairs, of Education, Culture and Sciences, and of Agriculture, Conservation and Fisheries (1995), *Kennis in beweging. Over kennis en kunde in de Nederlandse economie*, Ministries of Economic Affairs, of Education, Culture and Sciences, and of Agriculture, Conservation and Fisheries: The Hague.
Odink, J.G., and Breemen, R. van (1983), 'Studeren of niet? Alternatieve stelsels van studiefinanciering en de gevolgen voor het private rendement van studeren', *Economisch Statistische Berichten*, 68, pp. 568-572.
Oosterbeek, H., (1992), *Essays on Human Capital Theory*, Dissertation, University of Amsterdam: Amsterdam.

Oosterbeek, H., and Odink, J.G. (1990), 'Onderwijs, lonen en rendementen', in Schippers, J.J. (ed.) *Arbeidsmarkt en maatschappelijke ongelijkheid*, Groningen, pp. 41-71.

Psacharopoulos, G. (1981), 'Returns to Education: an Updated International Comparison', *Comparative Education*, pp. 321-341.

Psacharopoulos, G. (1985), 'Returns to Education: a Further International Update and Implications', *Journal of Human Resources*, 20, pp. 583-604.

Romer, P.L. (1986), 'Increasing Returns and Long-run Growth', *Journal of Political Economy*, 94, pp. 1002-1037.

Rosen, S. (1977a), 'Human Capital: Relations between Education and Earnings', in: Intrilgator, M. (ed.), *Frontiers in Quantitative Economics*, North-Holland: Amsterdam.

Schultz, T.W. (1960), 'Capital Formation by Education', *Journal of Political Economy*, 68, pp 571-583.

Spence, M.A. (1973), 'Job Market Signalling', *Quarterly Journal of Economics*, 87, pp 355-374.

Teulings, C. (1990), *Conjunctuur en kwalificatie*, Dissertation, Stichting voor Economisch Onderzoek, Universiteit van Amsterdam: Amsterdam.

Acknowledgement

I wish to thank Arie Gelderblom for his major contribution to a number of studies which constitute much of the basis for this Chapter.

4 Labour Market Forecasts and Choice of Education

Dinand Webbink

Introduction

What is the role of labour market expectations in the choice of education and what constitutes the basis of the labour market expectations of students? Do students use the most up-to-date information on the future labour market or do they base their decisions on the labour market experience of earlier cohorts of school-leavers? The answers to these questions are important to gain insight in the way in which the labour market works, and to be able to implement labour market policies. For the labour market to function properly, suppliers of labour must be informed adequately regarding their chances of obtaining jobs and the wages paid for various occupations. The structure of the supply of labour is determined by the education chosen by students. This means that students must have adequate information about the future labour market at the time when they decide what education to take, i.e. several years before they actually offer their labour to the labour market. If students base their choice of education on information from the labour market as it is at that particular time, there is a chance of the famous cobweb cycle. If students look at forecasts concerning the labour market situation at the time of their graduation, we may expect a labour market that functions much better.

Recent developments in the participation in Dutch education suggest that there is no relation between the choice of education and labour market expectations/forecasts. Three examples:

1 For the year 2000, the Research Centre for Education and the Labour Market (ROA) of the University of Maastricht predicted a shortage of academics (ROA, 1995); the number of college freshmen for the academic year of '95-'96 decreased by 10%, while the number of preregistrations for the '96-'97 academic year was down by approximately 15%. These decreases can only partly be attributed to demographic factors.
2 Research by the Foundation for Economic Research (SEO) of the University of Amsterdam as to the income position of visual artists in 1993 and 1994 showed that only 10% makes a good living. Most of the visual artists have an income at welfare level, while the income situation in 1994 had deteriorated compared to

1993 (Hopstaken et al., 1996). At the same time, the interest in art courses continues to exceed the capacity restrictions for such courses.
3 In spite of the very good labour market prospects for graduates of Higher Vocational Technical Education (ROA, 1995), preregistrations at the Technical University of Twente decreased by 25%, and those at the Technical Universities of Delft and Eindhoven by 20%.

Little empirical research has been done on the relationship between labour market expectations and choice of education. Moreover, such studies often focus on the role of subjective expectations in the process of choosing an education, rather than the direct influence of labour market forecasts. In this Chapter, we attempt to trace the influence of forecasts on the choices made by students of Higher Education in the Netherlands. As students have not been asked directly as to the role of labour market forecasts, such has been analysed indirectly. We will investigate to what extent the expectations of students correspond to labour market forecasts. If information about the labour market plays no role at all, we would expect that the consideration 'by completing this study programme, I am certain to obtain paid employment later' is equally important for students, irrespective of their studies. If information about the labour market does play a role in the choices that students make, we would expect students who find this aspect important to be overrepresented in the programmes that offer better chances of success. We will therefore investigate whether there is an above-average incidence of students who find it important to obtain paid employment in studies which offer good perspectives. For the analysis, we have used data on two cohorts of students, from 1991 and 1995 respectively. The classification of studies with good or bad labour market perspectives was done on the basis of forecasts made by ROA in the same years (de Grip et al., 1989; ROA, 1995).

We wish to stress at this stage that the results presented in this Chapter concern explorative analyses. We have not controlled for variables which may be of importance for the differences between studies. We will first give a summary of existing knowledge. Then we investigate to what extent data on the labour market, in the form of forecasts by ROA, can be traced in the choices made by students in Higher Education in the Netherlands.

Theory and empirical knowledge

By taking part in education, individuals invest in themselves. The return of such investment consists of higher wages, whereas the costs involved consists mostly of forgone earnings. This is the well-known idea from the human capital theory (see Becker, 1975, and others), which has been the dominant theory in educational economics since the sixties. If there is no balance on the labour market, the chances of work also play an important part, in addition to the above-mentioned cost and return of investments in education. This means that labour market expectations play a crucial role in the choice of education. Considering this pivotal role of labour market expectations in the choice process, one would expect that the expectations of pupils and students have been studied extensively. Such is not the case, however. After the classic studies by Freeman (1971, 1975, and others), only a few studies have been carried out in this field. Manski (1993) commented as follows: 'The profession has traditionally been sceptical of subjective data; so much that we have generally been unwilling to collect data on expectations. Instead, the norm has been to make assumptions about expectations formation.'

Freeman (1971) showed that the expectations of students correspond to a high degree with the performance of earlier cohorts on the labour market. This applies both to the initial wages for various occupations and to the wages after 15 years and at the end of the respective professional careers. The analysis also showed that income differences between occupations have an influence on the choice of education, assuming a limited set of educational alternatives. In other words, if an individual is trying to choose between a number of educational alternatives, the choice will be influenced by the expected income differences between occupations.

Dominitz and Manski (1994) recently asked students in the U.S.A. to complete a computerised questionnaire in order to obtain information about income expectations for various levels of education. The main conclusions drawn from this explorative study were that students are capable of making realistic estimates of future incomes, and that the general expectation was that more education leads to higher income. De Jong et al. (1996) investigated how realistic the income expectations of Dutch students were. The results of the latter study correspond to those in Dominitz and Manski's study. The average expected incomes per educational sector correspond with the incomes of graduates. At the same time, the dispersion of expectations is greater than the dispersion of realisations. This was also found by Dominitz and Manski. It is also important to note that 35 to 40 per cent of all students replied that they were unable to estimate the financial return of their studies. This is a clear indication of the uncertainty among students as to the return of their studies. Betts (1996) analysed the income expectations of undergraduates. The latter study also showed that there was not a great divergence between expectations and realisations. Students in higher years proved much better informed with respect to the labour market than college freshmen.

In the Netherlands, the influence of income expectations on the choices to start a study in Higher Education was analysed in detail by Kodde and Ritzen (1986). They asked students taking their final examinations which starting wages they expected to earn if they were to enter the labour market at that point in time (forgone earnings) and what income they expected upon completion of a Higher Education study (future income). The data concerned merely the perception of students taking their final examinations. The study provided all the results predicted by the theory. A higher expected future income provides a greater chance of further studies, whereas a higher expected forgone earnings provides a lower chance of further studies. These analyses were repeated in Webbink et al. (1993). The latter study showed that the influence of income expectations on the decision to start a study had decreased between 1982 and 1991.

The relation between chances of obtaining a job and the choice of education, i.e. the decision to study after completing Secondary Education, was analysed in Kodde (1985). This study also produced the results predicted by the theory. If the expected chances of work after Secondary Education are greater, the chances of studying decrease. If the expected chance of work after Higher Education is greater, there is also a greater chance of individuals continuing their studies. The second effect is stronger, which means that a general increase of employment (i.e. an equal increase for all levels) leads to increased participation in Higher Education. It may be concluded that participation in education is influenced in particular by differences in unemployment rates between various levels of education (Secondary versus Higher Education), rather than a high unemployment rate in itself.

Little research has been done after Freeman with respect to the extent to which labour market expectations affect the choice of education. Usually, assumptions are made about labour market expectations, or realisations are used for the analysis instead of expectations. An example is Berger (1988). This study aimed to find out to what extent predicted future incomes affect the choice of education. The study showed that the future income flow has a significant effect, but that the starting wages have no influence on the choice of education.

We may conclude that little research has been done as to the role of labour market expectations on the choice of education. Moreover, empirical research concentrated largely on the choice between studying and not studying, rather than the choice of a particular type of education or study. Little is known about the direct role of labour market forecasts in the choice process of students.

Labour market information and the choice of a particular study

Is the choice of a particular study affected by labour market information? This is the question that we wish to investigate in a simple way by determining how important the chance of work is for students in Higher Education in the Netherlands when they decide between a study which offers good labour market perspectives and one which offers less favourable perspectives. To this end, we have analysed data on two cohorts of students. The data on 1991 were derived from the 'Studying On' project, whereas the data for 1995 stems from the 'Determinants of Participation' project.[1] In 1991, SEO and SCO/Kohnstamm Institute started a longitudinal research project, entitled 'Studying On' (Verder Studeren). The study monitored the careers both within and outside education of pupils in their final year of secondary education and students of Higher Vocational and University Education up to the year 1995. Every year, a questionnaire was sent out. Nearly 4,000 students completed the first questionnaire. In 1995, the same institutes started the 'Determinants of Participation' project. One of the research items from this project concerned the effect of financial incentives on the choice of science studies in Higher Education. To determine this, the income expectations and the expected chances of work, both with and without a science study, were investigate in nearly 5,000 college freshmen from Higher Vocational Education (HVE) and University (UE). The project will be completed by early 1997.

In both studies, students were asked the following question:

When you chose your current study, a number of considerations may have played a role. Below, we have listed several considerations. Please indicate for each of these, how important that particular consideration was for your choice of the study you are now taking. (0: this consideration played no role at all; 10: this consideration played a very important role). I am taking this study because (.....) by taking this study, I expect to be sure of a paid job later.

From both samples, as many studies as possible were selected with either good or bad labour market perspectives. In a dichotomous separation of studies (as to good or bad perspectives), we expect much greater differences between studies, allowing better testing. In 1995, it is difficult to make such a dichotomous classification because of the improvement of the perspectives of practically all studies. The classification as to good and bad perspectives was derived from predictions by ROA for these years. The selection of studies was partly determined by the overlapping areas of the ROA classification and the SEO/SCO classification.

The sample years (1991 and 1995) and the years for which the forecasts were made do not match exactly, but they correspond to a great extent. For the sample year 1991, we used the forecasts from 1989, and for the sample year 1995 the forecasts from 1995.[2] The forecasts from 1989 and 1995 had been published at a time when the sample populations completed the questionnaires. However, the 1995 sample had already chosen their studies prior to publication of the forecasts.

A test for the role of current labour market information

To determine whether current labour information has an influence on the choice of education, we have analysed the scores with respect to the above-mentioned consideration obtained from students from different studies. We have two possible results:

1 The average score for said consideration is not higher in studies with good labour market perspectives than in studies with bad perspectives.
2 The average score is higher in studies with good labour market perspectives.

Conclusion for result 1: Labour market information plays no role in the choice of education. Conclusion for result 2: Labour market information does play a role in the choice of education. If labour market information does play a role, we would expect students who rate chances of work high, to be overrepresented in studies with good perspectives.

The choice of studies in 1991

The results for 1991 have been listed in Table 1. Column 2 gives the characterization of the labour market perspective of the study concerned (de Grip et al., 1989). Columns 3 and 4 respectively, contain the average and the standard deviation of the

Table 1
The importance of the chance of work (0-10 scale) for the study chosen in 1991

Study	ROA characterization	aver.	std. dev.	%≤2	%≥8	number
Higher Vocational (HVE)						
Teacher Training PE*	very bad	5.8	3.6	24.6	42.1	114
Social	very bad	5.7	3.2	20.9	35.7	182
Arts	very bad	4.4	3.6	35.5	26.9	93
Technical	reasonable	7.8	2.4	5.2	69.3	251
Teacher Training SE**	good	6.7	2.9	10.3	44.1	68
Economic/administrative	good	7.6	2.5	6.4	60.3	141
Laboratory	good	7.3	2.5	7.5	60.8	186
University (UE)						
Languages/Arts	bad	5.5	3.0	21.2	27.6	123
Social sciences	very bad	5.3	3.3	2.2	30.2	139
Law	bad	6.8	2.8	9.7	51.3	195
Economics	reasonable	7.2	2.5	9.0	56.4	166
Medicine (no numerus clausus)	reasonable	6.6	2.3	7.0	38.6	57
Medicine (numerus clausus)	reasonable	6.2	2.6	9.9	38.1	181
Management	good	7.4	2.5	8.3	60.0	60

*   PE = Primary Education
** SE = Secondary Education
Source: ROA/Studying on

score regarding the consideration 'by taking this study, I expect to be sure of a paid job later'. Columns 5 and 6 contain the percentages of students who had either a very low or a very high score for this consideration. This is the percentage of students in a study who consider the chances of work either of very little importance or very important.

The first impression that Table 1 gives, is that labour market information is an important factor for the choice of education. We can see, for example, that the average score for HVE students at the School of Arts was the lowest of all studies (4.4). The labour market perspectives of this study in 1990 were classified as 'very bad'. Apparently, students who valued paid employment opted less for the Arts in HVE. In HEAE ('Economic/administrative'), a study with good labour market perspectives in 1990, we find a considerably higher score of 7.6. Students who value the chance of paid employment, have a greater preference for HEAE. In general, the average scores are lower for studies with bad labour market perspectives and higher for studies with good perspectives. This applies to both HVE and UE.

Exceptions

In UE we find one exception: Law. The average score is higher than in studies which offer better chances of work. We here find the strange phenomenon that many students who said that the chance of finding paid employment played an important role in their choice of education, nevertheless opted for a study with bad perspectives, which Law is. This becomes even more clear if we look at the extreme scores. More than one in every two Law students (51.3%) said that obtaining paid employment was very important when they chose their current study. However, the chances of finding paid employment with their current study (Law) were at that time characterized as low.

In other studies, the extreme scores were also surprising. More than one in every four Arts students in HVE, for example, stated that they chose their current study because they believed that finding paid employment very important. For students of the Teacher Training study for Secondary Education and the Social Science studies, this score was even higher. This seems paradoxical, but these may be the very few students who, in spite of the unfavourable perspectives for their studies, manage relatively easily to find employment.

The choice of studies in 1995

Table 2 shows the results for 1995. We have attempted to use the same studies as those used in Table 1. An important difference compared with 1991 concerns the fact that the forecasts in 1995 (for the year 2000) were much more favourable. In accordance with the improved labour market perspectives, the average valuations of the importance of the chance of finding work have increased.

Table 2
The importance of the chance of work (0-10 scale) for the study chosen in 1995

Study	ROA characterization	aver.	std. dev.	%≤2	%≥8	number
Higher Vocational (HVE)						
Teacher Training PE*	good	7.6	2.3	3.0	56.4	133
Teacher Training SE**	good	7.2	2.9	8.0	61.1	113
Personnel and labour	good	8.1	2.2	1.1	71.9	89
Social and educational	good	7.1	2.2	6.0	48.0	100
Laboratory	good	8.0	2.1	2.6	68.1	116
Electrical engineering	good	8.5	1.3	0.0	79.2	120
Business administrative	moderate	8.4	1.9	1.0	78.0	100
University (UE)						
Languages/Arts	moderate	5.2	2.9	18.8	22.7	128
Psychology	good	5.7	2.9	17.6	25.3	91
Sociology	good	6.1	2.6	9.6	32.7	104
Law	moderate	7.8	2.3	4.3	67.4	141
Economics	good	7.9	2.2	4.2	65.3	95
Medicine	good	6.8	3.0	13.2	55.8	129
Management	reasonable	8.5	1.4	0.0	82.4	91

*   PE = Primary Education
** SE = Secondary Education
Source: ROA/Determinants of participation

In 1995, there was no clear pattern in the scores. This suggests that labour market information does not have a strong influence on the choice of education. Some studies offer moderate to reasonable perspectives of work. Many HVE students of Business Administration said that finding paid employment was important, but chose a study with only moderately good perspectives. In UE, the perspectives were moderate for Languages and Law, and reasonable for Management. In Language studies we find many students for whom finding a job does not score high among the reasons for choosing a study. In Law, on the other hand, as was the case in 1991, there are many students who opted for Law because they find it important to obtain a paid job. This is even more the case for students of Management, where finding a paid job played a very important role in the choice of study for many students. Also surprising is the fact that students of Psychology and Sociology put little value on finding employment, while their perspectives are good.

The differences in the scores for the various studies appear to relate to a kind of 'traditional image' of the chances on the labour market: according to this, scientific studies, such as Technology and Economics, offer better chances of work, whereas more academic studies, such as Sociology, Education, and Languages, have more problems on the labour market. This may be an important indication that current labour market information only reaches students slowly and that students therefore make their choices primarily on the basis of older data. The latter corresponds to the findings of Freeman (1971), and this is important if we wish to avoid cobweb cycles.

Changes in forecasts and the importance of work in the choice of education

For a number of studies, we have data for both years (see Table 3). It is striking that the student scores are clearly higher in 1995. This suggests that for the latest generation of students, labour market considerations are more important than was the case for the previous generation. As we have already said, this is related to the

Table 3
The importance of the chance of work (0-10 scale) for the studies chosen in 1991 and 1995, with the rating for each education level between brackets

Study	1990 characterization	average (rank)	1995 characterization	average (rank)
Higher Vocational (HVE)				
Teacher Training PE*	good	6.7 (3)	good	7.6 (3)
Teacher Training SE**	very bad	5.8 (4)	good	7.2 (4)
Laboratory	good	7.3 (2)	good	8.0 (2)
Business administration	good	7.6 (1)	moderate	8.4 (1)
University (UE)				
Languages	bad	5.5 (5)	moderate	5.2 (6)
Social/Cultural	very bad	5.3 (6)	good	5.9 (5)
Law	bad	6.8 (3)	moderate	7.8 (3)
Economics	reasonable	7.2 (2)	good	7.9 (2)
Medicine	reasonable	6.4 (4)	good	6.8 (4)
Management	good	7.4 (1)	reasonable	8.5 (1)

* PE = Primary Education
** SE = Secondary Education
Source: ROA/Studying on
ROA/Determinants of participation

improved labour market perspectives. For students at Teacher Training colleges for Secondary Education, the perspectives have improved greatly. In 1995, this study therefore seems to attract more students who value paid employment highly than was the case in 1991. In UE, the perspectives have improved for Languages and for the Social and Cultural sectors. This seems to have had little effect, though, on the choices made by students, as the scores have not changed a great deal. For Business Economics and Management, the perspectives have deteriorated, whereas the student scores have increased.

The order of studies in the two years may be an indicator of the relative labour market position of studies according to students.[3] Note that in both years, the order of student scores in HVE and UE is almost identical. This suggests that students had the same ideas in both years about the various labour market opportunities for different studies.

We may conclude that the results do not indicate a strong relation between labour market information and the choice of education. Rather, the results seem to suggest the existence of a 'stereotype view' of labour market opportunities in both years.

Expectations and forecasts

In 1995, students were also asked about their expectations of work after graduation. In addition, they were asked to indicate for three considerations what the importance was for the study chosen. Students did so by dividing 100% among three general considerations:

    ....% income and work after graduation
    ....% the chance of passing the final examination
    ....% the topic of their study
    ____ +
    100%

In Table 4, the scores for these variables have been set off against the labour market forecasts. On average, students believe that after graduation, they have about a 72% chance of finding a job. The labour market forecasts and expectations of students do not show a clearly corresponding pattern. This also applies to the labour market forecasts and consideration of the importance of income and work. We do find a positive, albeit not too high a degree of correspondence between the expected chance of work and the importance of income and work in the choice of education (R= 0.14). The more important students find 'the income and work after graduation', the more chance they give themselves of actually finding work after graduation. Here too, the order of expectations regarding the chances of work corresponds more to the 'stereotype' image of the chances on the labour market.

Table 4
Expectations and forecasts per study in 1995

Study	ROA characterization	Expected chance of work %	Importance for choice of study		
			Income and work %	Passing final exam %	Topic of study %
Higher Vocational (HVE)					
Teacher Training PE*	good	69.5	30.5	27.1	42.9
Teacher Training SE**	good	73.5	26.6	23.6	50.7
Personnel and labour	good	71.7	39.2	25.9	35.5
Social and educational	good	75.7	30.2	26.7	46.1
Laboratory	good	74.3	32.2	24.3	43.4
Electrical engineering	good	76.2	39.9	25.9	36.0
Business administration	moderate	73.6	45.3	25.9	28.7
University (UE)					
Languages	moderate	63.7	21.9	17.1	60.8
Psychology	good	60.5	24.5	19.7	57.4
Sociology	good	64.1	27.8	22.7	50.2
Law	moderate	70.0	39.8	22.3	40.0
Economics	good	72.8	39.5	23.2	38.3
Medicine	good	79.4	31.4	15.5	54.2
Management	reasonable	77.9	38.7	20.4	42.6

*   PE = Primary Education
** SE = Secondary Education
Source: ROA/Determinants of participation

Conclusions

Before we present our conclusions, we must add the following comments:

- the analyses have an exploratory character;
- the fine-tuning of the classification of studies used is not perfect; and
- at the time of they studies, the labour market forecasts were in principle available; for students in 1995, the labour market forecasts of 1995 were not yet available at the time when they chose their studies.

Below are the major findings:

1 We have not found a clear relationship between the latest labour market information and the choices made by students in Higher Education in the Netherlands. In 1991, the pattern of choices made by students largely corresponds to the latest labour market information available at that time. Students who value finding work, more often choose studies with good perspectives. Students who find work less important, more often choose studies with less favourable perspectives. This pattern could not be found in 1995.
2 The 'stereotype image' of labour market chances: 'scientific studies offer better chances, humanities offer less chances of finding employment,' corresponds better to the pattern in the considerations of students to choose a particular study. In other words, choosing a study seems to be determined more by the 'stereotype image' of the labour market chances than by the latest information available on this topic. This may be an important indication that labour market information only reaches students with some delay. This is particularly important if we wish to prevent cobweb cycles. This finding corresponds to the results found by Freeman (1971).
3 The latest generation of students seems to find its chances on the labour market more important when they choose their studies than the previous generation, and this corresponds to a clear improvement of the average labour market perspectives.

Notes

1 Both projects were carried out by SEO and SCO/Kohnstamm Institute at the request of the Ministry of Education, Culture and Science.
2 For the forecasts from 1989, see de Grip et al. (1989); for those from 1995, see ROA (1995).
3 Freeman (1971, pp. 214-217) used this interpretation in his comparison of income expectations in various studies.

References

Becker, G. (1975), *Human Capital, a Theoretical and Empirical Analysis with Special Reference to Education*, National Bureau of Economic Research: New York.

Berger, M.C. (1988), 'Predicted Future Earnings and Choice of College Major', *Industrial and Labor Relations Review*, 41 (3), pp. 418-429.

Betts, J.R. (1996), 'What do Students Know about Wages? Evidence from a Survey of Undergraduates', *Journal of Human Resources*, 31 (1), pp. 27-56.
Dominitz, J., and Manski, C.F. (1994), 'Eliciting Student Expectations of the Returns to Schooling', *NBER Working Paper Series*, no. 4936.
Dominitz, J., and Manski, C.F. (1996), 'Eliciting Student Expectations of the Returns to Schooling', *Journal of Human Resources*, 31 (1), pp. 1-26.
Freeman, R.B. (1971), *The Market for College-Trained Manpower*, Harvard University Press: Cambridge Mass.
Freeman, R.B. (1975), 'Legal Cobwebs: A Recursive Model of the Market for New Lawyers', *Review of Economics and Statistics*, 57 (2), pp. 171-179.
Grip, A. de, Heijke, J.A.M., Dekker, R.J.P. (1989), *The Labour Market by Education and Occupation in 1992*, Research Centre for Education and the Labour Market: Maastricht.
Hopstaken, P., and Meulenbeek, H. (1996), *De financiële positie van beeldend kunstenaars II*, Ministerie van Onderwijs, Cultuur en Wetenschappen: Den Haag.
Jong, U. de, Webbink, H.D., and Roeleveld, J. (1996), *De subjectieve factor, commitments en academische integratie in de studieloopbaan*, series 'Verder Studeren, een panelstudie onder scholieren en studenten', vol. 42, Ministerie van Onderwijs, Cultuur en Wetenschappen: Den Haag.
Kodde, D.A., (1985), *Micro-Economic Analysis of Demand for Education*, Ph.D. thesis, Erasmus University Rotterdam: Rotterdam.
Kodde, D.A., and Ritzen, J.M.M. (1986), *Vraag naar hoger onderwijs, eindrapport*, Series Beleidsgerichte Studies Hoger Onderwijs en Wetenschappelijk Onderzoek, nr. 6, Ministerie van Onderwijs en Wetenschappen: Den Haag.
Manski, C.F. (1993), 'Adolescent Econometricians: How do Youth Infer the Returns to Schooling?', in: Clotfelter, C.T., and Rothschild, M. (eds.), *Studies of Supply and Demand in Higher Education*, University of Chicago Press: Chicago, pp. 43-57.
ROA (1995), *The Labour Market by Education and Occupation to 2000*, ROA-R-1995/3E, Research Centre for Education and the Labour Market: Maastricht.
Webbink, H.D., de Jong, U., Oosterbeek, H., and Roeleveld, J. (1993), *Studiekeuzen van scholieren en studenten in 1991*, series 'Verder Studeren, een panelstudie onder scholieren en studenten', vol. 2, Ministerie van Onderwijs en Wetenschappen: Den Haag.

Acknowledgement

The author wishes to thank Hessel Oosterbeek for his comments on an earlier version.

Part Two
FLEXIBILITY

5 A Job to Match your Education: Does it Matter?

Joop Hartog and Nicole Jonker

Introduction

All over the world, the human capital revolution has left its mark. The Mincerian earnings function stands as a memorial needle in every country that has data on individual earnings. Since the revolution started in the United States in the 1960s, it has become the standard of reference for expressing the relation between *Schooling, Experience and Earnings*: the title of Jacob Mincer's seminal book on the topic (Mincer, 1974). In the standard specification, the logarithm of earnings per hour are related to years of schooling, experience and experience squared. The archivist of such studies is George Psacharopoulos, who collects and summarizes estimates on the rate of return to education from around the globe (e.g. Psacharopoulos, 1985).

As with all revolutions, the radical stage in which the establishment was completely brushed aside, was followed by a period of restoration with reflection on the good things in the old system. After focusing almost completely on the earnings consequences of schooling, attention returned to other benefits of education, which were – at least implicitly – an important element in the old consumption view of schooling. An education is indeed an asset for life, opening up a wide array of benefits, ranging from the joy of intellectual and cultural development, improved health and life expectancy to better jobs and better marriage partners. In this Chapter, we take a position between the revolutionary and the renegade. We follow the revolutionaries in singling out the effects of schooling on earnings, and measuring the effect as the return on an investment. But we modify the earnings function slightly, enough to break away from the world of homogeneity that lies behind the classical earnings equation, and to allow for a labour market where the matching of workers and jobs is important. This provides a link with the pre-revolutionary worlds of Roy (1951) and Tinbergen (1956). It also gives access to the immediate observation that earnings for individuals with a given education are not identical, but vary systematically with the work that the individual performs.

This Chapter will focus on the match between an individual's education and the job that is performed. In the next Section, we will present and discuss the conceptual framework, and give references to the literature. In the third Section we will present measurements of the match quality between individual education and the job held. The measurements refer to the Netherlands and allow an assessment of the development of the match quality over time. In the fourth Section we seek to establish the earnings consequences of the match quality. The last Section contains our conclusions.

Concepts

A job is a set of activities to be performed by a worker. The basic assumption of the human capital theory is that whatever job a worker performs, productivity equals the market return on the worker's investment in education.[1] This implies that human capital is homogenous, generating the same return no matter where it is employed. Stated otherwise, workers with different levels of schooling are perfect substitutes, with a rate of substitution that is identical throughout the economy. There is an alternative approach that we may call the theory of comparative advantage in the labour market. It has roots in the work of Roy (1951) and Tinbergen (1956), and it was beautifully surveyed in Sattinger (1993). The basic assumption of the theory of comparative advantage holds that productivity differentials between individuals with different capabilities depend on the job to which they are assigned. There may or may not be an absolute advantage; in the case of an absolute advantage, an individual with a higher level of some capability is more productive in every job. Only in the case of a comparative advantage is there a relevant assignment problem as an efficiency problem. Without a comparative advantage, there is only a distribution problem: national income is independent of the assignment of workers to job slots.

Write productivity of individual i in job j as:

$$q_{ij} = f(a_i, r_j) \qquad (1)$$

where a_i is the individual's capability level and r_j is an index of the job. Individual capabilities are well-known and frequently used variables like IQ, schooling, training, experience, etc.; r_j is less standard: job indexes are not routinely used in earnings functions. Often used job indexes are the so called *job requirements*: those characteristics required of the worker for adequate performance. Job requirements can be assessed by trained job analysts, job supervisors or personnel departments, or by the worker who holds the job. Job analysts have developed systems such as the *Dictionary of Occupational Titles* in the US, gratings of job requirements by *job level* in countries like the Netherlands and Portugal, and systems of job evaluation as a basis for company pay structures, or structures subject to collective bargaining. Self-assessment by workers may in principle refer to any type of capability. Mostly, applications in worker surveys focus on required education; sometimes, workers are asked to indicate the utilization of their schooling or their abilities in general, thereby implicitly specifying the job requirement.

If the productivity equation was additively separable, i.e. if we could write:

$$q_{ij} = f(a_i) + g(r_j) \qquad (2)$$

then a worker's effort would generate a return to individual capabilities and a return to the requirements of the job. The national product would be independent from the assignment of workers to jobs, as for any assignment, total productivity would be the sum of returns to the individual capabilities and to job requirements. Depending on the distribution of productivity between worker and employer, labour market participants would have an interest in job assignment, but the only relevance would be distributional. If any two workers were to switch jobs, total productivity would remain unchanged.

If we assume wages to reflect productivity, we can translate productivity considerations directly into wage consequences. A simple specification of (1) as a wage equation was developed in the literature on overschooling (see the references below):

$$w_{ij} = \beta r_j + \gamma (a_i - r_j) \qquad (3)$$

where w_{ij} is the logarithm of the wage rate and a_i and r_j refer to schooling levels. Equation (3) specifies that log wages relate to required schooling in the job and that there is a separate payment for deviations between required schooling and the worker's actually attained level of schooling. The wage equation reflects the notion of matching: adequate performance in a job requires a specified education r_j, and deviations will have consequences for productivity and earnings (for elaboration, see Hartog, 1992, Chapter 2). A refinement in applied work, also used below, distinguishes γ for situations of overeducation (attained schooling level higher than required in the job) and undereducation (the reverse). Equation (3) is a very condensed way of reflecting the relevance of job assignment. Mirroring worker heterogeneity expressed in schooling (years, or levels), job heterogeneity is expressed in required schooling (again in years, or levels). Specification (3) entails a restricted form of comparative advantage. Levels of productivity vary with job and worker, but the log specification implies that ratios are constant. The productivity ratio between different individuals depends on the difference in attained schooling levels, independent of the job, while the productivity ratio for the same individual in different jobs depends on the difference in required schooling levels, independent of the worker's level of schooling:

$$w_{ij} - w_{lk} = (\beta - \gamma)(r_j - r_k) \qquad (4)$$

$$w_{ij} - w_{hj} = \gamma(a_i - a_h) \qquad (5)$$

In the literature on overeducation (and undereducation), required schooling has been measured in three different ways:

1 From *job analysis*: systematic evaluation by professional job analysts who specify the required level (and type) of education, for the job titles in an occupational classification. The most elaborate example is the United States *Dictionary of Occupational Titles*. The information was used by Thurow and Lucas (1972) and by Hartog (1980).
2 From *worker self-assessment*: the worker specifies explicitly the education required for the job or indicates whether, compared to his or her actual education, a higher or a lower (or a different) education is needed. This method was applied by Duncan and Hoffman (1981) and by Sicherman (1991).
3 From *realized matches*: required education is set equal to the mean or the median education of workers observed in the job or occupation; overeducation (undereducation) is in such cases sometimes only defined as actual education at least one standard deviation above (below) the observed mean or median. This method was applied by Verdugo and Verdugo (1989).

Conceptually, systematic job analysis is the most attractive source for defining job requirements, because of its explicit goal of objectivity, clear definitions and detailed measurement instructions (see for example the discussion in the *Dictionary of Occupational Titles*). Even the scope for substitution of different levels and types of education (and other traits) can be indicated. Job analysis starts from the technology of the job, the type of activities to be performed. However, the desire for careful, systematic work may also lead to significant lags of information in case of rapid developments in technology and work organization. Worker self-assessment has the advantage of drawing on all local, up-to-date information, but lacks rigorous instructions. Individuals may easily overstate the requirements of their job or simply reproduce actual hiring standards. Using realized matches is far from any ambition to uncover the technological requirements of a job. It simply reflects actual assignment practice as determined by hiring standards and labour market conditions. It is well known that labour market conditions affect hiring standards; such fluctuations contaminate the measurement of technological characteristics of jobs.

Specification (3), distinguishing under- and overeducation, was introduced by Duncan and Hoffman in 1981 for the United States. Similar specifications have been estimated by others, both for the United States (Verdugo and Verdugo, 1989; Sicherman, 1991) and for other countries (Alba-Ramirez, 1993, for Spain, Kiker and Santos, 1991, and Santos, 1992, for Portugal). It is most common to find that overeducation has positive returns, but less than required education. This means that an individual with 11 years of education working in a job that requires only 10 years, gets a return on the eleventh year of education that is positive but smaller than the average return on the 10 years that are required for the job. Undereducation often has a negative effect: if a worker's education falls short of the required level, earnings in a given job are lower than for workers with just the required years of education. Broadly, such results have been found for the United States, Spain, Portugal and the Netherlands. However, sometimes negative returns to years of overeducation are reported (for the United States, see the discussion in Cohn and Khan, 1995, for the United Kingdom, see Groot and Maassen van den Brink, 1995).

For the Netherlands, the equation was first estimated by Oosterbeek in his graduation thesis (and reported in Hartog and Oosterbeek, 1988). The data were taken from the nationwide NPAO survey held in 1982.[2] The standard Mincer earnings equation yields a rate of return to schooling of 6.1%. Using the 'matching' specification, it turned out that required education commanded a return of 7.1%, years of overeducation only 5.7%, and that years of undereducation generated a penalty of 2.5%. All these rates were higher for men than for women, except for the penalty for undereducation.

Groot (1993) uses the Brabant data for 1983 (see below) and a different definition of under/overeducation, and distinguishes between employees with and without additional training. The former have a return of 4.0% and the latter of 6.1%. Both under- and overeducation reduce earnings. Groot focuses his analysis on the role of training programs, an issue to which we will return later.

Match quality measurement

Hartog and Oosterbeek (1988) presented four measurements of worker-job matching for the period 1960-1977; Groot (1993) presented two measurements for 1982-1983. Groot and Maassen van den Brink (1996) present yet another measurement. They use different definitions, so comparison implies both comparison over time and between definitions. Obviously, both are useful, but they serve different purposes.

Table 1 is copied from Hartog and Oosterbeek (1988). The comparison used there has the advantage of using a consistent data set and consistent definitions. The results are based on Dutch Census and Labour Force Surveys. The match quality is derived from a measure of the worker's job level, defined by job analysts' grading of job titles referring to the level of education considered necessary for proper performance.[3] Between 1960 and 1977, when the education level of the labour force rose substantially, overeducation strongly increased, undereducation fell and the incidence of proper matching was almost constant.

Table 1
The utilization of education (percentages of workers); job grading

	1960* %	1971* %	1971** %	1977** %
Overeducation	7.0	13.6	15.4	25.7
Job level matching level of education	57.5	59.3	55.2	53.6
Undereducation	35.6	27.1	29.5	20.6

* Labour force by education and job level, based on Conen and Huygen, 1980
** Labour force by education of job level, based on Huygen et al., 1983
Source: Hartog and Oosterbeek; 1988

Worker assessment of the match quality is also available for different years, but it is based on unrelated worker surveys. In a number of surveys, workers have been asked to state the level of education that they think is necessary for proper performance of their jobs. The results, collected in Table 2, point to an increase in the incidence of overeducation, particularly after the early eighties, and an increase in the incidence of proper matching, in particular during the seventies. Undereducation has steadily fallen over the two decades.

Table 2
The utilization of education (percentages of workers); worker self-assessment

	1974 %	1982 %	1995 %
Overeducation	17	16	24
Job level matching level of education education	53	62	63
Undereducation	30	22	12

Sources: 1974 *Kwaliteit van Arbeid*, Hartog, 1985
1982 *NPAO-survey*, Hartog and Oosterbeek, 1988
1995 *Taakverdeling en Tijdsbesteding*, Groot and Maassen van den Brink, 1996

The effect of different definitions is studied in Table 3. The left-hand panel shows a comparison between job grading and worker self-assessment in the early seventies. The results are comfortably close. The right-hand panel shows a comparison between self-assessment and observed matches. In the latter case, the reference match is defined as the mean years of education observed in the worker's job level, plus or minus one standard deviation. The job level is taken from the standard scale developed by job analysts, covering 7 levels. Thus, overeducation occurs if the worker's attained education is more than one standard deviation above the mean education for the job level. Now the differences are larger, but certainly not alarmingly so.[4]

Table 3
Different measures of match quality (percentages of workers)

	Job grading 1971* %	1971** %	Self-assessment 1974 %	Observed matches 1983 %	Self-assessment 1982 %
Overeducation	14	15	17	16	16
Job level matching level of education	59	55	53	68	62
Undereducation	27	30	30	16	22

Sources: 1971*, 1971** Hartog and Oosterbeek, 1988
1974 Hartog, 1985
1983 Groot, 1993
1982 Hartog and Oosterbeek, 1988

The results in Table 3 provide no strong argument against combining the information from Tables 1 and 2. We may therefore conclude from Tables 1 and 2 that the incidence of overeducation has increased between 1960 and 1995. The incidence of undereducation has decreased. If we merge Tables 1 and 2, the observations for 1977 have the character of an odd jump in an otherwise regular development. Whether this is a real non-monotonicity in the labour market or some peculiarity in the data, is not clear at this stage.

The Brabant-survey has two waves with labour market information. In 1983, individuals who were in the sixth grade of the elementary school in the province of Noord-Brabant in 1952, were reinterviewed. Another reinterview took place in 1993 (the data are documented in Jonker, 1995; an overview of empirical results is given in van Praag, 1993). All individuals in the survey have about the same age, having been born around 1940. An attractive trait of the data set is the information on childhood variables, such as IQ at age 12, family background and school results. From the original 5800 observations in 1952, some 2600 were retrieved in 1983 and some 2000 in 1993. Both in 1983 and in 1993, respondents were asked to state the most desirable education for their job. Using the full samples of workers in 1983 and 1993, we can deduce that the incidence of overeducation was 1.3% in 1983 and 7.3% in 1993. Undereducation was 19.0% in 1983 and 19.3% in 1993. The remainder of the workers were properly allocated:

79.7% in 1983 and 73.4% in 1993. These scores are best compared to the self-assessment scores reported in Table 2 for 1982 and 1995. The incidence of overeducation is remarkably low, while the incidence of proper matching is remarkably high for the Brabant cohort, in both years. This cannot be caused by the wording of the survey question, as this is similar to other surveys. Groot and Maassen van den Brink (1996) demonstrate that with rising age, overeducation falls and undereducation increases, in particular for men, which could explain part of the difference: the Brabant cohort, aged 42 in 1982, is well under way on its career profile. But the fall in overeducation does not fit in this explanation. Perhaps selective retreat from the labour force is a more important factor.

A key feature of the Brabant-survey is the longitudinal character of the observations. Hence, we can see what happened to the improperly matched individuals of 1983 in the decade that followed. In Table 4, we give a cross-tabulation for match quality in 1993 against match quality in 1983, while we also allow for exits. Exits appear to be very frequent: of the workers observed in 1983, 31% has left the labour force by 1993. This reflects the low participation rates that emerged during the eighties. The percentage of employees in the sample fell from 67 to 51, the percentage of the unemployed increased from 1 to 4, of the disabled from 3.4 to 10.4, while the percentage of housewives/housemen increased from 14 to 18. Exits are not markedly different for the properly allocated and the undereducated in 1983. Among the properly allocated, some move towards undereducation (15%), among the 1983 undereducated a fair share remains undereducated (41%), but more than half move towards a proper match. Clearly, match quality can change substantially over a period of ten years.

Table 4
Match quality; dynamic observations

	1983 Over-education	Proper match	1993 Under-education	Exit	Total
Overeducation	1 *(8)* *(14)*	5 *(42)* *(71)*	1 *(8)* *(14)*	5*(42)*	12
Proper match	45 *(5)* *(7)*	469 *(54)* *(78)*	88 *(10)* *(15)*	274*(31)*	876
Undereducation	5 *(2)* *(3)*	82 *(40)* *(56)*	60 *(30)* *(41)*	56*(28)*	203
Total	51 *(5)* *(7)*	556 *(51)* *(74)*	149 *(14)* *(20)*	335*(31)*	1091

Source: Brabant-survey, self-assessment
In parentheses: row percentage,
row percentage, excluding exits

Table 5
Self-assessed match quality; ordered probit estimates (t-values)

	Education 1983		Education 1993		Capabilities 1983		Capabilities 1993	
interval boundary	3.58	(25.47)	2.72	(25.53)	2.69	(37.70)	3.12	(28.44)
intercept	3.84	(6.28)	1.89	(2.88)	0.85	(1.70)	2.12	(3.07)
female	-0.05	(0.33)	0.18	(1.04)	0.13	(1.05)	-0.01	(0.05)
IQ/100	0.57	(1.67)	-0.42	(0.94)	-0.54	(1.80)	-0.01	(2.76)
married	0.03	(0.21)	0.05	(0.29)	0.05	(0.43)	0.26	(1.46)
schooling (years)	-0.23	(9.37)	-0.17	(7.05)	-0.02	(0.86)	-0.02	(0.85)
education father	0.03	(0.46)	0.05	(0.55)	-0.08	(1.27)	-0.06	(0.63)
education mother	0.00	(0.03)	0.13	(1.18)	0.07	(0.92)	0.20	(1.75)
job level father:								
- intermediate	0.15	(1.07)	-0.09	(0.52)	-0.01	(0.09)	-0.16	(0.93)
- high	0.01	(0.02)	-0.04	(0.11)	-0.42	(1.87)	-0.07	(0.15)
- independent	0.12	(1.26)	0.03	(0.23)	0.04	(0.46)	-0.11	(0.88)
job level	0.17	(5.49)	0.31	(5.21)	0.14	(5.24)	0.14	(2.25)
experience	-0.01	(0.86)	0.01	(1.53)	0.00	(0.18)	0.02	(2.00)
hours worked	0.00	(0.85)	0.01	(1.01)	0.01	(1.85)	-0.01	(1.08)
training	-0.29	(2.71)	0.05	(0.30)	-0.02	(2.48)	-0.30	(1.75)
firm size 25-500	0.42	(3.88)	0.11	(0.91)	0.09	(1.00)	-0.08	(0.59)
firm size > 500	0.47	(3.95)	0.18	(1.13)	0.05	(0.49)	-0.25	(1.51)
public sector	-0.00	(0.01)	-0.30	(2.00)	0.05	(0.52)	-0.08	(0.65)
trade	0.14	(0.92)	0.05	(0.30)	0.04	(0.29)		
business service	-0.00	(0.00)	-0.10	(0.44)	0.22	(1.22)		
other	-0.10	(0.86)	0.18	(1.20)	-0.07	(0.70)		
training '83-'93			0.08	(0.49)			0.11	(0.65)
job change '83-'93			-0.01	(0.10)			-0.04	(0.35)
employer change '83-'93			-0.23	(1.87)			-0.19	(1.44)
additional schooling '83-'93			0.03	(0.28)			-0.14	(1.07)
undereducation '83			0.61	(4.84)				
overeducation '83			-0.53	(0.85)				
underutilization '83							-0.38	(2.65)
overutilization '83							1.00	(4.20)
loglikelihood	-631.33		-450.14		837.52		-368.59	
observations	1243		714		1344		753	

Source: Brabant-survey

Since the Brabant-survey is an individual survey with observations on many individual characteristics, we can also investigate to what extent the incidence of over- and undereducation is related to other variables. In Table 5, we relate the match quality to individual characteristics with an ordered probit model. An ordered probit model explains the probability that an individual will be observed in any of a set of ranked intervals of some variable of interest (see Maddala, 1983, Section 2.13). A criterion function is estimated, relating explanatory variables to the value of the criterion function; an individual is assigned to an interval if the criterion value lies between the boundaries of the interval (which are also estimated). If a variable X has a positive coefficient, the probability of ending up in a higher interval of the dependent variable increases with increasing values of X.

In the first two columns, we report results for a model with three intervals: overeducation, proper match, and undereducation. The measurement is based on self-assessment: respondents themselves indicate whether their job requires more or less education than they have actually attained. We will refer to the results as explaining (the probability of) undereducation, meaning that a positive effect of an explanatory variable increases the probability of having a job with required schooling above the attained level. The interval boundaries have been normalized with the boundary between overeducation and proper matching at 1. We included schooling and job level to test whether the incidence of undereducation varies with these variables: there is no reason to expect independence. Undereducation clearly decreases with schooling[5] and increases with job level, in both years (or, at both ages of observation). Gender and family background have no effect, which testifies to the open, meritocratic character of allocation in the Dutch labour market. There are no strong effects of the industrial sector in which the individual works. Most interesting is the comparison between the two years (ages). IQ increases undereducation in 1983, but the effect has disappeared in 1993. The effect of experience on undereducation is larger in 1993 than in 1983. Training had a negative effect in 1983: individuals who had participated in training programs at some stage were less likely to be undereducated, or stated conversely, more likely to be overeducated. This suggests that training is given to those who already have a high level of schooling, relative to their job level as measured by required schooling. This effect has disappeared in 1993. Individuals who had their last training between 1983 and 1993 have no different match quality. Additional schooling in that period or job changes are also irrelevant. An employer change, however, reduces undereducation. This may be due to involuntary changes of employers: a loss in job level for workers who were forced to seek a new employer after the shake-out of the 1980s, a period with high unemployment. If the individual was undereducated in 1983, the probability of undereducation in 1993 is higher: undereducation persists. In 1983, undereducation was more likely if the individual worked in a larger firm, but this effect has disappeared in 1993. It should be noted that the results are not a longitudinal analysis on the same set of individuals: it is just a first analysis of the overlapping but not identical samples in the two years.

In the last two columns we analyze the utilization of capabilities, again based on self-assessment. In both survey years, individuals have been asked to indicate whether their jobs match their capabilities, whether they are underutilized or whether their jobs require higher capability levels than they actually possess. In 1983, 18% indicated underutilization, 5% indicated overutilization, 64% felt properly matched, while 13% did not reply. In 1993, under- and overutilization both scored 5%, 49% felt properly matched, and 41% did not reply. For those who responded, we estimated an ordered probit model for underutilization, proper match, and overutilization. We will refer to the results as explaining (the probability of) overutilization. We now find that IQ reduces overutilization, whereas job level increases it and training reduces it. Gender and family background again have no effect. Also, paralleling the results for undereducation, there are no systematic differences between industries. The size of the firm has no significant effect either. There are no substantial differences between 1983 and 1993. Experience increases overutilization in 1993 and this is an increase relative to the zero-effect in 1983. Additional training or schooling, or mobility between 1983 and 1993, have no effect on capability utilization. Overutilization and underutilization both persist, but persistence is stronger for overutilization than for underutilization. A further analysis of the match between a job and a worker's education and capabilities as a dynamic adjustment process is certainly a challenging topic.

Earnings and match quality

For the Netherlands, there are three sets of estimates of earnings functions (3). Hartog and Oosterbeek (1988) use the NPAO survey 1982, Groot (1993) uses the 1983 Brabant data, and Oosterbeek and Webbink (1996) use the IALS data 1995 (a survey of literacy simultaneously held in a number of countries). In the Section 'Concepts', we reported that Hartog and Oosterbeek (1988) found that in 1982 the rate of return to required education was 7.1%, for overeducation it was 5.7%, whereas the penalty for undereducation was 2.5%. Required education is measured through worker self-assessment. Oosterbeek and Webbink (1996) have add estimates from the IALS survey with required education measured through job analysis. Their comparison over time is based on two different measures of required education: worker self-assessment in 1982, and job analysis in 1995. They found, first of all, that for both men and women the return to required education had increased between 1982 and 1995 (by 1.6 and 2.7 percentage points, respectively).[6] Earlier work, not extending beyond the late eighties, did not detect such an increase, although this was observed in many countries (Hartog, Oosterbeek and Teulings, 1993). The return to overeducation dropped for men and increased for women. The penalty for undereducation became larger for men and smaller for women. Groot (1993) estimated earnings functions separately for workers who participated in company training programs and for workers who did not. Years of overeducation were measured as the number of years that actual education surpasses the mean education for the job level augmented by one standard deviation (undereducation is measured analogously). Note that this involves a scale with a kink: as long as years of actual education are below the job level mean education plus one standard deviation, overeducation is set equal to zero. Required education has a return of 6.1% for non-trained workers and 4.0% for trained workers. This could be explained from a truncation of the sample by level of actual education, as training is relatively more prominent among the lower educated. Both undereducation and overeducation have a negative effect on earnings; this is rather unexpected in view of the results commonly reported in the literature.[7] For workers who have participated in a company training program, the effect of overeducation is very small.

We start our own investigation of the earnings effect of the match between worker and job with a simple characterization. To provide a background, we first estimate a standard Mincer earnings function, relating the logarithm of net hourly wages (earnings per period divided by hours worked per period) to attained years of schooling. We also include experience and experience squared even though this variable naturally has little variation in a cohort like this. The rate of return in 1983 is 7.3%, (6.6% if we also include gender, IQ and a non-graduation dummy) and 7.4 % in 1993 (6.0% in the extended specification). To investigate the effect of match quality, we start with an earnings function in which we relate the natural logarithm of net hourly earnings to the individual's education and to the education that the individual considers necessary for the job. We estimate the relation both for all individuals in each sample and for the subset of individuals included as an observation in both 1983 and 1993. Education is represented with a set of dummies. We started with a full dummy specification for all combinations of attained and required levels of education (not reproduced here) and we added two restricted specifications. In the first, we have five dummies for each level of education: provided, attained, and required level are equal (level 3 being the omitted reference category), plus two separate dummies for overeducation and undereducation. In the second, we define such over- and undereducation dummies separately for each level of required education. Note that this specification does not yield the extra earnings that an individual receives for education surpassing (or falling short of) the required education. Individuals only score on one of the dummies, and, for example, the single dummy for overeducation gives the average earnings of overeducated individuals relative to the reference case (attained education equals required education at level 3). Results are presented in Table 6.

A Job to Match your Education 111

Table 6
Earnings and match quality; regression coefficients (t-values)

	Full samples				Only individuals observed in 1983 and 1993			
	1983	1993	1983	1993	1983	1993	1983	1993
intercept	2.37	2.69	2.38	2.69	2.37	2.68	2.44	2.68
	(73.97)	(111.77)	(74.57)	(119.05)	(73.98)	(95.36)	(60.08)	(103.22)
education								
2	−0.07	−0.07	−0.076	−0.074	−0.07	−0.06	−0.11	−0.06
	(0.92)	(0.54)	(1.04)	(0.57)	(0.93)	(0.47)	(1.14)	(0.51)
3	-	-	-	-	-	-	-	-
4	0.22	0.22	0.22	0.22	0.22	0.19	0.14	0.19
	(3.34)	(4.67)	(3.26)	(4.94)	(3.35)	(3.70)	(1.72)	(3.98)
5	0.50	0.50	0.45	0.50	0.50	0.52	0.42	0.52
	(7.83)	(12.69)	(7.78)	(13.44)	(7.83)	(11.89)	(5.50)	(12.78)
6	0.92	0.73	0.91	0.73	0.92	0.71	0.84	0.71
	(9.13)	(10.56)	(9.15)	(11.16)	(9.13)	(9.19)	(6.84)	(9.86)
overeducation	−0.44	0.19			−0.44	0.20		
	(1.93)	(2.70)			(1.92)	(2.42)		
undereducation	0.19	0.23			0.19	0.24		
	(3.40)	(6.95)			(3.49)	(6.32)		
overeducation								
2			n.a.	n.a.			n.a.	n.a.
3			−0.65	−0.03			−1.23	−0.12
			(2.51)	(0.29)			(3.07)	(0.88)
4			−0.41	0.27			−0.73	0.28
			(1.57)	(2.41)			(2.33)	(2.27)
5			−0.29	0.70			−0.35	0.70
			(0.42)	(4.46)			(0.50)	(4.15)
undereducation								
3			0.48	−0.01			0.08	0.01
			(0.36)	(0.01)			(0.36)	(0.07)
4			0.04	0.09			−0.12	0.08
			(0.56)	(2.52)			(1.36)	(1.83)
5			0.38	0.42			0.30	0.42
			(4.21)	(9.11)			(2.79)	(8.60)
6			0.91	0.80			0.78	0.85
			(4.61)	(8.87)			(3.52)	(8.94)
$\bar{R}^2$	0.11	0.20	0.13	0.28	0.11	0.21	0.13	0.31
N	1146	927	1146	927	737	720	737	720

Source: Brabant-survey

Between 1983 and 1993, the earnings for properly allocated individuals with the highest level of education lagged behind. In 1983, they were 2.5 times the earnings of the reference individual (exp 0.92) and in 1993 only twice as high (exp 0.72). This is remarkable, as generally earnings differentials between individuals tend to widen with age. Peak earnings are generally reached between age 45 and 50, so this would suggest that the highest educated have a relatively steep drop in earnings once they are over the hill. It is more likely, however, that individuals with the highest level of education are subject to the decrease in the returns to education that has been observed for many developed countries, but so far not for the Netherlands (Oosterbeek and Webbink, 1996, with different data, do not find a decrease between 1982 and 1995, but stability for men and an increase for women). In both years, undereducated individuals earned more than the reference individual. However, overeducated individuals earned less in 1983 and more in 1993. The result for 1983 can hardly be trusted, however, as it is based on only 12 overeducated individuals (cf. Table 4). In 1993, we have 51 individuals reporting undereducation, and the earnings effect is positive. Whether we consider the 1983 and the 1993 samples separately or restrict the analyses to individuals included in both samples, does not really matter for these results. The positive effects of both overeducation and undereducation are to be understood from the fact that they measure the earnings differential compared to a properly allocated individual at education level 3. Hence, most information is in the relative magnitudes of the dummies. As may be expected, they increase by level of education and are higher for overeducation than for undereducation.

The results for the longitudinal subset are similar but not identical. The earnings structure by education appears to have flattened. There is not only a drop for earnings at the highest level of education, but there is also an increase at the bottom. The latter effect may be related to selective exits into unemployment and disability schemes.

After exploring changes in the data at the surface, we will now impose a little more structure and estimate an earnings function like (3) while adding other explanatory variables. Education will now be measured in years, rather than as an ordinal variable. For required education, we take the education that the worker states as required for the job and then translate that into nominal years needed to attain that level (the translation is given in appendix A). For under- and overeducation we take the difference between required and actual education.

Actual education is measured as nominal school years needed to complete the highest school level that the individual attended, plus a separate dummy for non-graduation from this schooling level (this specification is indicated as 'nominal'). Again, we give results for the separate samples and for the longitudinal sample of individuals observed in both years. As additional control variables we use gender, participation in any training program, experience and IQ. IQ was measured in grade 6, when the individual was about 12 years old. We use two measures: PM and WS. PM is the Progressive Matrices Test, a series of figures containing some regularity, WS offers listings of six words from which a proper synonym had to be selected. Results are given in Table 7.

Table 7
Earnings and match quality; regression coefficients (t-values)

	Full samples				Only individuals observed in 1983 and 1993			
	1983	1993	1983	1993	1983	1993	1983	1993
intercept	1.76	1.83	1.29	1.46	1.83	1.83	1.35	1.42
	(24.70)	(25.79)	(4.09)	(7.53)	(19.85)	(23.67)	(2.99)	(6.74)
required schooling	0.07	0.08	0.06	0.01	0.07	0.08	0.01	0.08
	(11.72)	(16.80)	(8.38)	(12.85)	(8.84)	(15.53)	(6.09)	(12.25)
overeducation	-0.15	0.03	-0.13	0.00	-0.23	0.03	-0.20	0.03
	(-3.41)	(2.07)	(-3.17)	(2.05)	(-3.81)	(1.82)	(-3.57)	(2.02)
undereducation	-0.04	-0.03	-0.05	-0.00	-0.56	-0.03	-0.01	-0.03
	(-3.72)	(-5.07)	(-4.49)	(-5.07)	(3.83)	(-4.98)	(-4.59)	(-4.93)
non graduation	-0.08	-0.03	0.05	-0.03	-0.09	-0.04	-0.12	-0.03
	(-1.51)	(-0.58)	(-2.12)	(-0.56)	(-1.39)	(-0.89)	(-1.94)	(-0.65)
experience	-	-	0.01	0.02	-	-	0.02	-0.02
			(0.38)	(1.48)			(0.54)	(1.32)
experience^2	-	-	-0.00	-0.00	-	-	-0.01	-0.00
			(-0.64)	(-1.24)			(-0.77)	(-1.07)
training	-	-	0.12	0.02	-	-	0.13	0.00
			(2.90)	(0.56)			(2.29)	(0.07)
IQ-PM	-	-	-0.00	0.02	-	-	0.00	0.00
			(-0.09)	(1.35)			(0.51)	(1.44)
IQ-WS	-	-	0.01	0.00	-	-	0.01	0.01
			(4.29)	(1.09)			(2.34)	(0.87)
female	-	-	-0.67	-0.19	-	-	-0.66	-0.21
			(-15.86)	(-4.76)			(-11.90)	(-4.59)
SER	0.68	0.38	0.60	0.37	0.69	0.37	0.62	0.36
$\bar{R}^2$	0.11	0.28	0.30	0.33	0.11	0.29	0.27	0.32
N	1154	746	1154	746	745	619	745	619

Source: Brabant-survey

We find that between 1983 and 1993 the return to required education increased; the magnitude of the increase depends on the specification, but it is at least one percentage point. There is a penalty for undereducation, but it is smaller than the return to required education. Moving to a job that requires more education, pays off, even if the worker does not have the extra education. For example, in 1993 for the full, non-longitudinal sample, the return for an extra year of education required by the job is 8.4%. If the individual does not provide that extra year of education, the penalty is 3.2%, leaving a wage gain from moving to the more demanding job of 6.2%. For overeducation in 1983, we see again the negative wage effect, but as noticed before we should discard this on account of the small number of observations. The result in 1993 conforms to the usual findings in the literature, with a return that is positive but smaller than that on required education. The effects of experience are small, but this is to be expected, as the sample shows very little variation in experience values. Leaving school without the associated diploma reduces wages by some 4 to 6%. This is a plausible result. Hartog (1983) has shown how this effect may vary for different types of education. Here we find the interesting result that training only has a positive effect in 1983, not in 1993. This might be related to the nature of the training and to the way careers proceed. It may very well be that training received up to age 42 was career-oriented training, and may even be a requirement set by the employer for promotion to a better job. Later in their careers, when the workers are in their forties, the courses may reflect gross investment to beat depreciation, without net effects. It may also be that at this advanced stage, employers bear the cost and hence recoup the benefits, whereas in the earlier stages, with less information on worker qualities and dependability, the investment was shared between employer and employee. Training, of course, will be endogenous and full investigation requires a more structured model. Groot (1993) is an example, using the 1983 data set of the Brabant-survey. Among the IQ variables, only the verbal test score IQ WS has a significant effect, and even then only in 1983. Adding the controls reduces the returns to education by about one percentage point. Women earn dramatically less than men in this data set, but this is an issue we will not pursue in this Chapter.

Conclusions

If our objective was merely to provide an answer to the question raised in the title, the conclusion would be simple: yes, it does matter where in the labour market an individual ends up. A job that does not fully match a worker's education pays less, and if a worker manages to secure a job that requires a higher level of education than attained, his (and her) wages increase. A highly relevant implication of these results is the profitability of overschooling: even years of education that are not required for the job have a rate of return that is both statistically and economically significant: a real return of 3.5% is quite a fair rate.

Of course there are many caveats in this kind of research. Measuring job requirements and required education for a job is a difficult task. Not only should one acknowledge sizable measurement errors, one should in an ideal situation also consider potential substitutes for undereducation and possible explanations for overeducation. Particular types of experience, as reflected in work histories, may be relevant, but we have not investigated this possibility. Other potential intervening variables, such as training and intellectual ability have been included.

In particular, including the latter variable is a strong point for the results presented above. But the relation with training deserves more attention. The present data set is less than ideal for this purpose, however, as we have no information on the timing of the training prior to 1983. For training in the period 1983-1993, we have more detailed information. Further analysis using those observations would seem a worthy research target for the near future.

Notes

1. Throughout this Chapter, we use the terms education and schooling interchangeably, ignoring the wider connotations of education as compared to schooling.
2. NPAO is the acronym of Nationaal Programma Arbeidsmarkt Onderzoek (National Program Labour Market Research), a government program that funded labour market research and data collection.
3. The second column for 1971 is based on a revision of the data by one of the initial authors; see Hartog and Oosterbeek (1988) for references. Assignments of job level rankings to jobs were made separately for each year, thus allowing for jobs to be upgraded or downgraded.
4. However, for the United States Cohn and Khan (1995) report substantial differences between measurement through worker self-assessment and through realized matches.
5. To some extent this is obvious, as undereducation is impossible for individuals who have completed the highest level of education. Of course, this does not eliminate the need to allow for variations across schooling levels. A flexible dummy specification might be useful: in this exploration we only allow for a linear effect on the criterion function.
6. In a traditional Mincer earnings equation with actual education, returns for men increase from 6.5 to 6.8% and for women from 4.7 to 6.2%.
7. Groot reports positive coefficients for undereducation, but for comparability his estimates have to be adjusted. He specifies an earnings equation based on *actual* education and over/undereducation, rather than starting from *required* education as in (3). For comparability with specification (3), the coefficient for overeducation is to be calculated as the sum of Groot's coefficients for actual and overeducation. The comparable coefficient for undereducation is found by subtracting his actual-education coefficient from the undereducation coefficient.

References

Alba-Ramirez, A. (1993), 'Mismatch in the Spanish Labor Market?', *Journal of Human Resources*, 28 (2), pp. 259-278.
Cohn, E., and Khan, S. (1995), 'The Wage Effects of Overschooling Revisited', *Labour Economics, an International Journal*, 2 (1), pp. 67-76.
Conen, G.J.M., and Huijgen, F. (1980), 'De kwalitatieve struktuur van de werkgelegenheid in 1960 en 1971', *Economisch Statistische Berichten*, 3251, pp. 480-487; 3253, pp. 546-554; 3255, pp. 612-618; 3257, pp. 661-668.
Duncan, G., and Hoffman, S.D. (1981), 'The Incidence and Wage Effects of Overeducation', *Economics of Education Review*, 1 (1), pp. 75-86.
Groot, W. (1993), 'Overscholing, onderscholing en het rendement op bedrijfs opleiding', *Mens en Maatschappij*, 68 (4), pp. 386-405.
Groot, W., and Maassen van den Brink, H. (1995), *Allocation and the Returns to Overeducation in the United Kingdom*, Tinbergen Institute Discussion Paper TI 3-95-205, Universiteit van Amsterdam: Amsterdam.
Groot, W., and Maassen van den Brink, H. (1996), 'Overscholing en verdringing op de arbeidsmarkt', *Economisch Statistische Berichten*, 81 (4042), pp. 74-77.
Hartog, J. (1980), 'Earnings and Capability Requirements', *Review of Economics and Statistics*, 62 (2), pp. 230-240.
Hartog, J. (1983), 'To Graduate or not: Does it Matter?', *Economics Letters*, 12, pp. 193-199.
Hartog, J. (1992), *Capabilities, Allocation and Earnings*, Kluwer Academic Publishers: Boston.
Hartog, J., and Oosterbeek, H. (1988), 'Education, Allocation and Earnings in the Netherlands: Overschooling?', *Economics of Education Review*, 7 (2), pp. 185-194.
Hartog, J., Oosterbeek, H., and Teulings, C. (1993), 'Age, Wage and Education in the Netherlands', in: Johnson, P., and Zimmermann, K. (eds.), *Labour Markets in an Aging Europe*, Cambridge University Press: Cambridge.
Huijgen, F., Riesewijk, B.J.P., and Conen, G.J.M. (1983), 'De kwalitatieve structuur van de werkgelegenheid', *Economisch Statistische Berichten*, 4302, pp. 361-369; 3404, pp. 416-422; 3406, pp. 464-469.
Jonker, N. (1995), *Vervolgonderzoek Noordbrabantse zesdeklassers*, Universiteit van Amsterdam, vakgroep Algemene Economie: Amsterdam.
Kiker, B.F., and Santos, M.C. (1991), 'Human Capital and Earnings in Portugal', *Economics of Education Review*, 10 (3), pp. 187-203.
Maddala, G.S. (1983), *Limited-Dependent and Qualitative Variables in Econometrics*, Cambridge University Press: Cambridge.
Mincer, J. (1974), *Schooling, Experience and Earnings*, Columbia University Press: New York.

Oosterbeek, H., and Webbink, D. (1996), 'Over scholing, overscholing en inkomen', *Economisch Statistische Berichten*, 81 (4049), pp. 240-241.

Praag, C.M. van (1993), *Zomaar een dataset: De Noordbrabantse zesdeklassers, een presentatie van 15 jaar onderzoek*, Universiteit van Amsterdam, vakgroep Algemene Economie: Amsterdam.

Psacharopoulos, G. (1985), 'Returns to Education: a Further International Update and Implications', *Journal of Human Resources*, 20, pp. 583-604.

Roy, A.D. (1951), 'Some Thoughts on the Distribution of Earnings', *Oxford Economic Papers*, 3, pp. 135-146.

Santos, M.C. (1992), *An Exploration of Different Measures for Job Requirements: Over- (Under) Education on the Portuguese Labor Market*, Working Paper Faculdade Economia de Porto, Presented at the EALE meetings: Warwick.

Sattinger, M. (1993), 'Assignment Models of the Distribution of Earnings', *Journal of Economic Literature*, 31 (2), pp. 851-880.

Sicherman, N. (1991), 'Overeducation in the Labor Market', *Journal of Labor Economics*, 9 (2), pp. 101-122.

Thurow, L.C., and Lucas, R.E.B. (1972), *The American Distribution of Income: a Structural Problem*, a Study for the Joint Economic Committee, US Congress, Government Printing Office: Washington DC.

Tinbergen, J. (1956), 'On the Theory of Income Distribution', *Weltwirtchaftliches Archiv*, 77, pp. 156-175.

United States Department of Labor (1965), *Dictionary of Occupational Titles*, Government Printing Office: Washington DC.

Verdugo, R., and Verdugo, N. (1989), 'The Impact of Surplus Schooling on Earnings', *Journal of Human Resources*, 24 (4), pp. 629-643.

Acknowledgement

We are grateful for the comments given by Lex Borghans, Hessel Oosterbeek and participants in the ROA 10th Anniversary Conference.

Appendix A: Schooling levels and schooling years

1983

Schooling is defined according to the standard classification of the government statistical agency CBS, the 1987 S.O.I. Levels and years are related as follows:

1 = below primary level (kleuterschool)	0	years
2 = primary level(lagere school)	6	years
3 = secondary level, first step (LAVO, VGLO, MAVO)	9	years
4 = secondary level, second step (HBS, MMS, HAVO, VWO)	12	years
5 = third level, first step (HBO)	16	years
6 = third level, second step (WO)	18	years

1993

The classification for 1993 is as follows:

1 = primary education	6	years
2 = lower vocational	9	years
3 = intermediate general	10	years
4 = intermediate vocational	13	years
5 = higher general education	12	years
6 = higher vocational and university (kandidaats: bachelor's)	16	years
7 = university	18	years

6 Flexibility and Structure of the Dutch Labour Market

Lex Borghans and Hans Heijke

Introduction

The labour market is not completely subdivided into separate submarkets for each category of educated labour. In practice, occupations can be fulfilled by individuals with different educational backgrounds. As a result of the similarities and differences of qualifications, two different types of education may have a joint occupational domain, but may also have occupational opportunities that are mutually exclusive.

This overlapping structure of the labour market makes it possible to adjust the employment of individuals with a particular educational background to the changing needs of society. If the relationship between occupation and education were a one-to-one relationship, the available supply of workers in the labour force with a particular educational background would be the only factor determining the occupational structure of the labour force. Due to overlap in the occupational domains of various types of education, however, adjustments in the educational background of the workforce in a certain occupation are possible, even indirectly, by employment changes of types of education that are not primarily suited for the occupation concerned.

Imagine, for example, that lawyers find work as civil servants, while economists become both civil servants and computer programmers, and technically skilled individuals also become programmers and can find work in technical jobs. If there is an increasing demand for technicians, the overlapping structure of the labour market might make it possible for workers with a technical educational background to move to the technical jobs, leaving the programming jobs for the economists. Similarly, the economists may leave the civil service jobs to the lawyers, of whom there may not be such a shortage on the labour market. The overlapping structure of the labour market therefore enables flexible adjustment to changing needs by possibly long chains of occupational job-to-job mobility.

A similar adjustment potential would be created if education had a very general nature, focussing on general abilities as is often propagated. The disadvantage of such an approach, however, would be that in this case flexibility would lead to a great decrease of productivity. The curriculum should then provide the skills that are suited for a large number of occupations, while only one occupation will actually be taken. Given the amount of time available for education, this implies a reduction of the depth of the study. There is therefore a trade-off between a general curriculum and the degree of specialisation.

In the labour market, many changes may occur in the structure of occupational needs. Two types of changes can be distinguished. Firstly, the volume of certain occupational groups may increase while that of others shrinks. Since all types of education focus on specific occupations, this immediately implies a changing demand for education. Secondly, changes with respect to the qualifications required may take place within specific occupations. On the one hand, these changes of the required qualifications may be due to an upgrading process in which employers require higher skill levels because of the increased complexity of the technology used. On the other hand, these shifts may be caused by a change of the character of certain occupations. In certain logistic occupations, for example, technical knowledge is becoming less important, while economic qualifications are gaining importance, because the available equipment requires less knowledge, while at the same time the value of the capital involved increases. Finally, shifts of required qualifications may be caused by changes in the scarcity of different groups of workers, making it more attractive for employers to recruit workers with an educational background that is more prevalent and whose wages can be lower.

This chapter investigates the changes in the structure of the Dutch labour market between 1981 and 1993. Attention will be focussed on the occupational structure of the labour force with a certain educational background. The occupational domain of types of education and their mutual overlaps will be investigated for both 1981 and 1993, and we will analyse how the educational structure has been adjusted to the changing needs of the labour market in this period.

The remainder of the chapter is structured as follows. The second section gives a brief overview of the quantitative changes between 1981 and 1993. The third section investigates the measurement of the size of the occupational domain and the similarities between the occupational domains of different types of education. The fourth section provides an example of a changing overlapping structure. The fifth section describes the changes in the occupational structure, while the sixth section analyses the developments in similarity between types of education. Lastly, the seventh section contains some conclusions.

Changes in the Dutch labour market

In 1981 the Dutch working population consisted of 5.1 million people. In 1993 approximately 5.8 million people were employed. This implies an increase of 0.7 million people.[1] This increase is the result of both the entry of newcomers and the withdrawal of those employed in 1981. In addition, some changed occupations without leaving the labour market. These processes have led to increasing numbers of people working in certain occupational and educational groups and a reduction of employment in others. The educational groups which grew all together increased by 1.3 million people, while the others shrunk by 0.6 million. The growing occupations contain 1.2 million people more than in 1981, while there was an employment reduction of half a million for others. Occupational dynamics therefore, has been larger than educational dynamics.

Looking at each combination of type of education and occupation separately, there has been a total employment increase of 1.76 million people in some groups, while there has been a reduction of 1.09 million people in others. This means that there have been many more changes in the labour market than needed for a quantitative adjustment for the increase and decrease of occupations.

Table 1 provides an overview of the number of people in the workforce for different types of education. The table shows that there has been a major reduction of people with only Primary Education (PE). Also, some types of education at the Preparatory Vocational Education (PVE) level faced a small reduction in numbers of people. All other educational groups have been growing. In particular, some types of education at the academic level experience very large increases.

The changes of employment per educational category may correspond to the changes in the number of people required for specific occupations. In addition to the employment for all types of education in 1981 and 1993, the table therefore provides a calculation of the number of people required to cover the employment growth per occupation from 1981 until 1993, when the educational structure of all occupations was constant. This fixed structure projection for 1993, however, appears to be much more similar to the employment situation in 1981 than the educational distribution actually observed. Since the labour force grew between 1981 and 1993, more workers were required for most types of education, but this growth was not concentrated in certain types of education. PVE Agriculture and Technical were the only exceptions, facing a decline of the demand based on this fixed structure forecast, while at Intermediate Vocational Education (IVE) level Nursing and Paramedic Services and Commerce and Administration, at Higher Vocational Education (HVE) level Commerce and Administration, and Social and Cultural, and at University Education (UE) level Mathematics and Natural Sciences, Engineering, Medical Sciences, Pharmacy, Economics and Law

Table 1
Employment in 1981 and 1993 per educational category, and a comparison between actual employment and projected employment based on the educational structure in 1981

	Employment 1981 × 1,000	Fixed struct. projection 1993 × 1,000	Employment 1993 × 1,000	'Excess supply' persons × 1,000	%'81
PE	986	995	586	-410	-42
Lower General Secondary Education	418	455	399	-56	-13
PVE					
Agriculture	115	111	95	-16	-14
Technical	557	553	512	-42	-7
Transport & Harbour	12	12	39	27	223
Commerce & Administration	102	112	131	20	19
Community Care, Hotel & Catering	231	233	209	-24	-10
Security	3	4	7	3	102
Higher General Secondary Education	217	272	279	7	3
IVE					
Agriculture	89	92	122	30	34
Non-Medical Laboratory	5	6	13	7	160
Engineering	505	548	679	131	26
Transport & Harbour	44	49	44	-6	-12
Medical Laboratory	17	22	22	0	1
Nursing & Paramedical Services	113	170	173	3	3
Commerce & Administration	482	568	666	99	20
Administrative, Legal & Fiscal	40	50	46	-4	-9
Social & Cultural	26	33	44	11	43
Community Care	120	136	212	76	63
Hotel, Catering & Hairdressing	35	36	47	11	33
Police, Fire & Defence Forces	55	57	87	30	53
HVE					
Teacher Training	209	234	243	8.5	4
Interpreter & Translator	4	5	6	1	22
Theology	3	3	4	0.5	20
Agriculture	8	10	16	6.5	85
Non-Medical Laboratory	14	20	29	9	63
Engineering	89	141	118	-22.5	-25
Transport & Harbour	20	26	26	-0.5	-2

Table 1 (continued)
Employment in 1981 and 1993 per educational category, and a comparison between actual employment and projected employment based on the educational structure in 1981

	Employment 1981 × 1,000	Fixed struct. projection 1993 × 1,000	Employment 1993 × 1,000	'Excess supply' persons × 1,000	%'81
Medical Laboratory	13	16	19	3	24
Nursing & Physiotherapy etc.	34	56	78	22	65
Commerce & Administration	66	114	172	59	88
Business Administration Technology	1	2	11	9	777
Administrative, Legal & Fiscal	11	17	20	4	34
Social & Cultural	45	71	104	33	73
Hotel & Catering Industry	3	4	4	0	-3
Fine Arts	23	30	34	4	17
Police, Fire & Defence Forces	6	7	10	3	43
UE					
Teacher Training	12	14	20	6	46
Arts	14	18	36	18	130
Theology	6	6	7	1	17
Agriculture	4	6	10	4	94
Mathematics & Natural Sciences	21	32	39	8	35
Engineering	31	52	55	3	10
Veterinary & Medical Sciences & Dentistry	33	47	48	2	5
Pharmacy	2	4	5	2	95
Economics, Econometrics & Busin. Admin.	22	40	50	10	44
Law & Public Administration	23	41	50	9	41
Social Sciences	28	38	74	37	132
Fine Arts	2	2	5	3	222

experienced a large increase of the demand in the occupations which were relevant for them in 1981.

The last two columns of the table indicate the absolute and relative surpluses if only this fixed structure demand were relevant. The table shows that if we only count the changes in occupational structure, there would be large shortages for primary education and some other educational types at lower levels. Excess supply appears for relatively new types of education, such as PVE Security, HVE Business Administration Technology and UE Social Sciences.

As mentioned before, it is unlikely that these new types of education are the ones facing most of the excess supply. The table indicates that, besides occupational shifts, changes in employers' requirements with respect to the educational background required to fulfil an occupation are highly relevant. These changing requirements may be caused by exogenous shifts of the skills needed, due to technological changes, but are of course partly also caused by market reactions. As a result of the relatively high level of supply of higher levels of education, these groups became less scarce and therefore it became easier for employers to recruit people at higher skill levels for the same job.

Measuring switching opportunities and educational similarities

In order to investigate the extent of the occupational domains and the overlaps in the occupational domains between types of education, we need measurements. In this chapter, the extent of the occupational domain is measured by an index which is closely connected to the indicator for switching opportunities introduced by Warnken (1986) and de Grip and Heijke (1988). The overlap in the occupational domain is measured by the similarity index introduced in Borghans (1992). In this section, both measurements will be explained and attention will be paid to the way in which these indices can give additional information about the developments in the occupational structure of types of education.

The extent of the occupational domain

As mentioned above, although vocational education is sometimes focused on a specific category of jobs, in actual practice individuals with a certain educational background are employed in a range of occupations.

According to Warnken (1986), the extent of an occupational domain can be measured by the Gini-Hirschman index. This index is based on the probability that two individuals with the same educational background are in the same occupational group. If f_{ij} reflects the fraction of people with an educational background i in occupation j (and therefore $\sum_i f_{ij} = 1$), then this probability equals:

$$P_i = \sum_j f_{ij}^2 \tag{1}$$

The probability equals 1 if everyone is in the same occupational group, while it equals $1/m$ – where m denotes the number of occupational groups – if all workers are spread equally over all occupations. The following transformation of P_i:

$$K_i = \frac{1}{P_i} \tag{2}$$

has the property that if people with an educational background i are occupied in n occupations, where in all these occupations the fraction equals $1/n$, then $K_i = n$. This index can therefore be interpreted as the *equivalent number of occupations* of the occupational domain.[2]

A stylised example

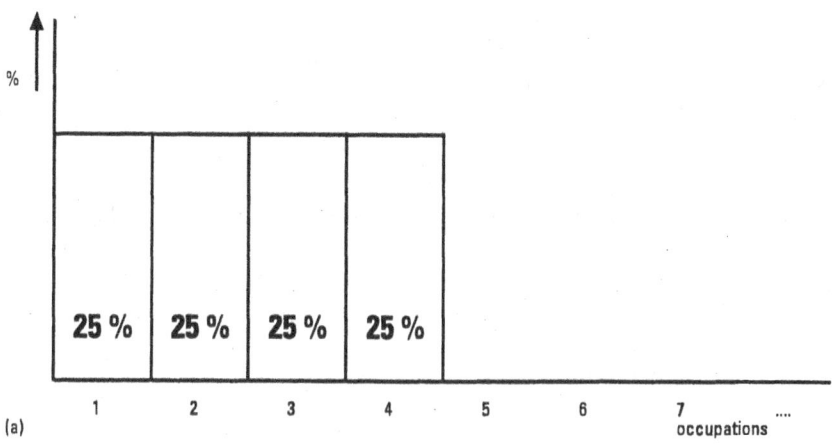

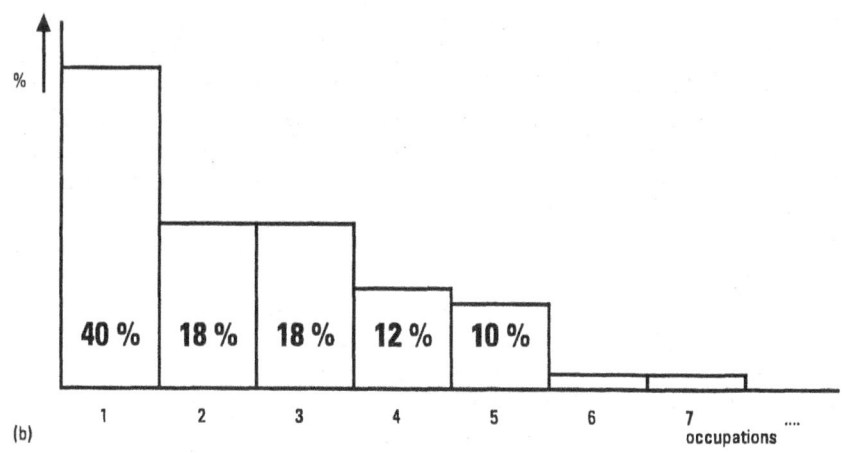

Figure 1 Example of two occupational distributions (a) with a uniform spread and (b) with occupations of different importance, both of which have an extent of the occupational domain of 4

Figure 1a gives an example of this. It shows an imaginary type of education. The individuals in the working population with this educational background are spread equally over four different occupations. This implies that the probability that two people with the same educational background work in the same occupation equals 0.25. There is a probability of 1/4 × 1/4 = 1/16 that both work in occupation 1, and also a probability of 1/16 that they both work in occupation 2, 3 or 4. This implies that the measure of the extent of the occupational domain equals 1/0.25 = 4, i.e. the number of occupations involved.

In practice, of course the occupational spread of a type of education will be less uniform than in this example. Figure 1b gives an example of this. By merely counting the number of occupations in which the individuals in the working population with this educational background work, the importance of the smaller occupations would be overemphasised. The index used, however, gives more weight to the larger occupations since the probability that two workers with the same educational background meet in this occupation is larger. Although the example of Figure 1b is on the one hand more concentrated in some occupations and on the other hand more spread over other occupations, the extent of the occupational domain is also measured as 4.[3]

Overlap in occupational domains

Besides the fact that most types of education have an occupational domain of more than one occupation, it will in general also be the case that within one occupation there will be individuals with different educational backgrounds. There is therefore a certain amount of overlap in the occupational domain of different types of education. To get an impression of the degree of overlap between educational types, we need to measure the similarity.

In the same way as measuring the probability that two individuals with the same educational background are in the same occupation, the probability that two individuals with different educational backgrounds are occupied in the same job can be calculated:

$$P(i,ii) = \sum_j f_{ij} f_{iij} \tag{3}$$

This probability gives insight in the degree of overlap between the occupational domains of two types of education. The similarity measurement (Borghans, 1992) equals this probability, relative to the probability that individual with the same educational background are in the same occupation:

$$Sim(i,ii) = \frac{P(i,ii)}{\sqrt{P_i P_{ii}}} \tag{4}$$

Flexibility and Structure of the Dutch Labour Market 127

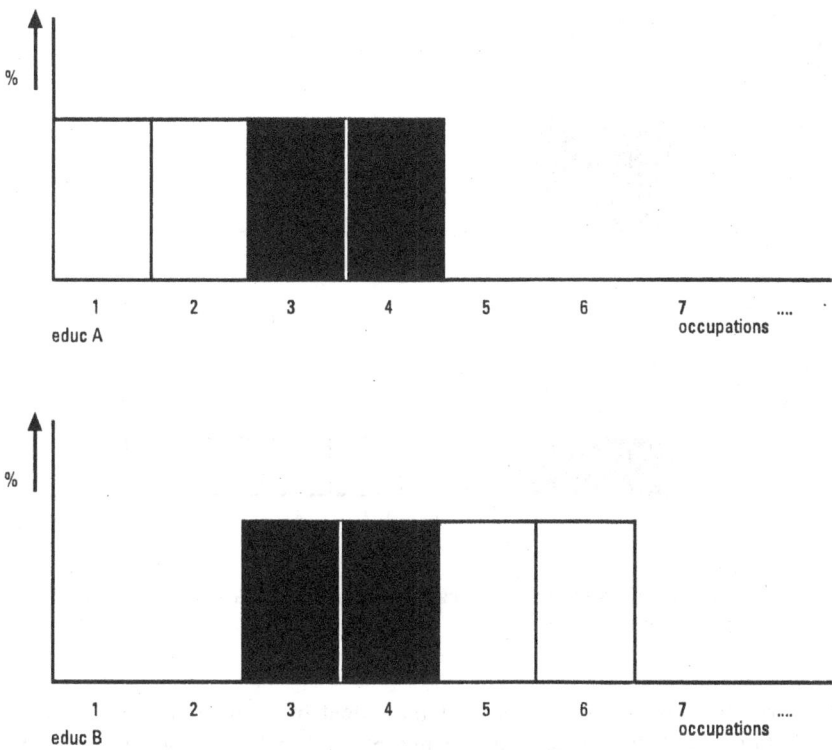

Figure 2 Example of two types of education with equally sized occupational domains, which have an overlap of 50%

This similarity equals 1, if i and ii have the same distribution across the occupations; it equals 0, if there is no occupation in which both a worker with the educational background i and one with the background ii is employed.

Figure 2 provides an example of this measurement. It provides the occupational distribution of two types of education, both of which have an occupational domain of 4. There are in this example two occupations in which both types of education meet each other. Therefore the probability that a worker with the one educational background meets a worker with the other educational background in the same occupation equals $1/4 \times 1/4 + 1/4 \times 1/4 = 1/8$. Since the probability that workers with the same educational background meet in the same occupation equals 1/4 for both types of education, the ratio between these probabilities equals 0.50, i.e. the two types of education share 50% of their occupational domains.

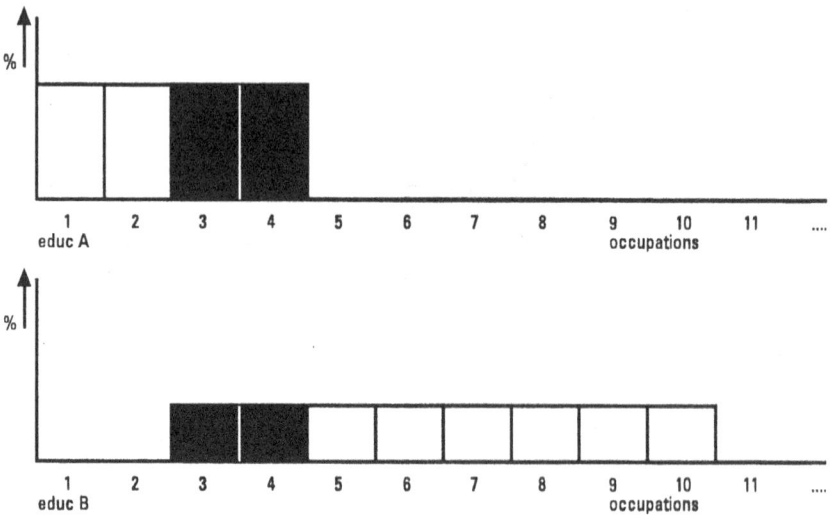

Figure 3 Example of two types of education with differences as to the extent of their occupational domains

As was the case in the example of the extent of occupational domains, the distribution across the occupations in this example is also more uniform than would be found in practice. The similarity measurement deals with the effects of larger and smaller jobs in a similar way, however. The example is also stylised since both types of education have occupational domains of equal size. Figure 3 provides an example in which two types of education share two occupations, but in which the number of the occupational domain is 4 for one and 8 for the other type of education. The probability that workers with these educational backgrounds meet is reduced to 1/16, due to the wider spread of the second type of education. Comparing this probability to the extent of the occupational domain of the first type of education would imply a similarity of 0.25, while the similarity would be 0.50 if the second type of education were used as a reference. These outcomes reflect the fact that the first type of education overlaps 0.25 of the second, but reversely the second overlaps 0.5 of the first occupational domain. The similarity measurement compromises between these outcomes and equals 0.35, which equals the geometric mean of 0.50 and 0.25.

Developments in occupational domains

In this chapter, the focus is on the development of the occupational domains over time. The measurements introduced also provide the possibility of analysing such developments. In the same way as the occupational overlap of two types of education at the same moment in time, the overlap of types of education at different moments of time can also be measured.[4]

Suppose, for example, that the third occupation in Figure 2 becomes much more important, e.g. 4 times as large as in the previous period. If both types of education react to this growth by also increasing their employment levels in this occupation by the factor 4, the extent of the occupational domain will reduce in both from 4 to 2.6.

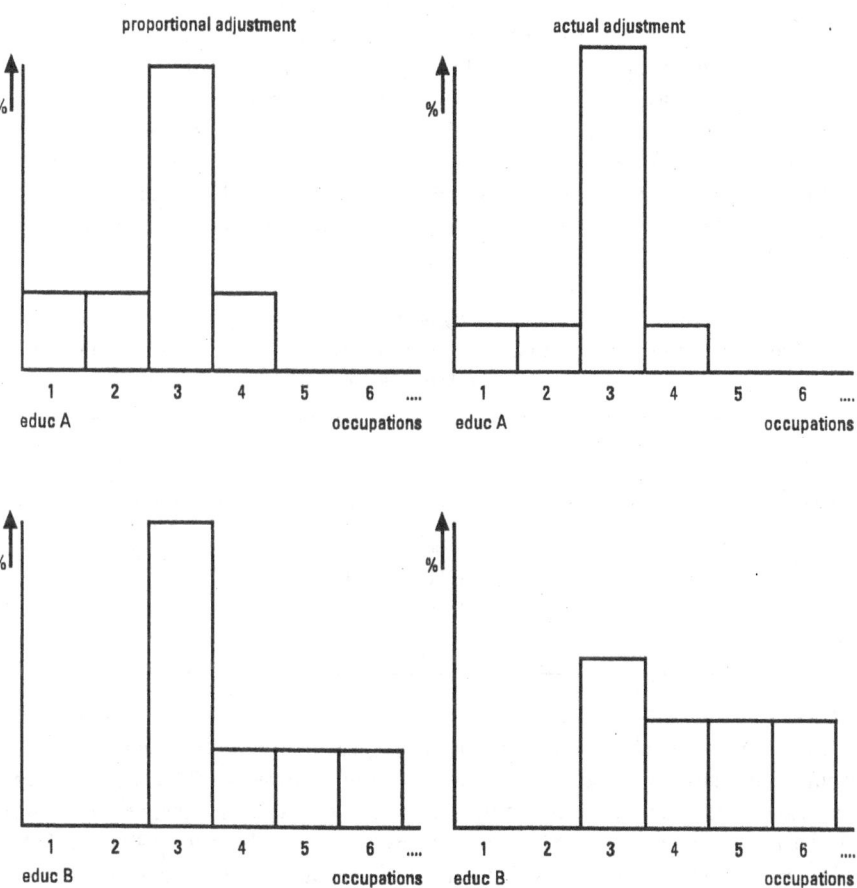

Figure 4   Example of the occupational structure of types of education in Figure 2 after the growth of occupation 3, with (a) a proportional adjustment of both types of education and (b) a more than proportional reaction of A and a modest adjustment of B

If, however, as indicated in Figure 4, the first type of education (A) grows even more than proportional in this occupation, while the growth of the second type of education is limited, the extent of the occupational domain for the first will decrease to 2.1, while for the second type of education the extent of the occupational domain equals 3.9.

Tables 2 and 3 show what happens to the similarities between the types of education. This is analysed by not only comparing the occupational domain of the two types of education in each year separately, but also by comparing the occupational domain of t with the occupational domain of $t+1$. Table 2 provides the projected changes in occupational overlap that would occur if both types of education reacted proportionally to this change of importance of the occupation involved. In that case, both types of education would become much more similar in 1993 than in 1981, due to the fact that this increasing occupation has become more important for both. This similarity would increase from 0.50 to 0.89. Furthermore, the character of both A and B would change. The similarity between the type of education A in 1981 and the type of education A in 1993 would then only be 0.80.

Table 2
Similarity between occupational structure in t and projected structure in $t+1$ between A and B of Figures 2 and 4

Type of education	A in t	B in t	A in t	B in t
A in t	1.00	0.50	0.80	0.57
B in t	0.50	1.00	0.57	0.80
A in $t+1$	0.80	0.57	1.00	0.89
B in $t+1$	0.57	0.80	0.89	1.00

Table 3 provides the actual similarity changes. Since B adjusts less to the new occupational structure than A, their similarity only grows to 0.70, i.e. 0.10 less than expected. In addition, the table shows that the type of education B is still similar to the situation in 1981, while the similarity of A between 1993 and 1981 is lower than expected. Therefore, the type of education B still has a similarity of 0.98 in 1993 with the situation in 1981, while proportional adjustment would have led to a similarity of 0.80. Therefore only 0.02/0.20= 10% of the projected change, based on a proportional adjustment to occupational growth, has been realised, while for type of education A 140% of the expected change has been realised. These ratios therefore show the underreaction and overreaction of both educational types. Lastly, the table shows that the type of education A in $t+1$ is more similar to B in t than reversely, indicating that A made a bigger move towards the new situation than B.

Table 3
Similarity between occupational structure in t and $t+1$ between A and B of Figures 2 and 4

Type of education	A in t	B in t	A in t	B in t
A in t	1.00	0.50	0.72	0.55
B in t	0.50	1.00	0.56	0.98
A in $t+1$	0.72	0.56	1.00	0.70
B in $t+1$	0.55	0.98	0.70	1.00

An example

The similarity index presented in the previous section provides detailed information about the labour market position of a type of education and its developments, in relation to the position of other ones. Since 49 types of education are distinguished, there are $1/2(49 \times 48) = 1,176$ similarities for each year in the analyses, so by distinguishing two different years $3 \times 1,176 = 3,528$ similarities have to be taken into account. To get an impression of the structure and the developments on the labour market, it is therefore necessary to aggregate the available information. In the fifth and sixth sections, the structure of the labour market will be described using average tendencies in the similarities. In this section, however, the focus will be on an example, to illustrate the usefulness of the similarity index at micro-level.[5]

From this point of view, one of the most interesting developments during the eighties has been the rise of the computer programmer occupation. The growth of this occupation has been considerable, from 17,500 in 1981 to 73,500 in 1993, but at the same time, the main suppliers for this computer programmer occupation have been educational types which are relatively small. Hence the impact of this change on the occupational structure of UE Economics and UE Engineering is very large.

While in 1981 the main suppliers to this occupation were HVE Engineering and HVE Commerce and Administration, and at the academic level Mathematics and Natural Sciences, in 1993 these groups were supplemented by HVE Non-medical Laboratory, Business Administration Technology, and UE Engineering and Economics. In addition, some closely related occupations have also become more important for these educational groups.

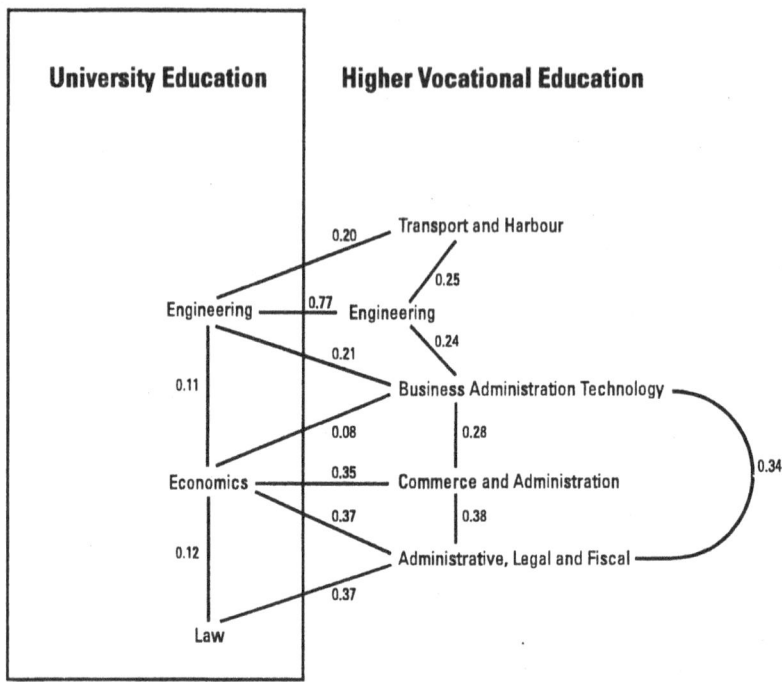

Figure 5   UE Economics and UE Engineering and similar types of education in 1981

Figure 5 illustrates the major labour market similarities of UE Economics and UE Engineering in 1981. The lines indicate the similarities, while the similarity index has been added to each line. The figure is complete from the point of view of UE Engineering and UE Economics, but all other types of education in the figure also have other neighbours, which have not been included. Adding all relevant relationships would lead to a map of the entire labour market. Such a map was presented in ROA (1995). The figure shows that the most important relationships of UE Economics are Commerce and Administration and Administrative, Legal and Fiscal, both at the HVE level. The similarities are 0.35 and 0.37 respectively. At university level, Engineering and Law are most closely related with UE Economics with similarities of only 0.11 and 0.12. UE Engineering has a very strong similarity with Engineering at HVE level, and moderate similarities with HVE Harbour and Transport and Business Administration Technology.

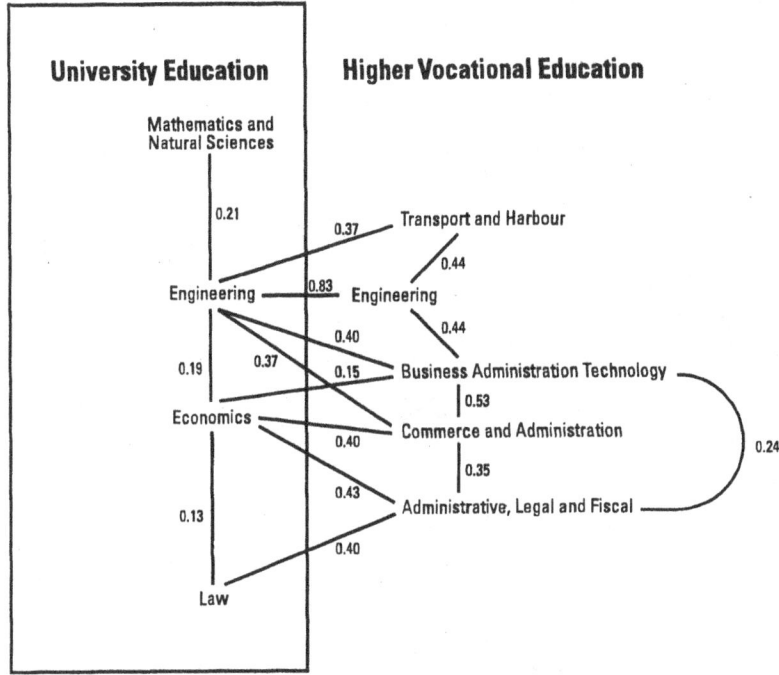

Figure 6 Projected changes of the labour market position of UE Economics and UE Engineering for 1993, based on occupational structure 1981

During the eighties, the rise of new computer technologies caused an increase of occupations which relied on both economic and technical skills. Figure 6 shows that this occupational growth would have led to larger similarities between the types of education involved. The figure presents the similarities that would have resulted from a proportional adjustment of the occupational structure for each type of education. Most obvious are the increases in similarity of UE Engineering with some of its neighbours. For UE Economics these changes are more modest. The reason for this is that in 1981 only a small fraction of the economists was working in computer occupations. At the beginning of the eighties, computer programming was mainly an engineering skill. For that reason, the increase of the number of computer programmers would mainly have led to more similarity between these technical types of education.

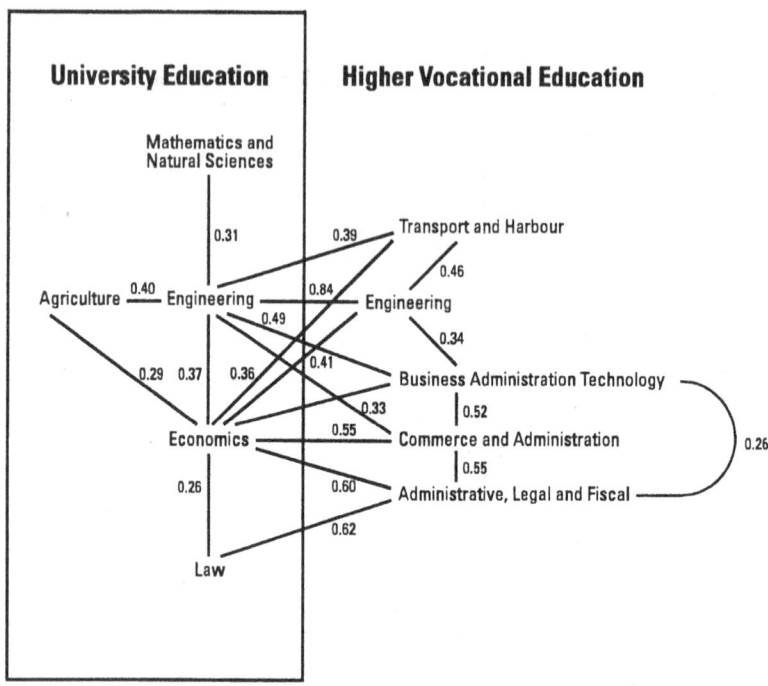

Figure 7 UE Economics, UE Engineering and similar types of education in 1993

Figure 7 provides the similarities actually observed in 1993. It shows that in practice the similarity of UE Economics and UE Engineering increased from 0.11 to 0.37. Other similarities also increased more than expected from an extrapolation of the educational structure of occupations. What actually happened was that on the one hand there has been a shift in the skills required, making computer work less technical and hence making economics a more appropriate educational background for such occupations, while on the other hand the scarcity of computer programmers forced employers to recruit personnel from alternative types of education to fill their vacancies.

Changes of the occupational structure

Table 4 presents the extent of the occupational domains for the various types of education. The occupational classification used distinguishes over 300 occupa-

Table 4
The extent of the occupational domain per type of education

	Extent of occupational domain	
	1981	1993
PE	42.0	45.1
Lower General Secondary Education	20.3	31.5
PVE		
Agriculture	6.1	9.8
Technical	42.1	49.3
Transport & Harbour	11.8	3.1
Commerce & Administration	12.9	20.1
Community Care, Hotel & Catering	14.6	19.8
Security	2.2	3.7
Higher General Secondary Education	19.4	29.5
IVE		
Agriculture	7.2	9.5
Non-Medical Laboratory	5.0	4.7
Engineering	50.9	60.2
Transport & Harbour	24.3	26.9
Medical Laboratory	4.0	4.4
Nursing & Paramedical Services	4.1	4.9
Commerce & Administration	20.3	25.2
Administrative, Legal & Fiscal	4.5	6.3
Social & Cultural	10.5	15.2
Community Care	9.1	12.1
Hotel, Catering & Hairdressing	8.1	10.1
Police, Fire & Defence Forces	3.7	7.4
HVE		
Teacher Training	5.2	7.1
Interpreter & Translator	8.3	11.7
Theology	1.7	3.1
Agriculture	14.7	16.8
Non-Medical Laboratory	4.5	7.3
Engineering	23.8	29.4
Transport & Harbour	18.4	23.4
Medical Laboratory	2.4	4.2
Nursing & Physiotherapy etc.	4.3	5.0

Table 4 (continued)
The extent of the occupational domain per type of education

	Extent of occupational domain	
	1981	1993
Commerce & Administration	11.9	17.4
Business Administration Technology	11.6	11.2
Administrative, Legal & Fiscal	9.2	13.1
Social & Cultural	4.9	9.5
Hotel & Catering Industry	12.3	11.1
Fine Arts	8.4	10.0
Police, Fire & Defence Forces	2.9	3.7
UE		
Teacher Training	2.9	4.8
Arts	2.9	6.8
Theology	2.1	4.0
Agriculture	6.7	16.1
Mathematics & Natural Sciences	6.8	11.6
Engineering	18.0	22.0
Veterinary & Medical Sciences & Dentistry	2.1	2.4
Pharmacy	2.6	3.3
Economics, Econometrics & Business Administration	7.8	14.2
Law & Public Administration	5.7	8.5
Social Sciences	4.7	14.1
Fine Arts	7.9	11.9

tions. The table shows that the similarity index of the extent of the occupational domain of the educational types varies from 1.7 for HVE Theology in 1981 to 60.2 for IVE Engineering in 1993. Other large domains are found for primary education (PE) and PVE Technical. Very restricted domains include Medical Sciences and Pharmacy at the UE level. It is interesting to note that almost all types of education experience an extension of their educational domain. There are only four exceptions. The decrease of the extent of the occupational domain of PVE Transport and Harbour is the largest, with a reduction of its occupational domain from 12 to 3 occupations. Huge increases of the occupational domain are observed for both the higher and the lower general secondary education, and for HVE Social and Cultural and UE Social Sciences, but also for UE Agriculture.

Table 5 summarises these results by presenting the average sizes of the occupational domains per educational level. An interesting aspect, also noticed by de Grip and Heijke (1989) and ROA (1995), is that the extent of the occupational domain decreases with the level.[6] This observation seems to imply that larger educational investments decrease rather than increase the extent of the occupational domain. The reason for this is of course that the higher levels of education lead to occupations in which people can less easily substitute one another. Learning another occupation on the job would require too great an effort.

Table 5
The extent of the occupational domain per educational level

	Extent of occupational domain		
	1981	projected '93	1993
PE	42.0	43.3	45.1
GE	20.0	25.0	30.8
PVE	28.4	30.7	34.6
IVE	26.0	27.5	31.4
HVE	9.7	10.1	12.9
UE	6.8	7.2	11.0

The developments of the occupational structure of the labour market have been such that the occupational domains would increase at all educational levels if their educational structure remained constant. This effect is most prominent for lower and higher general secondary education (GE) and HVE. Actually, the occupational domains increased even more than this. This additional increase of the extent of the occupational domain has been most prominent for GE, PVE, but most of all for university education (UE).

Due to the changes in the occupational structure and due to changes in required qualifications, there have been shifts in the occupational domains of types of education between 1991 and 1993. This can be observed in Table 6, which provides both the projected and the actual similarities between the occupational domains of the types of education in 1981 and 1993. The ratio shows to what degree the employment structure of types of education has been adjusted to new occupational developments. This ratio is extremely low for PE. This implies that, although there have been some shifts in the employment in the occupations which are relevant for PE, the workers with this educational background are still employed in the same jobs as in 1981. The same is the case for Commerce and

Table 6
Projected and actual similarity of occupational structure of types of education in 1981 and 1993

	Similarity projected	Similarity actual	ratio
PE	0.95	0.98	0.41
Lower General Secondary Education	0.98	0.93	3.41
PVE			
Agriculture	0.99	0.95	5.68
Technical	0.98	0.97	1.62
Transport & Harbour	0.99	0.69	34.25
Commerce & Administration	0.98	0.96	2.54
Community Care, Hotel & Catering	0.99	0.98	2.37
Security	1.00	0.98	14.45
Higher General Secondary Education	0.95	0.90	1.89
IVE			
Agriculture	0.99	0.98	1.68
Non-Medical laboratory	0.99	0.96	3.33
Engineering	0.95	0.96	0.88
Transport & Harbour	0.97	0.93	2.29
Medical Laboratory	0.99	0.99	0.93
Nursing & Paramedical Services	1.00	0.98	3.24
Commerce & Administration	0.96	0.97	0.84
Administrative, Legal & Fiscal	0.96	0.96	1.03
Social & Cultural	0.97	0.81	5.36
Community Care	0.99	0.97	1.99
Hotel, Catering & Hairdressing	0.95	0.91	1.69
Police, Fire & Defence Forces	1.00	0.99	2.79
HVE			
Teacher Training	0.99	0.99	0.70
Interpreter & Translator	0.98	0.68	18.37
Theology	0.99	0.97	5.82
Agriculture	0.96	0.88	3.17
Non-Medical Laboratory	0.98	0.93	3.18
Engineering	0.93	0.86	2.06
Transport & Harbour	0.88	0.84	1.35
Medical Laboratory	1.00	0.97	75.60
Nursing & Physiotherapy etc.	1.00	0.95	16.43
Commerce & Administration	0.87	0.96	0.27

Table 6 (continued)
Projected and actual similarity of occupational structure of types of education in 1981 and 1993

	Similarity projected	Similarity actual	ratio
Business Administration Technology	0.87	0.51	3.93
Administrative, Legal & Fiscal	0.95	0.86	2.98
Social & Cultural	0.98	0.96	2.53
Hotel & Catering Industry	0.96	0.83	3.97
Fine Arts	0.95	0.94	1.11
Police, Fire & Defence Forces	0.98	0.97	1.84
UE			
Teacher Training	0.99	0.98	1.20
Arts	1.00	0.96	17.56
Theology	0.98	0.96	2.68
Agriculture	0.98	0.83	9.40
Mathematics & Natural Sciences	0.95	0.92	1.71
Engineering	0.94	0.87	2.14
Veterinary & Medical Sciences & Dentistry	1.00	1.00	2.21
Pharmacy	0.99	0.97	2.98
Economics, Econometrics & Business Administration	0.99	0.88	9.46
Law & Public Administration	1.00	0.97	5.51
Social Sciences	0.99	0.87	12.95
Fine Arts	0.92	0.38	7.90

Table 7
Projected and actual similarity of occupational structure of types of education in 1981 and 1993 per educational level

	Similarity projected	Similarity actual	ratio
PE	0.95	0.98	0.41
GE	0.97	0.92	2.55
PVE	0.99	0.97	2.35
IVE	0.97	0.96	1.10
HVE	0.96	0.94	1.34
UE	0.98	0.93	3.74

Administration at HVE level. This type of education seems not to have followed the occupational trends of the eighties. Table 7 summarises these results per educational level. It shows that the most important occupational changes have been at PE level and HVE level. The first column shows that relatively few occupational changes are found at the PVE and UE levels. In fact, general secondary education and university education experienced the largest changes in their occupational domains. The ratio between the actual change and the projected change is small for PE, and relatively large for GE, PVE and UE. For IVE and HVE, employment changes were on average in accordance with the expected changes due to occupational shifts.

Developments of similarity

Table 8 shows for each type of education the type of education which is most similar according to its occupational structure. For 15 of the 49 educational types, the most related competitor on the labour market changed between 1981 and 1993.

Table 8
Most similar type of education in 1981 and 1993

Educational type	Most similar educational types	Similarity 1981	1993
PE	PVE Community Care, Hotel & Catering	0.69	0.71
Lower General Secondary Education	Higher General Secondary Education	0.95	0.93
	PVE Commerce & Administration	0.91	0.96
PVE Agriculture	IVE Agriculture	0.98	0.95
PVE Technical	IVE Engineering	0.77	0.79
PVE Transport & Harbour	IVE Transport & Harbour	0.68	0.65
PVE Commerce & Administration	IVE Commerce & Administration	0.92	0.90
	Lower General Secondary Education	0.91	0.96
PVE Community Care, Hotel & Catering	PE	0.69	0.71
	Lower General Secondary Education	0.59	0.74
PVE Security	IVE Police, Fire & Defence Forces	0.10	0.19
Higher General Secondary Education	Lower General Secondary Education	0.95	0.93
	IVE Commerce & Administration	0.89	0.95
IVE Agriculture	PVE Agriculture	0.98	0.95
IVE Non-Medical laboratory	HVE Non-Medical Laboratory	0.97	0.84
IVE Engineering	PVE Technical	0.77	0.79
IVE Transport & Harbour	PVE Transport & Harbour	0.68	0.65
IVE Medical Laboratory	HVE Medical Laboratory	0.21	0.19

Table 8 (continued)
Most similar type of education in 1981 and 1993

Educational type	Most similar educational types	Similarity 1981	1993
IVE Nursing & Paramedical Services	HVE Nursing & Physiotherapy etc.	0.56	0.71
IVE Commerce & Administration	PVE Commerce & Administration	0.92	0.90
	Higher General Secondary Education	0.89	0.95
IVE Administrative, Legal & Fiscal	Higher General Secondary Education	0.81	0.69
	HVE Administrative, Legal & Fiscal	0.62	0.70
IVE Social & Cultural	HVE Social & Cultural	0.89	0.76
IVE Community Care	PVE Community Care, Hotel & Catering	0.64	0.66
IVE Hotel, Catering & Hairdressing	HVE Hotel & Catering Industry	0.27	0.36
IVE Police, Fire & Defence Forces	HVE Police, Fire & Defence Forces	0.58	0.59
HVE Teacher Training	Higher General Secondary Education	0.06	0.10
HVE Interpreter & Translator	Higher General Secondary Education	0.30	0.39
	HVE Commerce & Administration	0.26	0.44
HVE Theology	UE Theology	0.97	0.95
HVE Agriculture	UE Agriculture	0.78	0.60
	IVE Agriculture	0.49	0.62
HVE Non-Medical Laboratory	IVE Non-Medical laboratory	0.97	0.84
HVE Engineering	UE Engineering	0.77	0.84
HVE Transport & Harbour	IVE Transport & Harbour	0.53	0.45
	HVE Engineering	0.25	0.46
HVE Medical Laboratory	HVE Non-Medical Laboratory	0.29	0.57
HVE Nursing & Physiotherapy etc.	IVE Nursing & Paramedical Services	0.56	0.71
HVE Commerce & Administration	IVE Commerce & Administration	0.71	0.78
HVE Business Administrat. Technology	Higher General Secondary Education	0.51	0.36
	HVE Engineering	0.24	0.64
HVE Administrative, Legal & Fiscal	IVE Administrative, Legal & Fiscal	0.62	0.70
HVE Social & Cultural	IVE Social & Cultural	0.89	0.76
HVE Hotel & Catering Industry	IVE Hotel, Catering & Hairdressing	0.27	0.36
HVE Fine Arts	UE Fine Arts	0.24	0.40
HVE Police, Fire & Defence Forces	IVE Police, Fire & Defence Forces	0.58	0.59
UE Teacher Training	UE Social Sciences	0.04	0.13
UE Arts	UE Social Sciences	0.11	0.19
	HVE Interpreter & Translator	0.08	0.24
UE Theology	HVE Theology	0.97	0.95
UE Agriculture	HVE Agriculture	0.78	0.60
UE Mathematics & Natural Sciences	UE Engineering	0.12	0.31
	HVE Business Administration Technology	0.08	0.32
UE Engineering	HVE Engineering	0.77	0.84
UE Veterinary & Medical Sciences & Dentistry	UE Economics, Econometrics & Business Administration	0.02	0.03
	UE Agriculture	0.00	0.08

Table 8 (continued)
Most similar type of education in 1981 and 1993

Educational type	Most similar educational types	Similarity 1981	1993
UE Pharmacy	IVE Medical Laboratory	0.06	0.02
	UE Agriculture	0.01	0.07
UE Economics, Econometrics & Business Administration	HVE Administrative, Legal & Fiscal	0.37	0.60
UE Law & Public Administration	HVE Administrative, Legal & Fiscal	0.37	0.62
UE Social Sciences	UE Fine Arts	0.40	0.31
	HVE Social & Cultural	0.33	0.64
UE Fine Arts	UE Social Sciences	0.40	0.31
	HVE Fine Arts	0.24	0.40

Table 9 summarises the structure of Table 8. It shows that for most types of education, the most similar competitor is one level above or below the type's own level. In 1981, it was only for general secondary education that the percentage of types of education which had the most similar competitor at the same level was 100% since lower and higher general secondary education were relatively similar, while this percentage was 56% for university level. In 1993, these high within-level similarities have disappeared, however, indicating that preparatory and higher vocational education grew away from each other, and more interestingly that the typical academic occupational domain seems to decrease.

It is also interesting to note that the main competitors of IVE in 1981 are at the PVE level. In 1993, this percentage of 81% has decreased to 49%. Partly, the competition with HVE became stronger, but most of all, general secondary education became a more relevant competitor for IVE.

This tendency of more similarity with general secondary education can also be seen at PVE level and HVE level. In 1981, 23% of the types of education at PVE level still had its main similarity with primary education, but in 1993 there were no longer any types of education for which primary education is the main competitor.

The results of Table 9 illustrate that the largest similarities between types of education are not within but between the different levels. Vertical similarity seems to be more important than horizontal similarity.

Table 9
Most similar type of education in 1981 and 1993 per educational level

	PE %	GE %	PVE %	IVE %	HVE %	UE %
1981						
PE	0	0	100	0	0	0
GE	0	100	0	0	0	0
PVE	23	0	0	77	0	0
IVE	0	3	81	0	16	0
HVE	0	39	0	36	2	22
UE	0	0	0	1	43	56
1993						
PE	0	0	100	0	0	0
GE	0	0	59	41	0	0
PVE	0	34	0	66	0	0
IVE	0	31	49	0	20	0
HVE	0	27	0	48	7	17
UE	0	0	0	0	82	18

Table 10
Average largest similarity within the same level

	1981	projected by fixed structure 1993	1993
GE	0.90	0.89	0.96
PVE	0.46	0.49	0.55
IVE	0.47	0.49	0.56
HVE	0.16	0.23	0.31
UE	0.14	0.17	0.26

Table 10 gives the average highest similarity within each level of education. This similarity clearly decreases with the level. At PVE and IVE levels, types of education have on average a competitor at the same level, with a similarity of more than 0.45 in 1981 and more than 0.55 in 1993. For HVE and UE this within-level similarity is much lower, although it also increased between 1981 and 1993. At these higher levels, the average highest similarity almost doubled. This increase of similarity is only partly explained by the changing occupational structure.

Tables 11 and 12 provide similar information for the average highest similarity at one level below and one level above the own level of education. Again, the data show that the similarities are to be found between levels and not within the level, reflecting the vertical structure of the labour market. Here too, similarities decrease with the level. At each level, these similarities increase between 1981 and 1993. At the same time, the growth of these inter-level similarities is only partly explained by the changing occupational structure.

Table 11
Average largest similarity with types of education at one level below the own level

	1981	projected 1993	1993
GE	0.66	0.66	0.74
PVE	0.58	0.59	0.65
IVE	0.72	0.69	0.72
HVE	0.36	0.35	0.39
UE	0.32	0.37	0.47

Comparing the figures of Tables 11 and 12, we can see that for PVE the similarities with types of education at a lower level (i.e. primary education) are less important than those with types above its level, but this difference is decreasing due to the increased similarities between PVE and primary education. IVE has higher similarities at PVE level than at HVE level, but these differences also tend to become smaller. Lastly, HVE is more closely related to IVE than to university education, but this difference has almost completely disappeared in 1993.

In the tables presented so far, similarities with most closely related competitors on the labour market have been considered. These figures showed that in most cases, the nearest competitors are types of education in the same or a related field of study, but at a different level. This picture changes if the average similarity with all types of education within a certain level is regarded. Table 13 provides these average similarities for 1981. The table shows that for each level, the highest average similarity is recorded for the types of education at the same level. Again, however, this similarity decreases with the level. The same is true for the average similarity between subsequent levels. General secondary education has relatively high average similarities with all levels of education. Only the average similarity with university education is below 0.20.

Table 12
Average largest similarity with types of education at one level above own level

	1981	projected 1993	1993
PE	0.69	0.66	0.71
GE	0.83	0.80	0.87
PVE	0.78	0.75	0.79
IVE	0.50	0.46	0.58
HVE	0.25	0.30	0.37

Table 13
Average similarity between all types of education at a certain level in 1981

	PE	GE	PVE	IVE	HVE	UE
PE	1.00	0.45	0.58	0.30	0.05	0.01
GE	0.45	0.98	0.35	0.45	0.15	0.04
PVE	0.58	0.35	0.51	0.31	0.05	0.01
IVE	0.30	0.45	0.31	0.34	0.10	0.03
HVE	0.05	0.15	0.05	0.10	0.24	0.06
UE	0.01	0.04	0.01	0.03	0.06	0.15

Table 14 provides the projected changes of average similarities based on actual employment growth in the occupations and the educational structure of 1981. Due to occupational growth, an increase of average similarity is projected only for HVE and university education and of the similarity between these two levels. Table 15 compares the projected occupational structure in 1993 with the one in 1981. The figures show that HVE in 1993 is expected to be closer to IVE in 1981 than IVE in 1993 to HVE in 1981. This implies that the growth of overlap between these two levels is in intermediate level occupations, rather than occupations at higher level. The same is true for IVE and PVE, in which the growth at the lower level also seems to contribute more to the expected increase of similarity than vice versa. This is, however, not the case for the similarity between UE and HVE and between PE and PVE.

Table 14
Average similarity between all types of education at a certain level, projection for 1993

	PE	GE	PVE	IVE	HVE	UE
PE	1.00	0.45	0.59	0.30	0.04	0.01
GE	0.45	0.96	0.35	0.44	0.14	0.06
PVE	0.59	0.35	0.52	0.31	0.04	0.01
IVE	0.30	0.44	0.31	0.34	0.11	0.05
HVE	0.04	0.14	0.04	0.11	0.27	0.09
UE	0.01	0.06	0.01	0.05	0.09	0.17

Table 15
Average similarity between all types of education at a certain level, 1981 compared with projection for 1993

'81	PE	GE	PVE	IVE	HVE	UE
'93						
PE	0.95	0.43	0.57	0.28	0.04	0.01
GE	0.43	0.94	0.34	0.41	0.11	0.04
PVE	0.56	0.36	0.50	0.29	0.04	0.01
IVE	0.30	0.45	0.31	0.32	0.08	0.03
HVE	0.06	0.21	0.06	0.13	0.22	0.07
UE	0.02	0.06	0.01	0.04	0.07	0.16

Table 15 gives the actual average similarities for 1993. The overall picture remains the same as in 1981, but almost all average similarities have increased. Remarkably high is the increase in average similarity of university education with other types of education at the same level, but also at all other levels.

Lastly, Table 17 compares the occupational structure of 1993 with the structure of 1981. It shows that due to the actual changes of the occupational structure, all levels became more similar to one level below in 1981 than reversely. For general secondary education, the employment structure became more similar to the structure of PVE in 1981 than the structure of PVE adjusted towards the 1981 situation of general secondary education. At the same time, general secondary education also became more similar to the employment structure of primary education in 1981.

Table 16
Average similarity between all types of education at a certain level, 1993

	PE	GE	PVE	IVE	HVE	UE
PE	1.00	0.56	0.64	0.35	0.08	0.04
GE	0.56	0.97	0.46	0.49	0.25	0.14
PVE	0.64	0.46	0.55	0.35	0.08	0.04
IVE	0.35	0.49	0.35	0.37	0.17	0.09
HVE	0.08	0.25	0.08	0.17	0.26	0.15
UE	0.04	0.14	0.04	0.09	0.15	0.23

Table 17
Average similarity between all types of education at a certain level, 1993 compared with 1981

'81 / '93	PE	GE	PVE	IVE	HVE	UE
PE	0.98	0.42	0.56	0.30	0.05	0.01
GE	0.56	0.90	0.41	0.45	0.15	0.05
PVE	0.63	0.36	0.51	0.31	0.05	0.01
IVE	0.34	0.45	0.33	0.34	0.11	0.04
HVE	0.08	0.22	0.07	0.14	0.22	0.07
UE	0.03	0.12	0.03	0.07	0.10	0.17

Conclusions

This chapter started with the observation that there is not a one-to-one relationship between type of education and occupation, but that most types of education give access to a range of occupations, while the occupational domains of different types of education seem to overlap. These switching opportunities and overlaps provide flexibility to the labour market to adjust supply to demand more easily. The aim of the chapter was to investigate which developments have occurred in this labour market structure between 1981 and 1993.

Firstly, although at all levels each type of education gives access to a range of occupations and at all levels there is overlap between the occupational domains, both the extent of the occupational domain and the similarities with others diminish with the level. The greatest gap in this respect is between IVE and HVE.

The closest competitor on the labour market is generally not found at the same educational level, but one level below or above the own educational level. The strongest labour market relationships are therefore vertical rather than horizontal. Again, the greatest gap is between IVE and HVE. If we consider not merely the nearest competitors, but all types of education at a certain level, average similarities become larger within than between different levels. There seem to be specific occupations that are typical for a certain educational level irrespective of the specific field of study concerned.

In general, both the extent of the occupational domains and the similarities between types of education increased between 1981 and 1993. The overall structure outlined above did not change, but all relationships became closer. This means that education has become less occupation-specific.

The largest occupational changes occurred at primary education level and for IVE and HVE. For the latter two levels, a large part of the changes of the occupational structure can be explained by changes of the relative importance of certain occupations. General secondary education, PVE, and most of all university education experienced a change of their occupational structures, which was much larger than needed to adjust for occupational shifts. Primary education, on the other hand, changed less with respect to its occupational structure than was needed to adjust for occupational shifts.

Both general secondary education and PVE seem to have taken over the role of primary education on the labour market. These types of education grew more into the direction of the role of primary education in 1981 than to the occupational distribution of primary education in 1993. University education clearly lost its special position on the labour market. In 1981, there still was a relative large proportion of university studies which had their closest competitor at university level. In 1993, this position has disappeared and the occupational structure of academics has become much closer to the 1981 position of higher vocational education graduates, while the similarities with lower levels also increased.

Today, university education is more similar to vocational education than in 1981, while special academic occupations have become less important for the labour market of university-educated individuals.

Notes

1. Due to differences in the sources for both years, these numbers are not completely comparable. The 1981 data, based on the 'Arbeidskrachtentelling' (AKT, or Workforce Count), contain more occupations of only a limited number of hours (<12 h) than the data for 1993, which are based on the 'Enquête Beroepsbevolking' (EBB, or Working Population Survey). Therefore, the actual growth will have been even larger.
2. Warnken (1986) and de Grip and Heijke (1988) used the Gini-Hirschman index, which can be calculated as:

$$GH_i = (1 - P_i) \frac{m}{m-1}$$

   This linear transformation of the variable P_i is such that GH_i equals 0 when every worker with the educational background i is in the same occupational group, while the index equals 1 if there is an equal spread over all occupations.
3. $1/(0.40^2 + 0.18^2 + 0.18^2 + 0.12^2 + 0.10^2 + 0.01^2 + 0.01^2) \approx 4$.
4. Borghans, Hughes and Smits (1997) used the same similarity index to compare Irish and Dutch types of education.
5. The analyses are based on data from the EBB mentioned in note 1. Occupations have been aggregated in 316 categories. A major source of overlap in the educational domain is the occupation of teacher. For example, many graduates from both arts and mathematics find work as teachers. However, this does not imply that these types of education can be regarded as substitutes. For that reason, the similarity between types of education from the teacher occupation is only counted for people with the same field of study.
6. The only 'exceptions' are lower and higher general secondary education (both combined in GE), but this level cannot really be treated as an intermediate level between primary education and PVE.

References

Borghans, L. (1992), *A Histo-topographic Map of the Dutch University Studies*, ROA-W-1992/5E, Maastricht University: Maastricht.
Borghans, L., Hughes, G., and Smits, W. (1997), *The Occupational Structure of Further and Higher Education in Ireland and the Netherlands*, ROA: Maastricht, ESRI: Dublin.
Grip, A. de, and Heijke, J.A.M. (1988), *Labour Market Indicators: an Inventory*, ROA-W-1988/1E, Maastricht University: Maastricht.
Research Centre for Education and the Labour Market (1995), *The Labour Market by Education and Occupation to 2000*, Maastricht University: Maastricht.
Research Centre for Education and the Labour Market (1995), *The Labour Market by Education and Occupation to 2000, Statistical Appendix*, Maastricht University: Maastricht.
Warnken, J. (1986), Zur Entwicklung der 'Internen' Anpassungsfähigkeit der Berufe bis zum Jahre 2000. Projektionen unter den Annahmen der Wachstumsszenarien der Prognos-Studie, *Mitteilungen aus der Arbeitsmarkt- und Berufsforschung*, no. 1, pp. 119-133.

Acknowledgement

The authors like to thank Bart Weerkamp for his computational assistance.

7 Asymmetric Skill Substitution, Labour Market Flexibility, and the Allocation of Qualifications

Adriaan van Zon, Joan Muysken and Huub Meijers

Introduction

One of Europe's most pressing problems of today is the relatively high level of unemployment especially among low-skilled workers, who generally suffer more and longer from unemployment than the rest of the working population.[1] The generic cure for this problem, which economists have a habit of promoting, is cuts in wage costs[2] and social benefits. The result of a reorganisation of the welfare state along these lines, however, may be high social costs. Before implementing such a reorganisation, one should at least be fairly sure about the size of the benefits involved, as well as their distribution over different skill groups in society. This would require at least a transparent labour market with respect to education and schooling.

This transparency of the labour market is related to an important, although often neglected, reason to believe that the benefits of wage-policy measures in terms of the envisaged effects on employment growth may be over-estimated.[3] This reason is that effective substitution possibilities between different skill levels of labour may be overrated by the inadvertent use of standard economic concepts such as (multi-level) production functions. These functions are often included in models used to quantify the expected employment effects of certain policy prescriptions, such as selective (i.e. skill-specific) cuts in wage costs.[4] It is then assumed that standard substitution features as they presumably apply at the aggregate level between labour and capital, also hold with regard to substitution between various skill groups of labour. These models therefore essentially assume that any skill group can be made to provide the services of any other skill group, if only the incentives for producers to make them do so are right. The logical conclusion following from this assumption is that the unemployment differences between skill groups, which can be observed in practice, exist only because of imperfections in the functioning of the wage-price system and/or other rigidities in the labour market. The remedy then is simple: remove (wage and other) rigidities.

This policy recommendation is completely in line with the assumption of symmetric substitution possibilities between skill groups, which actually means that one skill group can be interchanged for another. In our opinion, this implicit symmetry assumption neglects the fact that high-skilled people can generally perform a larger set of tasks at a positive efficiency level than low-skilled people. More in particular, high-skilled people could probably perform the tasks which low-skilled people could perform too, but not necessarily the other way around. Hence, a given number of tasks (i.e. jobs) offers more employment opportunities to the group of high-skilled people than to the group of low-skilled people. This feature of the labour market should be acknowledged in formulating employment policies.

In order to do so, we have constructed a model with *asymmetric skill-substitution*. This asymmetry has several important implications. (1) First, it is obvious that the number of jobs which can efficiently be performed by low-skilled people is essentially an upper boundary to employment of low-skilled workers. (2) The creation of jobs for the low-skilled does not necessarily have to coincide with an increase in employment for the low-skilled. High-skilled workers find their employment opportunities increased too, and may compete directly with low-skilled workers for the jobs of the latter, but not the other way around. (3) On the other hand, the creation of high-level jobs requires the input of high-skilled workers and hence this would free jobs to be filled by low-skilled workers, insofar as the high-skilled workers were taking up low-level jobs. This is the so-called 'chimney effect' of the creation of high-level jobs which draws the 'still smoking' low-skilled workers from the flames of unemployment.[5] (4) As a consequence, substitution between skills takes place in two different ways: *direct* substitution by means of the one skill replacing the other n low-level jobs, and *indirect* substitution of employment opportunities by means of changes in the job composition of employment. With respect to the latter one should realise that the job composition of employment is fixed to a large extent not only by the characteristics of the capital stock but also by the organisation of the production process as a whole. (5) This means that cuts in wage costs may have limited effects on the average job composition of employment, and mainly work through direct substitution. The resulting net effect on employment may therefore be limited.

These features of the model imply that in the short term, the employment effects of selective cuts in wage costs are bound from above, as far as old jobs are concerned. It also means that net creation of low-level jobs is required when direct substitution possibilities have been exhausted, in order to improve employment perspectives for the low-skilled. In times of a relatively large supply of skilled workers, however, the creation of high-level jobs may be more effective in alleviating unemployment problems for the low-skilled.

In this Chapter we will not focus on macroeconomic issues, but rather on the way in which the existence of asymmetric substitution possibilities influences the scope for wage cuts as an instrument to influence the distribution of unemployment over different skill groups. To do so, we define a framework with asymmetric substitution possibilities and add this to an otherwise standard (multi-level) production model, where we use made-up data and made-up parameters to implement the model. Before engaging in model simulations, however, we start with a description of the match between skills and jobs in the Netherlands in the next Section. The third Section describes the skill-substitution framework, while the fourth Section is devoted to a description of the production function framework and the way in which the skill-substitution framework is integrated with the rest. The fifth Section provides a description of the simulation experiments we have conducted with the model, while the final Section contains a summary and some concluding remarks.

The match between skills and occupations in the Netherlands, 1988-1994

In this Section we will analyse data for the Netherlands to get an impression of the utilisation of skills in that country and the mechanisms underlying some developments over time. Unfortunately the period for which data are available is

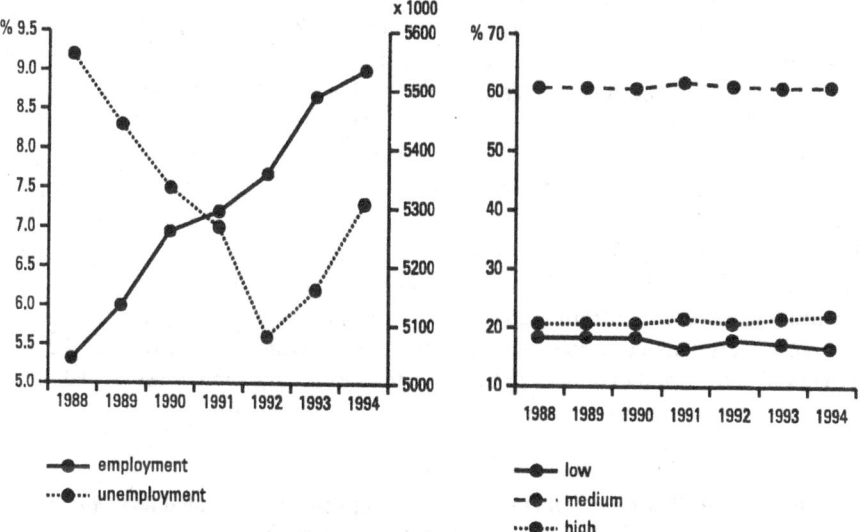

Figure 1 Employment and unemployment in the Netherlands, 1988-1994

Figure 2 Employment shares by skill in the Netherlands, 1988-1994

rather short, 1988-1994. Nonetheless some interesting observations can be made, which are also useful as a background for our theoretical analysis in the remaining part of this Chapter. We will first present some general features of the utilisation of skills in the Netherlands and then concentrate on the relation between the skill structure and job structure.[6]

To get an impression of the general situation in the period 1988-1994, aggregate employment and the rate of unemployment are presented in Figure 1. One can see that until 1992 the economic situation is prosperous: the rate of unemployment is declining and employment is increasing. From 1992 the economic situation deteriorates: the growth in employment slackens, while the rate of unemployment increases from 6 per cent to almost 8 per cent in 1994.

For our research we are particularly interested in a breakdown of these data with respect to skills and occupations. In the data available, skills refer to the highest level of education attained by workers.[7] We distinguish between a high, medium and low level of acquired education. The high educational level corresponds with high vocational and university education. The low educational level corresponds to primary school and low secondary school (up to age 16). Medium education is everything in between. The employment shares for these three skills are presented in Figure 2. Remarkable features are the high share of medium-level skills, about 60 per cent over the period and the low share of low skills, below 20 per cent over the period. As can be seen from Figure 3, the share of low skills in unemployment is very high, however, of over 50 per cent. And as a consequence, the rate of unemployment amongst low-skilled persons is over 25 per cent. This stresses the precarious situation of low-skilled people.

The data also allow us to look at occupational categories. Actually, two dimensions are given: occupational *types* and *levels*. We concentrate on the latter, since our analysis typically applies to the relation between skill levels and job levels.[8] The job level refers to the functional content of the jobs, and we distinguish between high-, medium-, and low-level jobs. The high job level requires professional or scientific skills at the level of high vocational or university education, whereas the low job level is characterised by simple routine tasks, which mainly require the use of hand-held tools and often some physical effort. Everything in between is labelled 'Medium', which means that at least some skill level is required.

Table 1
Percentage distribution of employment by skill and occupational level, the Netherlands, 1988-1994 (average)

Skill level	Occupational level		
	Low	Medium	High
Low	2.5	11.0	3.5
Medium	3.5	35.0	22.5
High	0.2	2.8	18.0

Source: Own calculations, based on Labour Force Survey data, Eurostat; cf. note 7

Figure 4 shows that over 50 per cent of employment is in jobs with a medium level, while the share of high-level jobs is almost 40 per cent. Employment in low-level jobs remains at a share of under 10 per cent over the whole period.[9] Hence comparing this result with Figure 2 learns that low-skilled employment must also be found in higher-level jobs. The share of workers with a certain skill level in a certain occupational level is presented in Table 1.

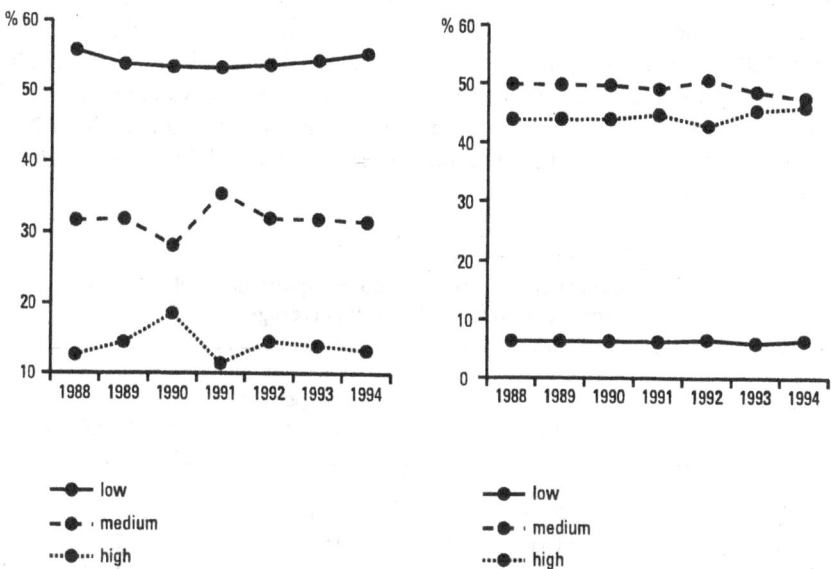

Figure 3 Unemployment shares by skill in the Netherlands, 1988-1994

Figure 4 Employment share by job-level in the Netherlands, 1988-1994

It is remarkable that about 35 per cent of all jobs are both of a medium level and occupied by persons with a medium skill. Moreover, over 10 per cent of all jobs are also of a medium level but occupied by workers with a low skill. This is inconsistent with our notion that higher level jobs cannot be occupied by lower level skills. The same holds for the substantial share of medium-skilled people in high-level jobs, which is over 20 per cent of all jobs.[10]

A possible explanation for the occurrence of these 'incorrect' shares is that skills are not properly measured by the highest level of education, and that job experience should also be taken into account. Actually, we have data on average job experience in all relevant dimensions, as can be seen from Table 2.

From these data we observe that low-skilled workers in high-level jobs have six more years of experience on average compared to those employed in medium-level jobs, i.e. 23.9 versus 18.0.[11] And they have also three more years of experience on average, when compared to medium-skilled workers in high-level jobs. This partly explains why relatively many low-skilled workers are employed in higher level jobs, as we observed above. Hence a better measurement of skills, which would take working experience into account, might lead to observations more consistent with our assumptions. Moreover, one should realise that the average level of schooling has increased rapidly over time. Hence, older generations of workers probably started in higher level jobs in their youth, than they would have nowadays with a similar age and level of schooling. Therefore, there may also be a vintage effect in the high share of low-skilled workers in higher-level jobs. In addition, the shedding of in particular these jobs and workers could also be an explanation for the observation that over 40 per cent of total unemployment is concentrated in low-skilled workers that where employed in medium-level jobs, i. e. about 80 per cent of low-skilled unemployment is in this situation.[12]

Table 2
Years of experience by skill and occupational level
the Netherlands, 1988-1994 (average)

Skill level	Years of experience		
	Low	Medium	High
Low	21.0	18.0	23.9
Medium	16.0	16.2	20.5
High	6.2	11.3	14.7

Source: Own calculations, based on Labour Force Survey data, Eurostat; cf. note 7

In conclusion, if we look at years of schooling as an indication of skill level, we do not find the asymmetries assumed by our model, whereas casual observation of our own workplace, for example, indicates that we should. In general, however, working experience is definitely an important factor in measuring skills. And taking this into account will probably lead to a picture which is much more consistent with the asymmetries assumed in our analysis. Moreover, one should be aware of the fact that the high, medium and low levels in the classifications of jobs and skills are actually ordinal measures rather than absolute ones. Therefore, the empirical correspondence between the two classifications does not necessarily have to be one-to-one. We note these observations as questions for further research, which, however, requires the availability of much more detailed data than we have at this moment.

Jobs, skills and asymmetries in substitution possibilities

Introduction

High-skilled people may in general be expected to perform better in low-level jobs than low-skilled people in high-level jobs. Hence, in terms of the assignment of skills to jobs there must be an intrinsic (more or less technical) bias against allocating low-skilled people to high-level jobs. Nonetheless, some kind of substitution between higher skills and lower skills should be possible, since empirical investigations in this area point to a substitution set-up where high-skilled people are complements of capital, and where low-skilled people in turn can be substituted for this high-skilled people/capital complex.[13] Broadening the skill spectrum to include intermediate skills, one finds relatively high elasticities of substitution between low and medium skills on the one hand, and a fair amount of substitution possibilities between the lower skill echelon and the high-skills/capital complex on the other.

In our model, a job is a set of tasks which need to be performed and which requires the people engaged in that job to have a certain minimum skill level in order to be able to perform the tasks concerned. These specific skill requirements define the level of the job. Moreover, a low-level job requires only low-level skills in order to be able to execute the tasks relating to that job.[14] Hence, everybody who has the minimum required level of skills available can actually be hired for that job. Therefore, generally speaking, high-skilled people can be hired for more levels of jobs than low-skilled people. This provides an asymmetry in employment opportunities for high-skilled and low-skilled people, which, given a certain lack of compensating asymmetries in wage formation, might lead to a bias in employment opportunities in favour of high-skilled people rather than low-skilled people.

Ex ante behaviour: choosing jobs

Let us assume that the design of a production process entails the definition of certain packages of tasks which require at least low skills and high skills, respectively – i.e. the combination of low-level and high-level jobs that are associated with the production process. Let us furthermore assume that technical constraints are such that a decrease in the number of high-level jobs must be compensated by increasing numbers of low-level jobs, and vice versa. These are the 'standard' substitution assumptions in the neo-classical production theory, and they are reflected in an isoquant like $j'j$ in Figure 5. In this figure the curve $j'j$ defines the number of low-level jobs and high-level jobs which are required to generate one efficiency unit of labour. Since the axes of this figure actually refer to the skills of workers, the isoquant is depicted as if all low-level jobs are filled by low-skilled people (L) and all high-level jobs are filled by high-skilled people (H).

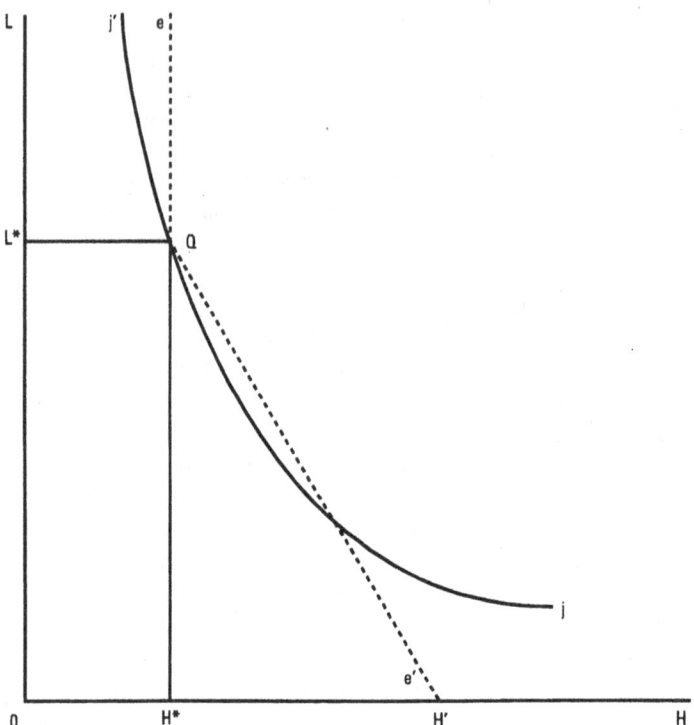

Figure 5 Substitution between jobs and skills

In our set-up the layout of the production process has been defined in terms of the number of high-skilled and low-level jobs required to generate one efficiency unit of labour, but the actual assignment of people to those jobs is a separate issue. Given the asymmetries described above, we know that low-skilled people can not efficiently perform in high-level jobs, whereas high-skilled people can perform efficiently in both low-level and high-level jobs. This means that the number of low-level jobs constitutes an upper limit for the number of low-skilled people which may actually be employed, while the number of high-level jobs is a lower limit to the number of high-skilled people which may actually find employment. Assuming that the efficiency of a high-skilled person relative to a low-skilled person in a low-level job is the constant number e', it follows that the framework sketched above can be pictured as in Figure 5.

Let us assume that point Q represents the optimum choice, where the optimum combination of jobs requiring only low skills and jobs requiring high skills is represented by the point (L^*, H^*). The dotted line eQH' then represents the combinations of low-skilled and high-skilled people which can generate an efficiency unit of labour. The slope of the line segment QH' represents the relative efficiency e' of high-skilled persons relative to low-skilled ones. The relative efficiency of low-skilled people in high-level jobs is equal to zero by assumption, as is indicated by the vertical line segment of the dotted line in Figure 5. Hence, on the unit-job isoquant, H cannot fall below H^*. When H is equal to H', then all low-skilled labour L is replaced by high-skilled labour H and still one labour efficiency unit is generated, i.e. $H'=H^* + L^*/e'$. Actually, all combinations of L and H on the line segment connecting points H' and Q are combinations of low-skilled and high-skilled people which generate one labour efficiency unit.

Given the location of H^* and L^* on the unit-job isoquant, and e', the location of the line segment QH' is determined too. Hence, the choice of H^* and L^* also defines the combinations of high-skilled and low-skilled people which may actually be observed to be employed. If we, for reasons of simplicity, were to ignore the possibility of supply constraints and costs of hiring and firing in this particular setup, then the combinations of low- and high-skilled people which may actually be observed at time t, for given levels of L^* and H^* which have been chosen at time zero, are given by:

$$L_t = L^* \exp(-\delta t) - e'\left(H_t - H^* \exp(-\delta t)\right) \tag{1}$$

where δ enters the analysis because we assume that the job design is embodied in machinery and equipment which is subject to (exponential) technical decay at rate δ. H' in turn is the maximum number of H people required to generate one labour efficiency unit. It can easily be determined from (1) by setting $L=0$:

$$H'_t = \left(\frac{L^*}{e'} + H^*\right) \exp(-\delta t) \tag{2}$$

It follows directly that for given wages by skill w_H and w_L, entrepreneurs can influence the cost of operating a labour efficiency unit in two different ways. Firstly they can do so by choosing a certain job combination (H^*,L^*) from the isoquant $j'j$ in Figure 5. This also determines the position of the line between Q and H' in the figure. Second they can choose workers with certain skills to fulfil this job combination (H^*,L^*) by selecting a skill combination (H,L) from the line between Q and H' in Figure 5 (cf. equation (1)).

We assume that entrepreneurs can determine the job layout of their production process (i.e. (H^*,L^*)) only when new capacity is installed. They will do so in such a way that the expected present value of the total operating cost of one labour efficiency unit installed at time zero is minimised. Given a nominal rate of discount of ρ, this present value declines with the progress of time at rate $\delta + \rho$. Hence, it is given by:

$$T = \int_0^\infty \left(w^e_{H,t} H_t + w^e_{L,t} L_t \right) \exp(-(\rho + \delta)t) \, dt \tag{3}$$

where $w^e_{H,t}$ and $w^e_{L,t}$ are the expected values of the wage rate for high-skilled and for low-skilled people at time t, respectively.[15] For reasons of simplicity, we assume that wages can be expected to grow at constant rates, $\hat{w}_H$ and $\hat{w}_L$, respectively.

We now will approach the problem of the minimisation of (3) subject to (1) recursively in two steps, analogous to the two possibilities sketched above. That is, we will first look at the allocation of skills to jobs, given a certain job combination. Then we will look at how this job combination is determined.

The allocation of skills to jobs

For a given job combination, i.e. given values of L^* and H^*, (3) describes the evolution over time of expected labour costs. In the absence of supply constraints and hiring and firing costs, there are no intertemporal connections between labour costs. Hence (3) can only be minimised when instantaneous labour costs are minimised at each moment in time, including the present, for a given initial job combination (L^*,H^*). In terms of Figure 5, this comes down to the choice of skill combinations from the line between Q and H'.

It can easily be seen from Figure 5 that the skill combination $(H=H', L=0)$ is the solution when $w^e_H/w^e_L < e'$, while the combination $(L = L^* \cdot \exp(-\delta t), H = H^* \cdot \exp(-\delta t))$ is the solution when the opposite is the case, because in these cases instantaneous labour costs, and hence total expected labour costs over the infinite lifetime of the jobs L^* and H^* under consideration, will be minimised. Using the shorthand notation $w_0 = w^e_H/w^e_L$ for time zero, i.e. the present time, and $\hat{w} = \hat{w}_H - \hat{w}_L$, for given and constant expected exponential growth rates $\hat{w}_H$ and $\hat{w}_L$, there are now four distinct possibilities to consider, depending on whether $w_0 < e'$ or $w_0 > e'$ and $\hat{w} < 0$ or $\hat{w} > 0$. These four cases are depicted in Figure 6.

In order to understand the difference between the four cases, one should realise that is, for instance, we have $w_0 < e'$ and $\hat{w} < 0$, the optimal solution will always be $(H=H', L=0)$.[16] In this case, low-level jobs will be filled by high-skilled persons from the beginning. When $w_0 < e'$ and $\hat{w} > 0$ there will be a moment when the other solution $(H=H^*, L=L^*)$ will be chosen. We assume the change to take place at time t^*. A switch between states will also occur when $w_0 > e'$ and $\hat{w} < 0$ which gives rise to the allocation of first $(H=H^*, L=L^*)$ and then $(H=H', L=0)$. The final case will always have $(H=H^*, L=L^*)$ since $w_0 > e'$ and $\hat{w} > 0$.

Asymmetric Skill Substitution 161

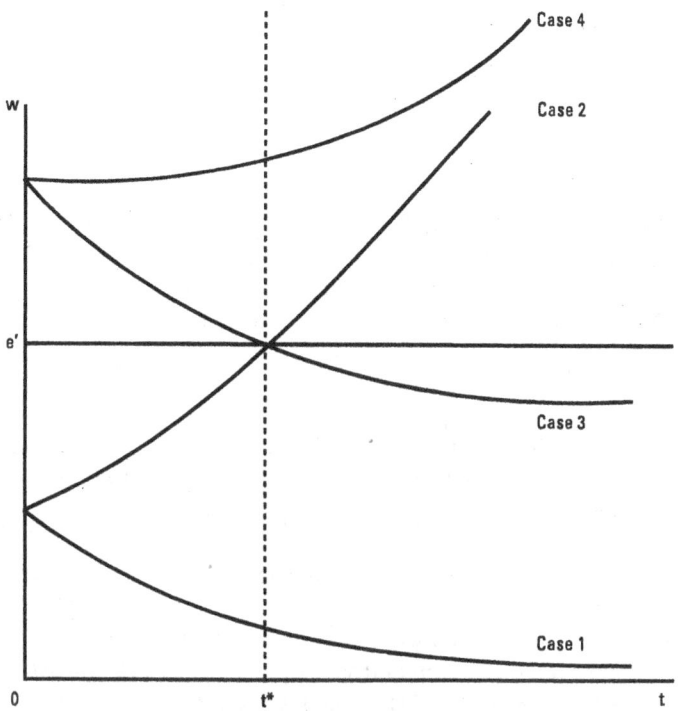

Figure 6 Expected wage growth and skill switching

Table 3
Optimum job-skill combinations

Case	wage/ efficiency ratio	growth rates wages	switching moment	$(L_1,H_1),(L_2,H_2)$[17]
1	$w \leq e'$	$\hat{w} \leq 0$	$t^*(L,H)=0$ [18]	$(0,H'),(0,H')$
2	$w \leq e'$	$\hat{w} > 0$	$t^*(H,L)=\ln(e'/w_0)/\hat{w}$	$(0,H'),(L^*,H^*)$
3	$w > e'$	$\hat{w} \leq 0$	$t^*(L,H)=\ln(e'/w_0)/\hat{w}$	$(L^*,H^*),(0,H')$
4	$w > e'$	$\hat{w} > 0$	$t^*(H,L)=0$	$(L^*,H^*),(L^*,H^*)$

In two of the four cases a switch from the one corner solution to the other will take place at time t^*.[19] Having determined t^*, the minimisation of the present value of expected labour costs over an infinite horizon can be defined as the solution to the problem of minimising unit operating costs over two consecutive horizons, namely 0-t^* and t^*-infinity. The solution for the optimal combination of skills, depending on the chosen job combination (L^*,H^*), is summarised for each case in Table 3.

The choice of jobs

Given the results in Table 3, the question remains what the optimal job combination (L^*,H^*) should be. Of course, this combination is chosen in such a way that equation (3) is minimised subject to equation (1), and given the results of Table 3. It can be shown that the solution in each case has the general form:

$$T_i = \alpha_i H^* + \beta_i L^* \tag{4}$$

T_i denotes the value of the objective function given by (3) for case i as described in Table 3. The coefficients α_i and β_i differ for each case, but are always positive. The resulting values of α and β are summarised in Appendix A.

Note that the objective function T_i is linear in L^* and H^*. Hence, maximisation of T_i by choosing (L^*,H^*) constrained by the unit job-isoquant $j'j$ should lead to a straightforward determination of L^* and H^* in terms of e', relative wages, relative growth rates in wages and the parameters of the job-isoquant. Since the α's and β's are positive, the intertemporal cost minimisation problem has a meaningful solution in all four cases – cf. Appendix A. This solution is implicitly given by the first-order condition:

$$\mathrm{MRS}(L_i^*,H_i^*) = \frac{\alpha_i}{\beta_i} \tag{5}$$

where L_i^* and H_i^* reflect the optimum values of L^* and H^* when case i is expected to hold, and MRS is the marginal rate of substitution. Note that equation (5) is totally comparable with the first-order conditions of a static cost minimisation problem, and hence we can conclude that a fall in the ratio α_i/β_i corresponds to a decrease in the slope of the isocost lines and hence to a movement down the unit job isoquant (see Figure 5) and therefore to a decrease in the L^*/H^* ratio. It is easy to show from the α/β ratios that case 1 will have the lowest value of the L^*/H^* ratio, while case 3 will have a larger L^*/H^* ratio than case 4. Case 2, in turn, will have a larger L^*/H^* ratio than case 1.

Switching thresholds

So far, we have implicitly assumed that switching workers on a job is costless. It seems reasonable, however, to assume that the act of switching entails costs, i.e. the costs of hiring and firing. These may act as a break on switching behaviour. Moreover, if expectations regarding the development of relative wages are uncertain, an unexpected reversal in the growth rate of relative wages may cause entrepreneurs to incur switching costs twice – instead of not at all if only one had waited a while. Hence, it stands to reason to introduce thresholds in order to account for uncertainties in expectations in combination with (implicit) switching costs. However, only if entrepreneurs have already decided on a certain allocation of skills towards jobs, potential switching costs come to bear on the decision-making process: in the set-up we have chosen, switching costs are only incurred ex post.[20] We assume that switching is always perceived as costly regardless of the direction of switching. We may implement this idea by defining 'threshold wage rates' at which a switch may actually be implemented. In case 2, for instance, in which a switch from $(H=H', L=0)$ to $(H=H^*, L=L^*)$ is expected to occur at time t^*, it stands to reason to switch only when the wage ratio has risen above the efficiency ratio by a certain percentage Δ: $w_{t^*} = e'.(1+\Delta)$.[21] Similarly, case 3 may be redefined in terms of switching costs by assuming that a switch takes place only when the relative wage ratio falls below the efficiency ratio by a certain margin: $w_{t^*} = e'.(1-\Delta)$.[22]

Only cases 2 and 3 are affected by the introduction of switching thresholds, for only in these cases a switch is expected to be necessary in the future relative to the initial situation which is optimal at the ruling w_0/e' ratio. So, only β_2 and β_3 can change and it is fairly easy to show that for $0 \le \Delta < 1$, all β's are positive again so that meaningful solutions to the intertemporal cost minimisation problem can be obtained, as is shown in van Zon and Muysken (1996).

The introduction of a switching threshold implies that, ceteris paribus, switching takes place at a later date. This implies too that the initial situation will have a greater weight in determining the present value of unit labour costs. This by itself would provide an incentive to change the job composition in a direction which makes the initial job composition more cost-effective relative to the 'end composition' after switching. This is elaborated in van Zon and Muysken (1996). With respect to case 3, similar conclusions can be drawn.

Threshold distributions

We now assume that entrepreneurs differ only with respect to their switching thresholds, and that these thresholds are uniformly distributed over the range $0 - \Delta$. A high value of signals a producer which is somewhat reluctant to switch, whereas a low value signals the opposite inclination. However, after a switch has taken place, we assume that the remaining entrepreneurs will become uniformly distributed over the entire threshold range at their side of the e'-mark (see Figure 6), in order to avoid the occurrence of 'gaps' in the threshold distribution.[23]

Given these assumptions, the population α's and β's can be obtained by aggregation over all individual entrepreneurs, leaving the α's unchanged, while only β_2 and β_3 change as indicated in Appendix A. The resulting parameters can be used to determine the demand for low- and high-level jobs by the entire population of entrepreneurs, while taking account of the impact of differences in risk aversion and perceived switching costs between entrepreneurs on the skill composition of employment.

The skill composition of employment

Our analysis now enables us to derive the development over time of the skill composition of employment. We define this composition by the ratio of employment by skill level over the number of jobs of the corresponding level. It is clear that at any point in time such a skill composition is essentially given by the initial skill composition and the effects of a series of skill switches (when applicable), between the present and the moment of the 'creation' of L^* and H^*. Hence, both L/L^* and H/H^* are essentially defined in a time-recursive way.

The assumption that entrepreneurs are uniformly distributed with respect to their switching thresholds is useful when specifying these time-recursive relations, because this assumption enables us to subdivide the population of entrepreneurs at any time into a subset which will change the skill composition existing at a certain point in time, and a subset which will not. This essentially depends on the ratio w_t/e'. More specifically, given the assumption of uniform distributions of switching thresholds, it follows that for a situation in which $w_t/e' > 1$ and $w_t > w_{t-1}$ a fraction $(w_t - e')/((1 + \bar{\Delta})e' - e') = (w_t - e')/(\bar{\Delta} e')$ of entrepreneurs would be satisfied with the state $(L=L^*, H=H^*)$, and hence the part of that fraction which had not yet switched from $(L=0, H=H')$ to $(L=L^*, H=H^*)$ would do so, while the part of that fraction which had already attained the state $(L=L^*, H=H^*)$ in the past, would be satisfied to stay in that state. Because of our assumption that the threshold distributions at both sides of the e'-mark remain uniform, individual entrepreneurs who are switching between states only change the densities of the distributions at both sides of the e'-mark rather than the distributions themselves. Moreover, as long as the wage rate is above the e'-mark, there is an incentive for the population in the state $(L=0, H=H')$ to switch to the other state.

Denoting the fraction of the population of entrepreneurs which is in the state $(L=L^*, H=H^*)$ at time t by μ_t^*, it follows that at any point in time:

$$\mu_t^* = \mu_{t-1}^* + \frac{w_t - e'}{\overline{\Delta} e'}(1-\mu_{t-1}^*) \quad \text{if} \quad w_t/e' > 1$$

$$\mu_t^* = \mu_{t-1}^* - \frac{e' - w_t}{\overline{\Delta} e'}\mu_{t-1}^* \quad \text{if} \quad w_t/e' \leq 1$$

(6)

The skill-composition of employment, as given by L/L^* and H/H^*, can now readily be obtained by using (6):[24]

$$\frac{L_t}{L_t^*} = \mu_t^* \tag{7}$$

$$\frac{H_t}{H_t^*} = \frac{\mu_t^* H_t^* + (1-\mu_t^*)H_t'}{H_t^*} = 1 + \frac{(1-\mu_t^*)(L_t^*/e')}{H_t^*} \tag{8}$$

Equation (6) shows the importance of thresholds in determining lags in switching behaviour. The higher the average switching thresholds ($\overline{\Delta}$) are, the lower the impact is of the current wage rate on switching and the higher will be the influence of the employment situation in the past. Note that a rise in $\overline{\Delta}$ would tend to defer the moment of switching, thus increasing the relative weight of the present value of the initial skill allocation in the objective function. Hence there should be an incentive to change the job composition in such a way that the costs of using those jobs with the initial skill allocation would become lower. And so, a change in average switching thresholds will have an impact on the job composition of employment too.[25] Finally, equations (7) and (8) show the asymmetry in skill employment because H can never fall below H^*, whereas L can decline to zero.

A multi-level putty-clay production model with substitution asymmetries

Introduction

As we have discussed above, the job composition of employment can only be altered by investing in new machinery and equipment. We should therefore include the investment decision in our analysis, in order to properly model the determinants of the skill composition of employment. For this purpose we will use a putty-clay vintage model based on Bischoff (1971), which by its very nature introduces an asymmetry in time of substitution possibilities between capital and labour. It should be noted that this production model, which we will use to run a number of simulation experiments, is highly stylised: we have left out every detail which is not directly connected to the representation of production technology as such, since we are at this stage only interested in the principal working of asymmetries in substitution possibilities between different types of labour given the asymmetries in substitution possibilities in time (i.e. differences in substitution possibilities ex ante and ex post) between capital on the one hand and labour on the other. More in particular, we will use a linear homogeneous production function, where labour and capital are the only factors of production. With regard to technological change, we only consider purely labour augmenting technical change, possibly biased against low-skilled labour.

Behavioural assumptions

Apart from the production function features mentioned above, we assume that producers will try to minimise production costs while producing an amount of output which is exogenously given. Since we use a linear homogeneous production function, this implies that producers try to minimise average production costs. As we have explained in the previous Section, producers making investment decisions take into account expectations regarding price developments and the consequences for future (discounted) production costs of the choice of a production technique. However, we assume that producers do not consider the consequences of their current investment plans for the formulation and realisation of plans for the not too distant future, which in turn influence the realisation of plans still further in the future, and so on. The solution to such an optimisation problem would have to be obtained by means of a dynamic optimisation procedure which takes into account all future effects of the decisions entrepreneurs have to make today. This goes beyond the illustration purposes which the vintage model is intended to serve.

We also assume that the supply of physical capital is infinitely elastic at the ruling price of capital goods. Furthermore, entrepreneurs share the same expectations regarding the development of prices.

Note that in the previous Section we have assumed that labour is a composite factor (or a 'complex' of different types of labour) rather than a purely homogeneous factor. The 'price' of a unit of such a complex then depends on its composition, but for the purpose of defining the production framework it can be assumed as given for the moment.

The putty-clay vintage production model

For the purpose of finding the cost minimising factor proportions on the newest vintage, it should be noted that factor proportions ex post are assumed to be fixed. Hence we assume, very much as in the job composition problem described in the previous Section, that entrepreneurs try to minimise the expected present value of the total costs associated with buying and using a new vintage over an infinite horizon. We furthermore assume that the ex ante production function is a linearly homogeneous CES function and that only embodied labour augmenting technical change occurs. The production structure of the vintage model can then be described by:

$$1 = B_N(e^{\gamma T} v_{T,T})^{-\rho} + B_K \kappa_{T,T}^{-\rho}$$
$$\kappa_{T,t} = \kappa_{T,T}$$
$$v_{T,t} = v_{T,T}$$
$$I_{T,t} = (1 - \delta)^{t-T} I_{T,T}$$

(9)

where $\sigma = 1/(1 + \rho)$ is the elasticity of substitution between capital and labour (i.e. jobs), B_N and B_K are distribution parameters and represents the rate of embodied labour augmenting technical change. $v_{T,t}$ and $\kappa_{T,t}$ represent the labour/output ratio and the capital/output ratio at time t of the vintage installed at time T, respectively.[26] Minimisation of the expected present value of the total cost per (initial) unit of output on the newest vintage over an infinite horizon then yields the optimum factor proportions on the newest vintage as a function of factor prices.[27] In the absence of disembodied technical change, total capacity output X_t, as well as total capacity labour demand N_t can now be obtained from:

$$X_t = \frac{I_{t,t}}{\kappa_{t,t}} + (1 - \delta)X_{t-1}$$
$$N_t = \frac{v_{t,t}}{\kappa_{t,t}} I_{t,t} + (1 - \delta)N_{t-1}$$

(10)

The vintage model now works as follows. Output is exogenously determined, as are wages. Together with prices, the latter determine optimum factor proportions on the newest vintage and therefore unit total cost on the newest vintage. Given the volume of capacity output associated with 'old' equipment which has not been completely worn down yet, this determines how 'large' the newest vintage should be. Total capacity labour demand then follows as the capacity labour demand associated with the existing capital stock and capacity labour demand associated with the new vintage.

Adding heterogeneous labour to the production function framework

In the previous Section we have postulated that employment is the result of a match between the demand for labour as reflected by the number of jobs on the one hand and the supply of labour in terms of skills on the other. We now assume that capacity labour demand within the context of the vintage model, refers to labour demand in terms of high-level and low-level jobs, which are combined into one job complex. That is, $v_{T,t}$ in the ex ante production function (9) represents the labour/output ratio in terms of job efficiency units per unit of output: it comprises both low-level and high-level jobs.

In order to model substitution possibilities between low-level and high-level jobs within the job complex, we have taken a linear homogeneous job-CES-function, with an elasticity of substitution equal to 0.5.[28] With regard to substitution between capital on the one hand, and jobs on the other, we nested the job-CES-function in another linear homogeneous CES function with elasticity of substitution equal to 0.25.[29]

In the absence of skill supply constraints, the optimum composition of the labour complex in terms of jobs and the allocation of skills to these jobs defines the expected present value of the total cost associated with using a job efficiency unit over an infinite horizon. Hence, this 'present value' price of a job efficiency unit serves the same function as the 'present value wage rate' in equations (4) and (5).[30]

With regard to allocating skills to jobs, a distinction should be made between existing capacity and new capacity. The reason is that, although ex post substitution is possible by assumption, switching costs may prevent this. By assumption the average employment state on old capacity is a weighted average of the states ($L=L^*$, $H=H^*$) and ($L=0$, $H=H'$) with weights μ^* and ($1-\mu^*$), respectively. New equipment starts out either in the state ($L=L^*$, $H=H^*$) or in the state ($L=0$, $H=H'$), depending on whether $w_0 \neq e'$ or $w_0 < e'$. Obviously, unit variable cost on the old vintages depends on this 'mix' of states too.

Adding wage and price responses

In standard macro-economic models, wage formation is influenced by labour productivity, inflationary expectations and labour market conditions. Usually an increase in the rate of unemployment decreases the rate of growth of wages, which in turn increases the demand for labour, ceteris paribus, which then lowers unemployment again. In our case direct substitution between L and H will occur as long as $w_0 \neq e'$, i.e. as long as the state which entrepreneurs are leaving has a cost disadvantage relative to the 'target' state.

For illustrative purposes we have specified a very simple wage adjustment equation consisting of a constant trend (equal to zero in most experiments) and a Phillips effect which is linear in the unemployment rate. We have added a uniformly distributed random component to the growth of wages in the range from −1 to 1 per cent. Let $\hat{w}_i$ refer to the value of the growth rate of the wage rate associated with skill i, then:

$$\hat{w}_i = \hat{t}_i - \theta_i u_i + \hat{e}_i \qquad (11)$$

where $\hat{t}_i$ refers to the constant trend term, and $\hat{e}_i$ refers to the random component in the rate of growth of relative wages. Assuming that the trend growth of the wage rates of both skills are the same, it follows from this specification that the ratio of the steady-state unemployment rates by skill is defined in terms of the relative strength of the Phillips effect. More in particular, a stable ratio of w_H/w_L for a given supply of labour implies that:

$$\bar{u}_L = \frac{\hat{t}_L - \hat{t}_H}{\theta_L} + \frac{\theta_H}{\theta_L} \bar{u}_H \qquad (12)$$

where $\bar{u}_i$ denotes the steady-state rate of unemployment of skill i.[31] Note that this equation implies that for symmetric trend growth of wages and symmetric speeds of adjustment of wage growth to unemployment, the steady-state unemployment rates for low-skilled and high-skilled workers are identical. However, if the symmetry were broken by, for instance, a decreasing low-skilled trend growth of wages for a given supply of low- and high-skilled workers, this would lead to an immediate disparity in the long-term rates of unemployment of low-skilled and high-skilled workers.

With regard to the price of output, we assume that it is equal to unit total cost on the newest vintage. The price of investment is assumed to be equal to the price of output in turn.

Supply constraints and the chimney effect

In order to be able to see the 'chimney effect' at work, it is necessary to define explicit supply constraints with respect to low- and high-skilled labour. Moreover, supply must be distributed over the various entrepreneurs who are in either of the two states associated with 'old jobs'. This is because one should realise that the skill composition of employment derived in the previous Section (cf. equations (7) and

(8)), essentially holds only for the old jobs. Hence the preferred skill for old low-level jobs may be either H or L, which are different by definition for the two groups of entrepreneurs. With respect to the latter, we assume that the distribution of supply by skill level over these two groups is proportional to the group sizes. That is, when total supply of low and high skills is L^s and H^s, respectively, the relevant supply for the group preferring low-skilled labour on low-level jobs is $\mu^*.L^s$ and $\mu^*.H^s$, while the relevant supply for the group preferring high-skilled labour on low-level jobs is $(1-\mu^*).L^s$ and $(1-\mu^*).H^s$.

With regard to 'new jobs', we have assumed that all entrepreneurs face the same hiring costs.[32] Hence, all entrepreneurs will have the same 'preferred' allocation with respect to new low-level jobs, which again may be either L or H. However, the preferred allocation may not be feasible due to the possible existence of supply constraints, i.e. supply of the 'preferred skill' may fall short of demand, in which case we assume that second best allocations will be made. As a consequence, we can distinguish between four different situations, which cannot occur simultaneously, however. The first two situations, A and B, occur when the preferred skill for new low-level jobs is L. In situation A the preferred skill for old low-level jobs is L too, while in situation B the preferred skill is H. The next two situations, C and D, occur when the preferred skill for new low-level jobs is H. The difference between C and D lies in the preferred skill for old low-level jobs which is L and H, respectively. Hence, denoting the skill combination which is preferred for old and new jobs by (Old, New), where both Old and New can be L and H, it follows that the situations A-D are given by $A=(L,L)$, $B=(H,L)$, $C=(L,H)$ and $D=(H,H)$.

The influence of supply constraints on the allocation process can now be introduced in a straightforward manner. First it should be noted that after installation of each vintage, the number of jobs on that vintage is fixed except for technical decay, which affects both types of jobs to the same extent. Secondly, because of the job complementarity ex post and because high-level jobs can only be filled by high-skilled workers, it follows that the maximum degree of 'high-level-job-utilisation' (i.e. q_{H^*}) which will be realised for a given supply of high-skilled labour H^s, is equal to:

$$q_{H^*} = \min\left(1, \frac{H^s}{H^*}\right) \qquad (13)$$

where H^s denotes the available supply of high-skilled workers. Obviously, if supply is larger than needed to fill H^* jobs, high-skilled workers may be used to fill L^* jobs as well in combination with the available supply of low-skilled workers. The maximum degree of low-level job utilisation is then equal to:

$$q_{L^*} = \frac{(H^s - q_H \cdot H^*)e' + L^s}{L^*} \qquad (14)$$

If $q_{L^*} < q_{H^*}$ then, because of the complementarity ex post between low- and high-level jobs, the maximum overall degree of job-utilisation is between q_{L^*} and q_{H^*}, and this level can be reached by reallocating some of the H workers who were initially allocated to H^* jobs to L^* jobs instead. The latter leads to a fall in q_{H^*} and a rise in q_{L^*}, in accordance with equation (14) above. This reallocation should continue until $q_{L^*} = q_{H^*}$, which, when substituted into (14), gives rise to the overall job-utilisation rate q^* as given by:[33]

$$q^* = \frac{H^s e' + L^s}{H^* e' + L^*} \qquad (15)$$

The allocation should now be such that first-best allocations are realised to the largest extent possible, whereas second-best allocations are used to fill the gaps in the first-best allocations resulting from the existence of supply constraints. Consider for instance the group A entrepreneurs, i.e. $A=(L,L)$. Denoting the amount of skills $S=L,H$ allocated to jobs $J=L^*,H^*$ by SJ, it follows that for group A entrepreneurs:

$$LL^* = \min(q^* L^*, \mu^* L^s)$$

$$HL^* = \min\left(\frac{q^* L^* - LL^*}{e'}, \mu^* H^s - HH^*\right) \qquad (16)$$

Something similar holds for group D entrepreneurs, who prefer high-skilled workers on both old and new low-level jobs. By contrast, group $B=(H,L)$ and group $C=(L,H)$ entrepreneurs have different preferences for old and new jobs. Group B entrepreneurs first fill new jobs with low-skilled workers, and use further low-skilled workers only when low-level jobs cannot be filled by the preferred high-level skill. The opposite holds for group C entrepreneurs.[34]

Simulation results

Introduction

In this Section we will present the results of some simulation experiments in order to illustrate the working of our model and to emphasise some interactions which might be relevant from a policy point of view. The experiments are:

1 a decrease in the barriers to firing (lower switching thresholds);
2 lowering the relative wage of low-skilled workers;
3 a lower demand for high-level jobs relative to low-level jobs; and
4 a higher demand for high-level jobs.

These experiments will be discussed after we have introduced the simulation set-up and presented the base run.

The simulation set-up

In this Section we will present the results of the simulations we ran with the putty-clay vintage model. To this end we have defined a very simple general framework with output growing at a fixed rate of 2.5 per cent per year. This also holds for the supply of both low- and high-skilled workers. We assume that at zero rates of unemployment, nominal wage rates grow with an average rate of 2 per cent per year with random fluctuations of 0.5 per cent on average. The sensitivity of the growth of wages with respect to the rate of unemployment by skill has been set to 0.25, which is roughly in line with the findings by van Zon et al. (1995) for the Netherlands. The interest rate is assumed to be equal to the nominal rate of discount ρ, which in turn is equal to 10 per cent. Technical decay has been set at 5 per cent. The elasticity of substitution between jobs and capital is 0.25, and 0.5 between low- and high-level jobs, as has been elaborated above. The price of output (which is equal to the price of capital goods by assumption) is set equal to marginal production cost. The parameter e' has been set at 1.25, which is in line with the wage ratio for high-skilled and low-skilled workers given in Nickell and Bell (1995). Hence, at this particular wage ratio entrepreneurs are assumed to be indifferent between hiring either low-skilled workers or high-skilled workers on low-level jobs. Finally, the threshold value of $\overline{\Delta}$ has been set at 0.75.

Starting values for the endogenous and exogenous variables were chosen in such a way that the distribution of jobs is 35 per cent in low-level jobs and 65 per cent in high-level jobs (in the sense of not low). This is an exaggeration of the actual distribution (compare for instance Figure 4 for the Dutch situation), but is used for illustrative purposes only.

In order to exclude the influence of the choice of initial values for the capital stock on the outcomes of the model, we let it run for 225 years and then applied a shock in accordance with the experiment under consideration. The simulation experiment always ends in year 300, although the shock is ended after 50 years, i.e. in year 275.

The base run

In Figures 7-9 below, we present the outcomes of the base run. The average rate of unemployment for both types of skill u_L and u_H, respectively, is about 7 per cent as can be seen from Figure 7. We see that the overall rate of unemployment u is

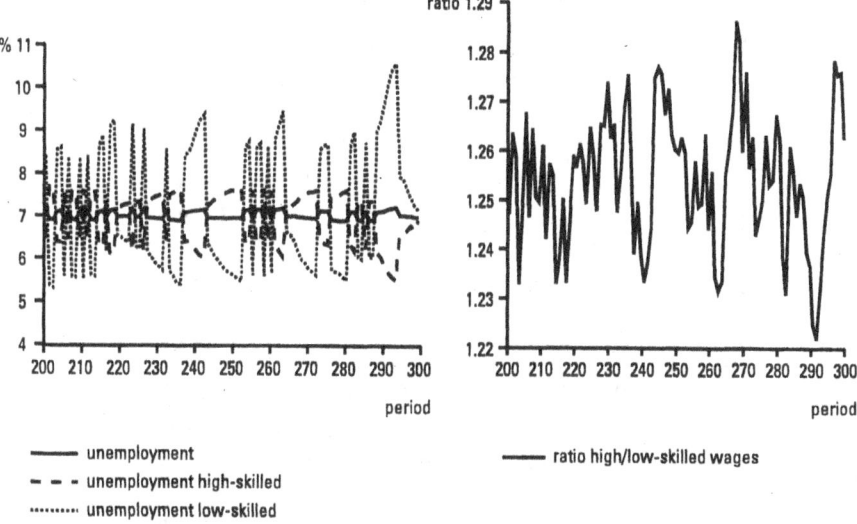

Figure 7 Unemployment of high- and low-skilled in base run

Figure 8 Ratio high/low-skilled wages in base run

more stable than u_L and u_H while in turn the fluctuations in u_L are roughly twice as large as those in u_H. Moreover the fluctuations in u_H and u_L are almost perfectly negatively correlated. The reason is that changes in employment are caused primarily by entrepreneurs switching between states rather than changing the job composition on the newest vintages. And since H^* (and H employment) is about twice as large as L^* (and L employment), replacement of a low-skilled worker on a low-level job by a high-skilled worker leads to a fall in the rate of high-skilled unemployment which is about half the corresponding rise in the rate of low-skilled unemployment. Note that on average both rates of unemployment are equal. This follows directly from equation (12), since we have $\hat{t}_H = \hat{t}_L = 2.5$ and $\theta_H = \theta_L = 0.25$, as mentioned above.

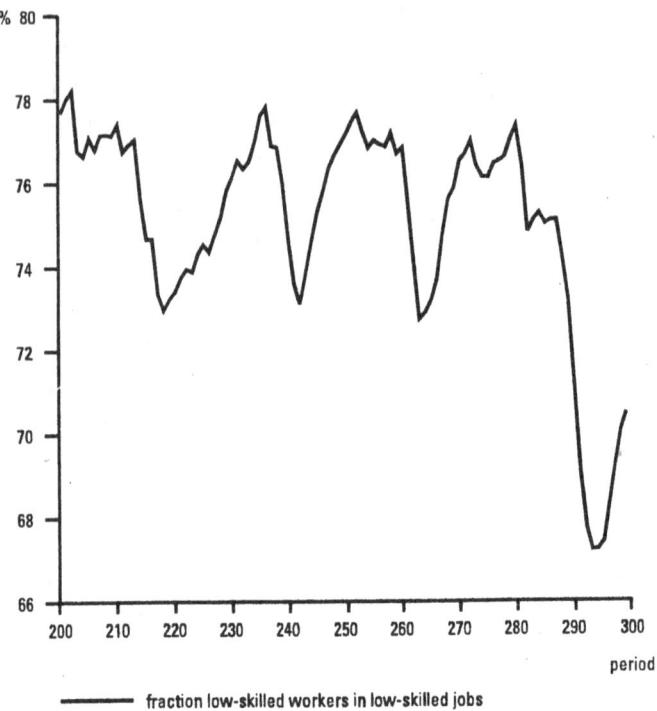

fraction low-skilled workers in low-skilled jobs

Figure 9 Fraction low-skilled workers in low-skilled jobs in base-run

The ratio of high-skilled wages and low-skilled wages, w_0, is on average equal to 1.25 as is shown in Figure 8. Fluctuations in this ratio are caused by random shocks on the one hand and fluctuations in u_H / u_L on the other. The share of employment in 'old jobs' in the state $(L=L^*, H=H^*)$ is given by μ^* which is depicted in Figure 9. μ^* fluctuates around 0.75 for most of the period 200-300 except for a 10 per cent drop of μ^* during the last 20 years of the simulation period. Note that there is a positive correlation between fluctuations in μ^* and fluctuations in w_0, although the former fluctuations are less volatile, due to the partial adjustment of μ^* to deviations between w_0 and e' (cf. equation (6) above).

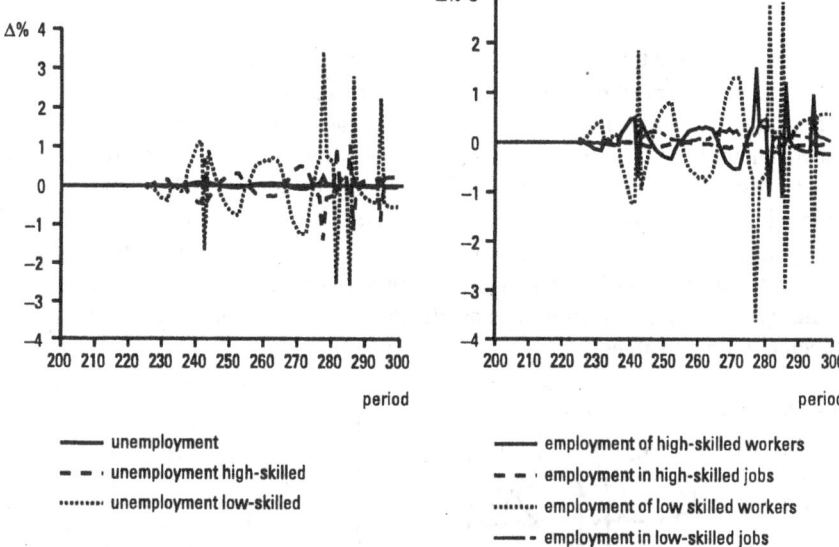

Figure 10 Changes in unemployment of high- and low-skilled with diminishing barriers to firing

Figure 11 Changes in employment of high- and low-skilled jobs with diminishing barriers to firing

Diminishing barriers to firing

In experiment 1, we have changed the threshold value of $\overline{\Delta}$ from its base-run value of 0.75 to a value of 0.375. One would expect a fall in switching thresholds to increase the intensity of the flows of labour from the one state into the other. Hence, the more flexible allocation of skills to jobs would tend to lower the effective user cost of a job-efficiency unit, and would therefore increase the labour/capital ratio. However, only the job composition on new vintages may profit from less costly reallocations, and hence the effects on the creation of new jobs are only marginally positive, as can be seen from Figure 11. Because of that, the overall employment rate is hardly affected at all (see Figure 10), while changes in unemployment rates by skill are far less outspoken than in the wage experiment. Moreover, these changes vary over time, sometimes increasing unemployment vis-à-vis the base run and sometimes decreasing unemployment. Hence, we conclude that a reduction in the cost of firing does not seem to have any net effects for particular groups of workers in the longer run.

Lowering the growth of low-skilled wages

In experiment 2, the trend growth of low-skilled wages is lowered from 2.5 per cent by 1 per cent, while that of high-skilled wages remains at 2.5 per cent. This reduction in trend wage growth leads to a decrease of the steady-state equilibrium rate of low-skilled unemployment by about 4 percentage points (i.e. the reduction in trend growth divided by the unemployment elasticity of wages, c.f. equation (12)). Although we do not show this here, the results are very similar to the ones obtained in an experiment with a higher wage flexibility where we doubled the speed of adjustment of low-skilled wages to unemployment conditions. However, this similarity does not result from the specification of the model, but is a result of the chosen numerical values.

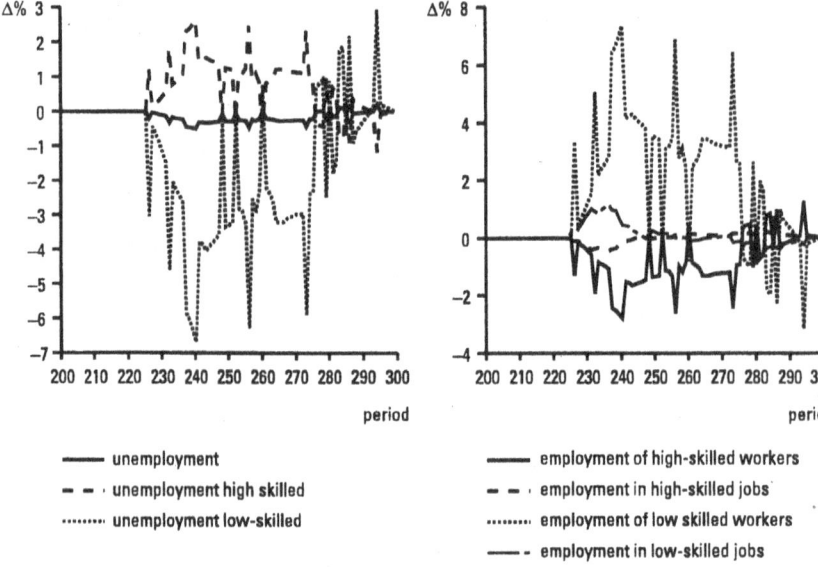

Figure 12 Changes in unemployment of high- and low-skilled with lower growth of low-skilled wages

Figure 13 Changes in employment of high- and low-skilled with lower growth of low-skilled wages

The background of the similarity of the results of both experiments is highlighted in Figures 14 and 15 which depict deviations of μ^* from its base-run value and the percentage deviations of w_0, respectively. From Figure 14 one sees that fluctuations in μ^* hardly occur in experiment 1, as might be expected, whereas μ^* rises by roughly

10 percentage points in experiment 2. This is a reflection of what happens to the relative wages in experiments 1 and 2 as is shown in Figure 15.

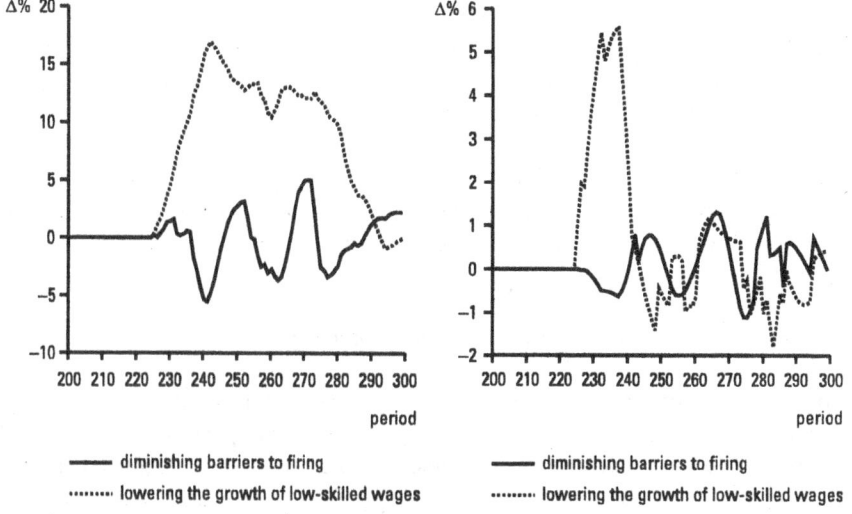

Figure 14 Comparison of the fraction of high-skilled workers in high-skill jobs in two scenarios

Figure 15 Comparison of the change in the relative wage rate in two scenarios

The relative wage rate, w_0, rises rapidly in a few years by about 5 per cent compared to the base run. After this year w_0 falls to its original value in roughly the same amount of time. Note that this leads the timing of the peaks in the changes in the unemployment rates, which reach their largest deviations in about period 240, when w_0 has more or less returned to its original level. But although changes in relative wages have led to fairly large changes in μ^*, one can observe again that there is hardly any net job creation and hence the overall employment effects are very limited indeed – although low – skilled workers will outcompete high-skilled workers on low-level jobs, for a while at least. This is apparent from Figure 12, where the overall rate of unemployment remains relatively unaffected, whereas changes in unemployment for the individual classes of low- and high-skilled workers are far more outspoken. The same picture emerges from Figure 13, where the job composition of employment changes only slightly in favour of low-level jobs. Actual employment, however, changes much more in favour of low-skilled workers, but at the expense of employment opportunities for the high-skilled.

The overall conclusion to be drawn is then that a change in the growth rate of low-skilled wages does not change the job composition of employment to a large extent, but affects the allocation of skills to jobs instead. More in particular, low-skilled workers are used more intensively in low-level jobs, and high-skilled workers who had displaced them become unemployed in turn. This is a consequence of the relatively low employment share of low-skilled workers,[35] which causes induced substitution effects between capital and labour to be of minor importance from an employment perspective. This is aggravated by the fact that the job composition of employment is for a large part embodied in already existing machinery and equipment, which causes 'on-the-job substitution' to be more relevant in the short and medium run than either substitution between jobs or substitution between capital and jobs.

Experiments concerning the working of the chimney effect

In order to simulate the working of the chimney effect, we have introduced a bias in job augmenting technical change, thus changing the job composition of the demand for labour. In experiment 3 we have assumed a 1 per cent high-level job saving rate of technical change and a 1 per cent low-level job using technical change. Hence, fewer high-level and more low-level jobs are needed to generate one job efficiency unit, and it is obvious that the job composition of labour demand shifts in favour of low-level jobs. Since the demand for high-skilled workers on account of high-level jobs is now diminished for a given supply of high-skilled workers, relatively more high-skilled workers will be available for low-level jobs. In this case, the creation of low-level jobs does not necessarily have to lead to an increase in low-skilled employment. Rather, the 'excess availability' of high-skilled workers may reduce the employment opportunities for low-skilled workers.

By contrast, experiment 4 assumes only a 1 per cent high-level job using technical change, thus creating the conditions for the chimney effect to occur. Now a given supply of high-skilled labour will be confronted with an ever growing number of high-level jobs, thus reducing the amount of high-skilled labour available for employment in low-level jobs.

Figure 16 shows the principal difference between the two experiments. In experiment 3, relative wages fluctuate around their base-run values, where the amplitude of the cycles increases during the experimental period 225-275 and decreases again after the experiment has ended. The reason is that the 1 per cent rate of high-job saving technical change increases the availability of high-skilled workers for low-level jobs. Moreover, the initial increase in u_H decreases w_0, but w_0 does not decrease enough to fully counter the increase in u_H. Also u_L starts to rise, which depresses low-skilled wages and hence increases w_0 again. The main effect is that changes in u_L and u_H fluctuate around an upward trend in the overall rate of unemployment, as can be seen from Figure 17.[36] The reason for this upward trend is that the additional availability of high-skilled workers makes them replace low-skilled workers in low-level jobs. However, the increase in the number of low-level jobs, as shown in Figure 18, still does not favour employment of low-skilled workers because high-skilled workers take over their jobs.

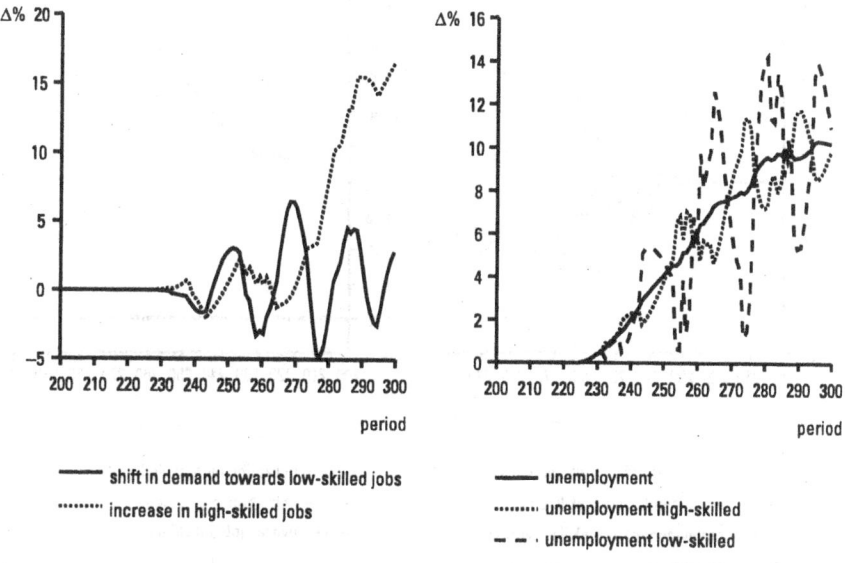

Figure 16 Comparison of change in relative wages in two scenarios

Figure 17 Change in unemployment of high- and low-skilled due to a shift in demand towards low-skilled jobs

The bias in technical change is illustrated quite clearly in Figure 18, where low-level jobs increase and high-level jobs decrease. Nonetheless, both high-skilled employment and low-skilled employment decrease (with fluctuations around this decreasing trend). This conclusion is corroborated by inspection of Figure 19, where q_{L^*} exceeds a value of 1, while q^* is equal to 1, indicating that there is no quantitative shortage of supply of both high-skilled and low-skilled workers. Hence, experiment 3 shows that the effectiveness of the creation of low-level jobs in alleviating low-level unemployment is negatively affected by the existence of an excess supply of high-skilled workers.

By contrast, experiment 4 shows that the introduction of high-level job using technical change, leading to the creation of additional high-level jobs, may be much more effective in creating employment opportunities for low-skilled workers than the creation of low-level jobs did in the context of experiment 3.

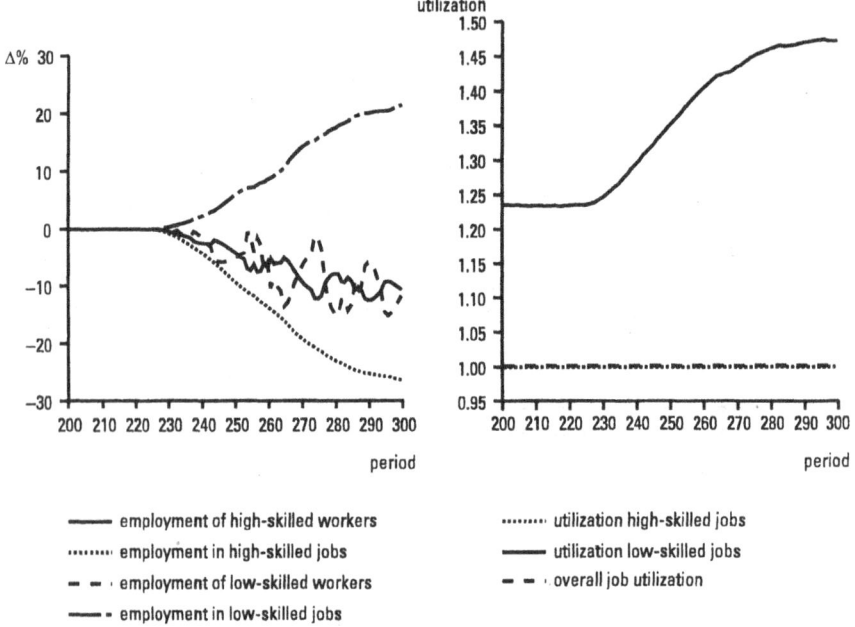

Figure 18 Change in employment due to shift in demand towards low-skilled jobs

Figure 19 Utilization of high- and low-a skilled jobs in experiment 3 which shifts demand towards low-skilled jobs

Figure 21 shows that the introduction of high-level job using technical change does not only increase the number of high-level jobs, but also the number of low-level jobs. The latter is caused by the phenomenon of substitution of low-level jobs for high-level jobs, which is induced by the increase in high-skilled wages following the reduction of high-skilled unemployment. Nonetheless, low-skilled employment is only positively affected for part of the experimental period, i.e. from 225-245 as indicated by the fall in q_L. which was the maximum rate of low-level job utilisation attainable for a given supply of low-skilled workers and supply of high-skilled

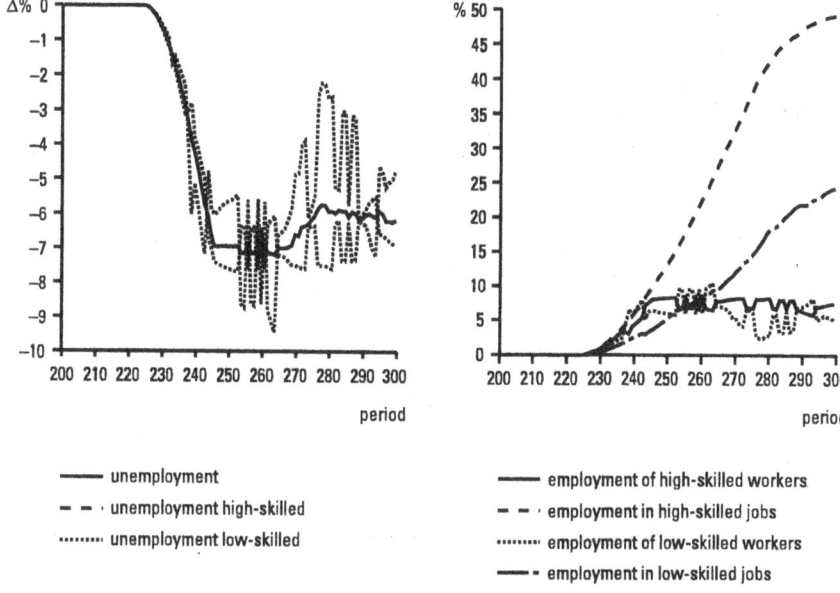

Figure 20 Change in unemployment of high- and low-skilled due to the working of the chimney-effect

Figure 21 Change in employment of high- and low-skilled workers due to the working of the chimney effect

workers available for employment on low-level jobs. Hence the increase in demand for high-skilled workers due to the increase in high-level jobs, extends employment opportunities for low-skilled workers. From Figure 20 one can see that this leads to a drop in the rates of unemployment for both skills until year 245. In 245 something interesting happens: q_{L*} falls below a value of 1. This means that the supply of labour available for employment in low-level jobs is insufficient to meet the demand. Hence, in the period between 245 and 265, we have a situation of a shortage of supply of low-skilled workers. However, from period 265 q_{H*} falls below q_{L*} which indicates that from period 265 the supply constraint with respect to high-skilled labour becomes more binding (i.e. high-skilled labour becomes relatively scarce again), and we see the rate of unemployment of low-skilled labour rising again from period 265. The overall unemployment rate rises too, but falls again after resetting the rate of high-level job using technical change in period 275. The latter would tend to alleviate the bottleneck character of the supply of high-skilled workers from period 265, thus allowing employment for low-skilled workers to increase too.

The main conclusions of experiment 4 are therefore firstly that the creation of high-level jobs may favour employment opportunities for low-skilled workers, and secondly that the occurrence of bottlenecks in the supply of high-skilled workers may also diminish employment prospects for low-skilled workers. Both conclusions point to the paradox of the need to monitor the high-skilled side of the labour market, especially in times of low-skilled unemployment.

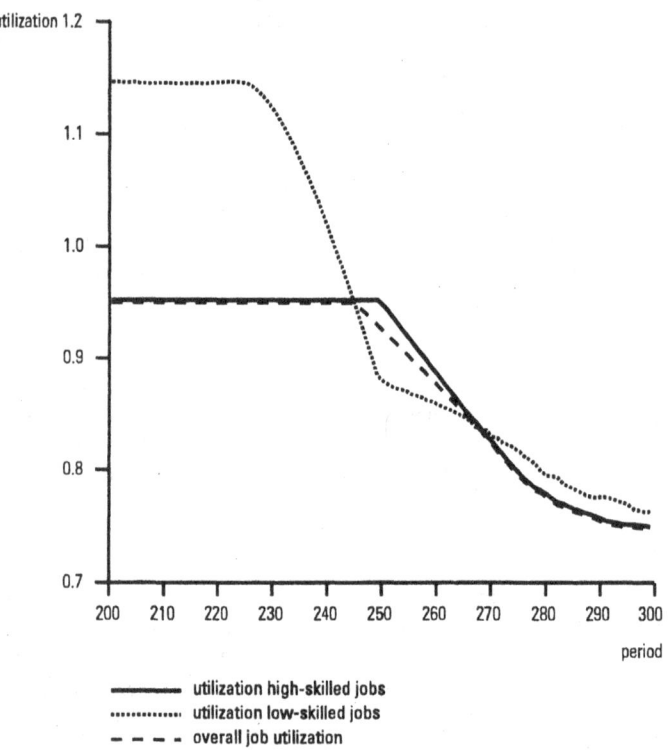

Figure 22 Utilization of high- and low-skilled jobs in the experiment concerning the chimney-effect

Summary and conclusion

In this Chapter we have presented the outlines of a labour allocation model which focuses on asymmetries in substitution possibilities between different types of labour. The general idea underlying this model is that high-skilled people can take over the jobs of low-skilled people but not necessarily the other way around. This implies that the number of low-level jobs is an upper limit to low-skilled employment, while the number of high-level jobs is a lower limit to high-skilled employment. We assume that a high-skilled person has a non-zero efficiency on a low-level job, whereas a low-skilled person has zero efficiency on a high-level job, which is an exaggeration of the actual immobility of skills between jobs.

We have assumed forward-looking behaviour for the firm. Entrepreneurs determine the job composition of employment, as well as the capital intensity of production, based on the expected growth of relative wages. Moreover, in deciding about the job composition of labour demand, they take account of future changes in the allocation of skills to jobs – when relative wages and relative efficiencies indicate that this would be the most profitable thing to do. However, we also introduced switching thresholds in order to model adjustment costs and uncertainty, and assumed that entrepreneurs are heterogeneous with respect to these thresholds. By using the assumption of a uniform distribution of these thresholds, we have been able to derive a simple skill allocation mechanism. This mechanism reacts to wage formation and to average threshold sizes, given the job composition of employment. However, the latter also depends on the average size of thresholds, although in a far more complex way than the skill allocation process itself.

Apart from specifying the model, we have also looked at labour force survey data for the Netherlands available from Eurostat. We found that the substitution asymmetries between high-skilled and low-skilled people are far less outspoken in the data than in our model. Since we measure skill levels as the educational level attained, this seems to point to on-the-job learning as a possibility to cross skill boundaries. The Eurostat data allow us to check this surmise in a tentative way. We noticed that the mobility of low-skilled people between low-skilled and medium-level jobs is considerable indeed. This is also the case with medium-skilled people between medium- and high-level jobs, which in our view stresses the necessity of defining skills in human capital terms rather than the last level of schooling attained. It is obvious that this requires a more transparent labour market, that is, one cannot solely rely on diplomas as an indicator of the relevant skills. Finally, the data did show us that the problem of unemployment of low-skilled people in the Netherlands is severe – as it is in most West-European countries.

A typical solution to the problem of the uneven distribution of unemployment across skills is to rely heavily on wage flexibility to alleviate this problem. However, we have run some simulations with our model using plausible parameter values – although output growth is assumed to be exogenous. One result is that asymmetries in substitution possibilities between low-skilled and high-skilled people imply that the employment response in terms of a change in the job composition in favour of low-level jobs may require quite a fall in low-skilled wages. But even then the largest impact on low-skilled unemployment is to be expected from diminishing the incentives for having high-skilled people replace low-skilled people on low-level jobs. Another result concerns the removal of barriers to firing. It turns out that this may not lead to any significant net benefits for a particular skill group. Rather, fluctuations in unemployment rates become more outspoken due to more frequent and more intensive direct substitution of low-skilled and high-skilled labour on low-level jobs.

Finally we presented a simulation experiment to illustrate the working of the so-called chimney effect. It was shown that the creation of low-level jobs in a situation of excess supply of high-skilled workers may not be an effective way of creating employment opportunities for low-skilled workers. Instead, the creation of high-level jobs which require reallocations of high-skilled workers from low-level jobs to high-level jobs may be much more effective in generating effective job openings for low-skilled workers than the direct creation of low-level jobs would be (this is the chimney effect). Moreover the creation of high-level jobs may lead to the creation of low-level jobs as a 'side-effect', which would essentially increase the effectiveness of the creation of high-level jobs in alleviating low-skilled unemployment problems.

These last conclusions point to the paradox of the need to monitor the high-skilled side of the labour market, especially in times of low-skilled unemployment. That is, transparency of the labour market is an important element – not just in identifying relevant human capital, as mentioned above – in the combat against low-skilled unemployment.

Notes

1. For the Netherlands this is recognised in, for instance, CPB (1996), pp. 77-79, and CPB (1996), Ch. 6.
2. In Nickell and Bell (1995, p. 51), the ratio of high-skilled wages and low-skilled wages for the US and the Netherlands are 1.51 and 1.22 respectively, which implies a 20 per cent drop in low-skilled wages in the Netherlands, if the ratio of high-skilled wages and low-skilled wages in the US was considered to be the benchmark.
3. A more common objection is of course that an increase of labour market flexibility insofar as such would lead to lower levels of private consumption, may be less effective in promoting employment for the low-skilled unemployed than expected.
4. Examples of such studies are Hamermesh and Grant (1979), Broer and Jansen (1989) and Hebbink (1990).
5. Cf. also van den Rijen (1996). Interestingly enough, there is a magnification effect involved in the creation of high-level jobs with respect to low-level employment opportunities when high-skilled workers would be more efficient in low-level jobs than low-skilled workers, since the creation of one high-level

job filled by a high-skilled worker who previously performed low-level tasks would offer employment opportunities for more than one low-skilled worker. Another possible 'magnification' effect could be present when productivity increases are indeed connected with the use of human capital, as suggested by Lucas (1986) and Romer (1990), for instance. The creation of an additional high-level job may then lead to overall efficiency increases, which may in turn favour employment in general and hence employment for the low-skilled too.

6   A similar, somewhat more elaborate analysis has also been performed for Germany, 1988-1994, in van Zon and Muysken (1996). In particular, more attention has been paid to the sectoral differentiation and the differentiation between types of jobs. It turned out that these dimensions were not very relevant for the analysis of the match between skills and occupations. Since the same holds for the Netherlands – cf. also Draper and Manders (1996), Appendix 1 – we ignore these dimensions below.

7   We have used Eurostat's Labour Force Survey data for employment and unemployment. The data are available by country (European Union), by sector of industry, occupation (ISCO 68/88), age and highest level of education attained. The latter dimension corresponds to the ISCED educational classification. (Further information on the Dutch educational system is provided in the Appendix to this book.)

The data have been provided only for the period 1988-1994, because Eurostat did not perform an educational desaggregation of (un-)employment data for earlier years. In 1992, two major changes occurred in the classification of the data. First, the classification of sectors of industry changed from NACE-CLIO to NACE-Revision 1. Second, the classification of occupations changed from ISCO 68 to ISCO 88.

8   In the empirical version of this model we distinguish between three different types of occupations: administrative-commercial, personal services and technical, however.

9   Similar observations can be inferred from Figure III.5.1 from CPB (1996), p. 77.

10 The observation that more higher-skilled workers than low-skilled workers are employed in low-level jobs is also made in CPB (1996), Figure III.5.2, p. 78. This is also seen as evidence for the 'chimney effect', mentioned in the first Section above. Cf. SoZaWe (1996), pp. 57-58.

11 A comparison with 21.0 years of average experience in low-level jobs not useful, since working experience of low-skilled people in low-level jobs may be quite irrelevant for the formation of human capital, when compared to working experience in medium- and high-level jobs.

12 This is also an explanation for the low participation rate of low-skilled persons, since most of the males in this category are either early retired (VUT) or disabled (WAO) – cf. SoZaWe (1996), p.59.

13 Many writers have investigated the possibility of direct substitution between skill-categories. A survey for the US is provided by Hamermesh and Grant (1979), while Hebbink (1990) and Broer and Jansen (1989) provide some results for the Netherlands. Kugler c.s. (1990) do the same for Germany. Mincer (1989) provides additional results for the US. The general conclusions which emerge from these studies are *firstly* that capital and high-skilled labour are complements, while *secondly* low-skilled labour and the capital/high-skilled labour complex are substitutes.

14 From our discussion in the second Section it is obvious that skills should be interpreted in a broad sense, including such aspects as experience.

15 Note that due to Hicks-neutral disembodied labour augmenting technical change, the effective discount rate of job operating costs rises with the value of the rate of disembodied technical progress. However, for the moment we disregard the influence of technical change.

16 Since high-level jobs always need to be filled by high-skilled workers, the four distinct possibilities can actually be defined in terms of the allocation of skills to low-level jobs only.

17 (L_i, H_i) is the combination of L and H during sub-period i. $i=1,2$ denotes the period before and after switching, respectively.

18 $t^* = t^*(x,y)$ defines the moment in time when a switch from type x employment to type y employment should be realised. Note that a switch with $t^*(L,H)=0$ implies that entrepreneurs would expect to allocate high-skilled workers to low-level jobs from the beginning.

19 Although this has not been indicated in Figure 6, t^* can of course be different for these cases. t^* itself is easily determined from the condition that: $w_{t^*} = w_{H,t^*}/w_{L,t^*} = (w_{H,0}/w_{L,0}).\exp\{(\hat{w}_H - \hat{w}_L).t^*\} = e'$. Hence: $t^* = \ln(e'/w_0)/\hat{w}$.

20 This assumes, of course, that there are no initial switching costs, which means that these costs should be interpreted in terms of the costs of firing rather than hiring. Note however, that when switching costs are defined in terms of on-the-job learning, switching costs may be incurred at each moment in time when a certain allocation of skills to jobs has to be made. This means that asymmetries in learning potentials/speeds between skills now determine how large the sunk costs will be for a certain allocation, and hence how these costs should actually be sunk. Indeed, for a simple implementation of costs in a switching setting, it is easy to show that the case of switching thresholds is but a particular case of a more general (but still simple) learning model (see van Zon and Muysken (1996), and van Zon, Meijers and Muysken (1997)). For reasons of simplicity we stick to the simple threshold case in this model, however.

21 i.e. switch at time t^* as it is implicitly defined by $w_{t^*} = e'.(1+\Delta)$, instead of at t' as given by $e' = w_{t'}$. Cf. also note 19.

22 Note that it is not absolutely necessary for the switching thresholds to be symmetric around e'. Rather, the $\Delta's$ could be different, indicating asymmetries in the costs of hiring and firing, depending on which skill is hired and which is fired. We will not pursue this potential asymmetry here, however. See van Zon, Meijers and Muysken (1997) on this subject.
23 These gaps would make it impossible to describe aggregate behaviour without tracking the behaviour of individual entrepreneurs. Obviously, we want to avoid the latter.
24 Note that substitution of equation (7) into (8) still implies that $H_t = H^*_t + (L^*_t - L_t)/e'$, which follows from the assumption that high-skilled people can replace low-skilled people, but not vice versa.
25 See Appendix D of van Zon and Muysken (1996).
26 The Bischoff approach disregards economic obsolescence.
27 The expected present value of the total cost per (initial) unit of output on the newest vintage over an infinite horizon (Λ_T) is equal to:

$$\Lambda_T = \frac{w_T}{\rho+\delta-\hat{w}} \cdot v_{T,T} + q_T \cdot \kappa_{T,T}$$

where q_t represents the price of investment at time t, w_t the wage rate and $\hat{w}$ the growth rate of wages. See van Zon (1990) for a derivation of this result. $v_{T,T}$ and $\kappa_{T,T}$ can now be obtained by minimising Λ_T conditional on the ex ante production function as given in equation (9).
28 This function is consistent with the isoquant $j'j$ in Figure 5. The value of the elasticity of substitution is consistent with that found in Hamermesh en Grant (1979) and Hebbink (1990). Note that we do not assume here that high-level jobs are complementary with capital. Rather, the job complex is a substitute for capital, while low-level and high-level jobs are substitutes within the job complex. The reason for doing so is that substitution reactions between high-skilled and low-skilled workers in response to changes in wage rates et cetera, should become more pronounced than if high-level jobs were complementary with capital.
29 The latter elasticity of substitution is the one found for the Netherlands by Kuipers and van Zon (1982) and Muysken and van Zon (1987), for instance.
30 The present value price of investment is equal to the price index of investment (see van Zon (1990) for a description of the assumptions underlying this result), while the present value price of labour is the initial value of the wage rate divided by the sum of the rate of discount and the rate of technical decay less the growth rate of wages.
31 Equation (12) follows from (11) and the assumption that w_H/w_L is constant in the steady state.
32 See note 20.

33 The reader can easily verify that the value of q^* given in (15) is consistent with H^s and L^s being completely exhausted at this value of the overall job utilisation rate, as required. Hence, q^* is the maximum rate of job utilisation which can be realised given the available supply of skills.
34 See Appendix A for a more detailed description of the various allocation processes.
35 Roughly one third of all jobs is low-level in our simulation experiments.
36 In period 275 the rates of job-saving/using technical change are set equal to zero again, and one sees the rise in the overall rate of unemployment coming to an end.

References

Bischoff, C.W. (1971), 'The effect of alternative lag distributions', in: Fromm, G. (ed.), *Tax incentives and capital spending*, the Brookings Institution: Washington.

Broer, D.P., and Jansen, W.J. (1989), 'Employment, Schooling and Productivity Growth', *De Economist*, 137, pp. 425-453.

CPB (1996), 'Macro Economische Verkenningen 1997', Centraal Planbureau: Den Haag.

Draper, N., and Manders, T. (1996), 'Structural Changes in the Demand for Labour', CPB Netherlands Bureau for Economic Policy Analysis, Research Memorandum 28.

Hamermesh, D.S., Grant, J.H. (1979), 'Econometric Studies of Labor-Labor Substitutions and Their Implications for Policy', *Journal of Human Resources*, 14, pp. 518-542.

Hebbink, G.E. (1991), 'Employment by Level of Education and Production Factor Substitutability', *De Economist*, 139, pp. 379-401.

Kugler, P., Muller, U., and Sheldon, G. (1990), 'The Labor Market Effects of New Technologies – an Econometric Study for the Federal Republic of Germany', in Schettkat, R., and Wagner, M. (eds.), *Technological Change and Employment Innovation in the German Economy*, Walter de Gruyter: Berlin.

Kuipers, S.K., and Zon, A.H. van (1982), 'Output and Employment Growth in the Netherlands in the Postwar Period: A Putty-Clay Approach', *De Economist*, 130, pp. 38-70.

Lucas, R.E. (1988), 'On the Mechanics of Economic Development', *Journal of Monetary Economics*, 22, pp. 3-42.

Mincer, J., (1989), *Human Capital Responses to Technological Change in the Labor Market*, NBER Working Paper 3207.

Muysken, J., and Zon, A.H. van (1987), 'Employment and unemployment in the Netherlands, 1960-1984: a putty-clay approach', *Recherches Economiques de Louvain*, 53, pp. 101-133.

Nickell, S., and Bell, B. (1995), 'The Collapse in Demand for the Unskilled and Unemployment across the OECD', *Oxford Review of Economic Policy*, 11 (1), pp. 40-62.
Rijen, P.J. van den (1996), 'Verdringing geen probleem op de Nederlandse arbeidsmarkt', *ESB*, 5-6, pp. 508-510.
Romer, P. (1990), 'Endogenous Technological Change', *Journal of Political Economy*, 98 (5), pp. 71-102.
SoZaWe, *Werkgelegenheidsnota 1996*, Ministerie van Sociale Zaken en Werkgelegenheid, Den Haag 1996.
Zon, A.H. van (1990), 'Vintage Capital and R&D Based Technological Progress', in: Freeman C., and Soete, L. (eds.), *New Explorations in the Economics of Technological Change*, Pinter Publishers: London & New York.
Zon, A.H. van, Janssen, M., Meijers, H., Meulen, J. van der, Muysken, J., Oude Wansink, M. (1995), 'Technical Change, Unemployment and Skill Mismatch', Report for DG5 of the European Commission.
Zon, A.H. van, and Muysken, J. (1996), 'MASS: A Model of Asymmetric Skill Substitution', MERIT Research Memorandum, RM2/96-016.
Zon, A.H. van, Meijers, H., and Muysken, J. (1997), 'On Trickling Chimneys and Other Unemployment Misery', MERIT Research Memorandum, RM2/97-006.

Acknowledgement

Special thanks are due to Maurice Oude Wansink for his help in preparing the data.

Appendix A: Solving the intertemporal cost minimisation problem

For cases 2 and 3, there are two periods to consider, i.e. the pre-switching period and the post-switching period. Case 4 is the case where both L and H skills are used to fill L^* and H^* jobs. The various objective functions associated with the cases mentioned above are given in equations (A1)-(A3).

$$T_2 = \int_0^{t^*} w_{H,t} \cdot (L^*/e' + H^*) \cdot \exp(-(\rho+\delta) \cdot t) \, dt + \int_{t^*}^{\infty} \left(w_{L,t} \cdot L^* + w_{H,t} \cdot H^* \right) \cdot \exp(-(\rho+\delta) \cdot t) \, dt \qquad (A.1)$$

$$T_3 = \int_0^{t^*} \left(w_{L,t} \cdot L^* + w_{H,t} \cdot H^* \right) \cdot \exp(-(\rho+\delta) \cdot t) \, dt + \int_{t^*}^{\infty} w_{H,t} \cdot (L^*/e' + H^*) \cdot \exp(-(\rho+\delta) \cdot t) \, dt \qquad (A.2)$$

$$T_4 = \int_0^{\infty} \left(w_{L,t} \cdot L^* + w_{H,t} \cdot H^* \right) \cdot \exp(-(\rho+\delta) \cdot t) \, dt \qquad (A.3)$$

The cost function parameters and presented in Table A.1, can be derived from for a given moment of switching t^*. These are presented in the table below, where z is defined as being equal to $z = (\hat{w}_L - \rho - \delta)/\hat{w}$.

In order for the cost-minimisation problem to have a meaningful solution, it follows that the α's and β's should be positive. This requires the growth rates of high-skilled wages and low-skilled wages to be less than $\rho+\delta$, which we have had to assume in the first place in order to obtain finite objective function values. Hence, all the α's are positive, while it is immediately clear that β_1 and β_2 are positive too. In order for β_3 to be positive, it is necessary that $(e'/w_0)^z < z+1$. Note that in case 3 $z>0$ and $e'/w_0 < 1$, which implies that $(e'/w_0)^z < 1 < z+1$ for $z>0$, as required. For case 2 similar results can be obtained. Defining $z'=-z$, the requirement that $\beta_2>0$ implies that $(w_0/e')^{z'-1} - z' < 0$, since $z+1<0$, by assumption. Because $w_0/e'<1$ in case 2, this only holds for $z'>1$, i.e. for $z<-1$.[*] Hence $\beta_2>0$ when $z<-1$. Using the definition for z (see above), this requires that $\hat{w}_L - \rho - \delta < \hat{w}_L - \hat{w}_H \rightarrow \rho + \delta - \hat{w}_H > 0$, which is true by assumption.

---

[*] For $z'=1$, it follows that $(w_0/e')^0 = z'=1$. For $0<z'<1$ $(w_0/e')^{z'-1}>1$, while $z'<1$, by assumption. Hence, $\beta_2>0$ for $0<z'<1$.

Table A.1
Cost function parameters

Case	α	β
1	$\dfrac{w_{H,0}}{\rho+\delta-\hat{w}_H}$	$\dfrac{w_{L,0}}{\rho+\delta-\hat{w}_L}\left(\dfrac{w_0}{e'}\right)\dfrac{z}{1+z}$
2	$\dfrac{w_{H,0}}{\rho+\delta-\hat{w}_H}$	$\dfrac{w_{L,0}}{\rho+\delta-\hat{w}_L}\left(\left(\dfrac{w_0}{e'}\right)\dfrac{z}{z+1}+\left(\dfrac{w_0}{e'}\right)^{-z}\dfrac{1}{1+z}\right)$
3	$\dfrac{w_{H,0}}{\rho+\delta-\hat{w}_H}$	$\dfrac{w_{L,0}}{\rho+\delta-\hat{w}_L}\left(1-\left(\dfrac{w_0}{e'}\right)^{-z}\dfrac{1}{1+z}\right)$
4	$\dfrac{w_{H,0}}{\rho+\delta-\hat{w}_H}$	$\dfrac{w_{L,0}}{\rho+\delta-\hat{w}_L}$

Cost function parameters and switching thresholds

When an individual entrepreneur, characterised by a certain value of, is assumed to take account of potential future switching costs, the revised cost function 'parameters' β_2 and β_3 are given by:

$$\beta_2 = \frac{w_{L,0}}{\rho+\delta-\hat{w}_L}\left((w_0/e')\frac{z}{1+z}+(w_0/e')^{-z}(1+\Delta)^z\left(\frac{1-\Delta z}{1+z}\right)\right) \quad (A.4)$$

$$\beta_3 = \frac{w_{L,0}}{\rho+\delta-\hat{w}_L}\left(1-(w_0/e')^{-z}(1-\Delta)^z\left(\frac{1+\Delta z}{1+z}\right)\right) \quad (A.5)$$

The requirement that all β's are positive has the same implications as before, provided $0 \leq \Delta < 1$, which seems to be a fairly unrestrictive assumption to make. Note that for $\Delta = 0$, the original no-threshold parameter values are obtained again.

Threshold distributions

Only β_2 and β_3 are changed due to the introduction of threshold distributions, since only in cases 2 and 3 a switch between states is expected to occur. Hence, only in these cases the population averages matter. The average values of the β's are given by:

$$\bar{\beta}_2 = \int_0^{\bar{\Delta}} \frac{\beta_2(\Delta)}{\bar{\Delta}} d\Delta = \frac{w_{L,0}}{\rho + \delta - \hat{w}_L} \left((w_0/e')\frac{z}{1+z} + \frac{(w_0/e')^{-z}}{1+z} \frac{(1+\bar{\Delta})^{z+1}(2-z\bar{\Delta})-2}{\bar{\Delta}(z+2)} \right) \quad (A.6)$$

$$\bar{\beta}_3 = \int_0^{\bar{\Delta}} \frac{\beta_3(\Delta)}{\bar{\Delta}} d\Delta = \frac{w_{L,0}}{\rho + \delta - \hat{w}_L} \left(1 - \frac{(w_0/e')^{-z}}{1+z} \frac{2-(1-\bar{\Delta})^{z+1}(2+z\bar{\Delta})}{\bar{\Delta}(z+2)} \right) \quad (A.7)$$

where a bar over a beta denotes a population average. Unfortunately, equations (A.6) and (A.7) cannot readily be interpreted.

Supply constraints and the allocation of skills to jobs

In the case of supply constraints, the preferred allocation of skills to jobs in old and new jobs may be different. This leads to the identification of four groups of entrepreneurs with their own preferences with respect to allocating skills to jobs. Group A entrepreneurs have a preference for low skills on both new and old jobs, and the allocation process is relatively straightforward. This also holds for group D entrepreneurs, who have a preference for high skills in both old and new jobs. Hence, the allocation process for group D entrepreneurs is described by:

$$\begin{aligned} HL^* &= \min\left(\frac{q^*L^*}{e'}, (1-\mu^*)H^s - HH^*\right) \\ LL^* &= \min(q^*L^* - e'HL^*, (1-\mu^*)L^s) \end{aligned} \quad (A.8)$$

Denoting 'new' low-level jobs by ΔL^*, the allocation process for group B entrepreneurs, who prefer high skills in new jobs and low skills in old jobs, can be described by:

$$H\Delta L^* = \min(q^*.\Delta L^*/e^I, H^s - HH^*)$$
$$LL^* = \min(q^*.L^* - e^I.H\Delta L^*, L^s)$$
$$HL^* = \min(q^*.L^* - e^I.H\Delta L^* - LL^*, H^s - HH^* - H\Delta L^*)$$
$$L\Delta L^* = q^*.\Delta L^* - \epsilon.H\Delta L^*$$

(A.9)

For group C entrepreneurs, who prefer low skills in new jobs and high skills in old jobs, the allocation process is given by:

$$L\Delta L^* = \min(q^*.\Delta L^*, L^s)$$
$$HL^* = \min((q^*.L^* - L\Delta L^*)/e^I, H^s - HH^*)$$
$$LL^* = \min(q^*.L^* - L\Delta L^* - e^I.HL^*, L^s - L\Delta L^*)$$
$$H\Delta L^* = (q^*.\Delta L^* - L\Delta L^*)/e^I$$

(A.10)

Part Three
CURRICULUM

8 Curriculum Characteristics and Labour Market Perspectives

Wim Nijhof

Introduction

This Chapter attempts to show and analyse the relationship between curriculum characteristics and labour market perspectives. The term curriculum is here defined as a learning path or learning route, which is the original meaning of the concept (Nijhof, 1993). A learning route may take a variety of forms. Some authors argue in favour of learning and working, some prefer learning by working, while others opt for traditional learning in schools only. Hence there may be a great variety, ranging from conventional school-type learning routes to more experience-oriented routes.

The question is whether curriculum characteristics play a relevant part. This concerns in particular the aspect of labour market perspectives: getting a job, keeping a job, developing a career, and the degree of access to the labour market in terms of visibility and recognisability of educational courses for the suppliers of jobs. A learning route should ensure that pupils or students can acquire skills which enable them to obtain a job.

It would be naive, however, to state that such perspectives can only be achieved by means of a well-organised curriculum. There are also other market conditions and various legal, economic and socio-political aspects. Nevertheless, we wish to discuss a number of studies dealing with different variants of learning routes, in order to determine whether – and if so, to what extent – curriculum characteristics do (or may) play a role in the realisation of opportunities, both within the learning process (in terms of the effectiveness of learning) and in terms of chances of work and a career.

We make use of a number of recent studies to illustrate the issues, but we will start with a description of curriculum characteristics. This is followed in the third Section by a discussion of labour market perspectives. The fourth Section combines the results of the two previous Sections into a model and attempts to analyse the different studies in order to determine whether the model has any validity. The Chapter concludes with a summary of the main conclusions.

Curriculum characteristics

In the previous Section, we defined a curriculum as a learning route. Curricula are often preplanned learning routes prepared and drawn on paper. For vocational education, such a learning route is often seen as a skills-oriented path. Skills are here defined as activities or abilities enabling one to create a product or render a service with which one can generate an income, prestige, or status. The concept of skills has different connotations and meanings in different labour organisation models. For example, the concept of the 'learning organisation' has recently placed an emphasis on the abilities of employees to consult with others, to negotiate, to share responsibility and knowledge, and to take individual responsibility. Such requirements are far removed from the traditional Taylorist and/or Fordist organisation models, where employees were instrumental extensions of the production machinery. Learning skills in a job therefore depends to a large extent on the present demands of the job involved.

We can also see that the policies of governments and enterprises are aimed not only at improving the 'performance' of the organisation at all levels in the light of a world economy (global competition), but should also contribute to the personal happiness of the people involved by allowing them to develop as a person. Governments often promote such an approach from the viewpoint of the human capital theory, but also because of pedagogical motives (Nijhof and Streumer, 1994). The preparation for an occupation, for further studies, and for a personal and social life, then extends the discussion of the skills deemed necessary to the question what the function is of vocational education to which the authorities are bound and for which it is responsible, also financially. In business managers, this discussion leads to different questions, such as the quality of supply, the screening and/or selection principles that can be applied to get the best person in the best place.

This gradually extends the issue from a specific question related to the first job, to a question relating to one's functioning in society, where recent developments have been creating the need for greater flexibility of time, tasks and future. The combination of high skills and low wages (Commission on the Skills of the American Workforce, 1994) is dominant here.

To be able to answer the question relating to curriculum characteristics, we must first deal with an organisational problem and then with an empirical one. Which characteristics have been studied and are relevant? Curriculum characteristics are the constituent characteristics that define and instrument a learning route. This concerns the input characteristics of the curriculum, process characteristics and results: skills.

Input characteristics constitute the main conditional and content criteria that can be imposed on a curriculum. These often determine its scope, content, duration and level. Process characteristics are often the characteristics of the learning route itself. In vocational education, these are defined in terms of learning and working, and combinations of these two, also called the relationship between theory and practice. The way in which the processes are coached or guided (with an emphasis on either the school or the work setting) determines the process. Output characteristics relate to the results of the learning route: the learning effects. In the case of vocational education, these concern the skills acquired to be able to start one's first job. But it is also possible to acquire skills that enable one to operate flexibly in the labour market, in occupations for which one was not specifically trained (transition skills). These characteristics can be represented in a model (see Figure 1).

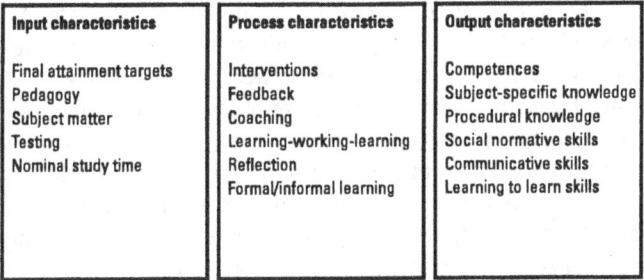

Figure 1 Input-process-output model

Input characteristics of the curriculum

The main input characteristics of a learning route include:

Final attainment targets. These can be regarded as the main control instruments, because they constitute the minimum standard for directing the educational learning process. Final attainment targets must also be operationalised in types of tests, so as to enable the measuring of skills (cognition, insight, and capabilities and attitudes). In a occupation-oriented setting, attempts are currently being made to represent attitude (level), transfer to the context (workplace), and degree of independence in the skills structure (Ministerie van Onderwijs en Wetenschappen, 1993). The national skills structure, with its different levels, plays an important role here (WEB, 1995). It is not clear how one should define final attainment targets. A number of alternatives are available, varying from behaviourist to constructivist ones.

Learning content, specific knowledge or declarative knowledge constitutes the second major input factor. Learning content in the form of knowledge areas (such as robotics, mechanical engineering, nursing, agriculture, economics). Final attainment targets are thus linked with content. Techniques to achieve this make use of concept maps, or V-maps (Novak and Gowan, 1990). These further the internal consistency between contents, final attainment targets and tests, often a major problem in curriculum development and the implementation of education (Nijhof, 1993). The transformation of final attainment targets into instruction and into learning results constitutes a serious consistency problem (Goodlad, 1984; Nijhof, 1983, 1995).

Pedagogy constitutes the third major input factor. In particular in vocational education, there is the important question of the relationship between learning and working, which also applies to in-service training: can a place of work be an adequate place of learning (de Jong, 1995; van der Klink, 1996), can a workplace or a virtual organisation be simulated? This concerns the question of which learning route is the most efficient and most effective one in order to acquire (occupation-oriented) skills. The robust introduction of modular education in Intermediate Vocational Education (IVE), in Higher Vocational Education (HVE), and in University Education, almost without pilot studies, and the discussion of the dualisation have shown that there may be many learning routes leading to occupational competence (Commissie Dualisering, 1992). There is, however, a striking lack of experimental, and international comparative research that may provide a satisfactory answer to the question of the most effective learning route.

The course duration is the important fourth component. The time factor has proved to be one of the best predictors of learning effects and returns. But the means which the government is capable of providing or prepared to provide, are limited. Those who wish to study longer, who choose more subjects at a higher level, may expect greater personal returns (Bishop, 1995; van Ingen, 1996), although there are limits to the employability or mobility of graduates.

The degree of achievement of the final attainment targets constitutes the important fifth component, because this measurement indicates the level at which students are expected to perform. Curricula which promote learning to master skills, for example by organising feedback, usually yield better results than those which fail to do so.

Process characteristics

A curriculum which is being implemented is often the real curriculum, i.e. the actual learning route. This route is then determined by the interaction between learner and learning environment. The learning environment includes the study materials, possibly a (virtual) workplace, a (virtual) learning place, and an instructor, coach or tutor. This learning environment steers, guides, coaches, co-ordinates, checks, provides feedback, motivates, or in short, performs all functions which are necessary to effectuate a learning process, either formal or informal. It is the learner who learns. In this sense, the curriculum is a true, authentic learning route.

The traditional route is that of a year group, which – on the basis of 'starting together, finishing together' – is offered the study material to process, disclose, and learn to master it. By means of modern information and communication technology, by means of simulations, by co-operative learning, many different combinations can be made, paving the learning route, both externally (by the school, teacher) and by the students themselves. It is difficult to identify relevant curriculum characteristics within these process characteristics. Studies often show that interaction between previous knowledge in students, the degree of structuring of the learning route, and motivation may play a relevant part (Cronbach and Snow, 1977). Whether such is always the case in vocational education is questionable. Vocational education has proved to be a second, often negative choice, which means that the motivation of pupils may be lower than average. Vocational education and in-service training do, however, have the intention of providing a strong relationship between the requirements as to skills of the workplace (e.g. by analysing occupational profiles) and learning content. The principle of similarity, which plays a major role in studies of the transfer (Gielen, 1995; den Ouden, 1993) is important here. Transfer principles and tactics are therefore important characteristics of a learning route. As the direct similarity between learning task and working task decreases, the learning principle generalises accordingly, but in principle the applicability to other tasks increases. Transfer capabilities and transition skills should then in principle increase (Nijhof and Remmers, 1989, 1990; Moerkamp, 1995).

Many interventions of an instructional or curricular nature, such as the organisation of feedback, co-operative learning, and expert-novice models, may influence the acquisition of skills. The essence of the process variables is that these may be combined into an intervention, and thus become an actual learning route. This applies to the dual system, where variants of learning and working can be addressed by means of all kinds of interventions, such as by means of the 'Leittextmethode' developed in Germany. The same is also true for modular education, which has been introduced in the Netherlands in a variety of forms. There is, however, little implementation research on the basis of which the 'real' curriculum for vocational education can be constructed.

Output characteristics

A curriculum can be regarded as a carrier of expertise and skills, which must be converted into professional capabilities by means of effective interactions. The results of a learning route are therefore occupational capabilities at a particular level. This is also referred to in the literature by means of starting qualifications or initial qualification, although some authors assign a more limited meaning to this concept. In this case, starting qualifications constitute the lowest quantifiable level of a vocational education system (the apprentice level) (Hövels, 1996). The occupational capabilities that can be acquired by an individual are strongly related to the way in which these are defined. This can be done in formal terms by pointing at terms often used in taxonomies: categories of learning results (Gagné, Briggs and Wager, 1991), or by using some of the taxonomies themselves as instrumental source, such as the one used by Bloom (1956) for the cognitive domain, the one used by de Block (1975), who focuses more on transfer skills, and the one by Romiszowski (1981), who emphasises the communicative and interactive skills. Narrowing skills down to taxonomic categories may result in loss of information. A taxonomy used by Olbrich and Pfeiffer (1980), for example, was developed from the perspective of labour activities, complexity levels and co-operation patterns in technical professions, and hence covers a particular set of activities and skills better. The selection of a taxonomy therefore determines the way in which results of learning routes can be represented validly and reliably. If these results consist not only of skills which are relevant in order to be able to perform an initial occupation, but also of results which are meaningful for further studies and personal development, then we also have to deal with qualifications relating to learning strategies, learning to learn, and motivational aspects, such as self-efficacy. In general, the discussion regarding the results then moves in the direction of general study skills, generic skills and basic skills.

Brown (1997) has made an analysis of effective characteristics of curricula for vocational education and has come to the conclusion that to achieve wide-ranging occupational skills requires a strong interaction between education, training and working by means of learning. He therefore argues in favour of developing effective learning strategies, i.e. that learning occupational skills in various contexts is of great importance for the transfer of what has been learnt. Reflective skills and process skills provide a further contribution to the development of 'occupational competence', but only if the condition is met that such are learnt in relation to and linked with occupational contexts. The development of a substantial knowledge base is important because the latter is a precondition for domain-specific expertise and because such knowledge is of great importance for further learning. The importance of this occupational link and capitalising on 'occupational competences' is also strongly supported by Bishop (1995), who believes that there has been too much and unjustifiable emphasis on 'academics' during the past few years. A great number of studies has shown that occupational skills are much more important for the acquisition of a job and an income. In their study of a broader vocational education, Nijhof and Streumer (1994, p. 137) emphasise the need of occupational skills which are learnt in a working context and decontextualised in the learning process. Competences which are regarded as important include: subject-specific expertise, knowledge of methodological procedures, social normative qualifications, communicative skills and abilities for further studies. All this leads to the model presented above (see Figure 1), in which input, process, and output are systematically linked.

In practice, combinations of input characteristics give rise to important variants of vocational education and occupation-supporting education, in such as way that one may conclude that these combinations define the set of learning routes:

- traditional school variants of vocational education (with simulations and/or apprenticeships, possibly in a modular form; with possibilities for horizontal and vertical advancement);
- dual learning routes: alternating between learning and working
- varying duration (short(er) or long(er)); and
- varying levels: Preparatory, Intermediate and Higher Vocational Education (PVE, IVE, HVE).

Labour market perspectives

Within the framework of the present Chapter, it is important to define labour market perspectives. After all, if we wish to create a link between characteristics of the learning routes and labour market perspectives, it is essential that we know what they are. We have already pointed out that acquiring skills is aimed at obtaining a (first) job, possibly at developing a career, while at the same time it must be viewed from a wider social perspective whether such is adequate. The issue here is therefore the chance of getting a job or work, and the factors affecting this chance. Does the curriculum play a role in this? If someone fails to find a job of his or her choice, the curriculum should enable such an individual to choose or take alternatives. The curriculum should therefore allow substitution between jobs, between what is required and what has been acquired, so that those who demand qualifications may choose from a wide range of competences. Polyvalence of learning routes may contribute to the solution of this problem. The relationship between mobility and substitution is evident in this case. The curriculum as a learning route must then provide a wide foundation on the basis of which students may avail of such characteristics as to also allow them a wide entry in the labour market. This is also referred to as extended vocational education. The fact that, on the other hand, forming a large reservoir of competences also refers to the need for an accurate assessment in the labour market, was shown by Wolf (1997).

Screening and selection

It is a known fact that screening and selection take place in the labour market. This phenomenon refers to the so-called credentials theory. This theory is a sorting theory. Companies make their choices from the available graduates on the basis of more factors than education alone, often on the basis of personality characteristics. The result of such a selection procedure may be that an imperfect match is made between work tasks and skills offered. In the case of overeducation, there is the risk of replacement or of frequent selection processes because, in the longer term, the overeducated will be dissatisfied with less ambitious jobs. Although screening and selection processes show how choices are made, they do not always make it clear why particular choices and selections were made and if these were justified. If courses are less clear and the supply of graduates is great, companies apparently tend to make more use of assessment and screening techniques. The acquired educational qualifications are no longer decisive. This brings us to a second element: the transparency problem.

Transparency, effectiveness and efficiency

In 1988, the Dutch Ministry of Agriculture and Fisheries introduced a procedure for the innovation of agricultural education by systematically starting from occupational profiles, from a qualification structure and from the possibility of organising curricular flexibility (Raffe, 1994) by means of modular education. In 1990, the Ministry of Education and Science followed a similar procedure. The starting point is a clear classification of skills levels and skills requirements, in line with the needs of the national organisations for vocational education. The recognition of diplomas and certificates is often influenced to a great extent by the way in which the qualification structure is organised. The modular structure, combined with premature leaving with a set of partial certificates, may lead to situations in which employers are unable to determine the value of such dossier certificates in the labour market. There are signals which indicate that the implementation of final attainment targets and modules is not a smooth process, and that the transparency of the qualification system in terms of recognisability of levels is causing problems (Brandsma, Thuring-van der Linden and Schuit-van der Linden, 1996).

If the recognisability is limited, this not only creates a communication problem between the supplying and the demanding party, but also a problem of legitimacy in terms of recognition of the requirements for an occupation or position. In this sense, flexible curriculum characteristics as further operationalisation of the aims of the qualification structure, may create a tension with respect to labour market perspectives: the chances of work, and hence the chances of mobility, decrease. Strangely enough, relatively little is known about modular systems. We know little about the effects, both internal and external ones. For the benefit of external effects, new indicators must be found within the new qualification structure, because year classes are no longer the starting point (Lokman, Woerkom and Bruin, 1996). The external effects, however, can be redefined relatively easily as finding or obtaining work on the basis of transfer, complexity and responsibility. Figure 1 can then be extended to include a cell for work, job, or employment (see Figure 2).

Input characteristics	Process characteristics	Output characteristics	Labour market perspective
Final attainment targets	Interventions	Competences	Transferability
Pedagogy	Feedback	Subject-specific knowledge	Transition skills
Subject matter	Coaching	Procedural knowledge	
Testing	Learning-working-learning	Social normative skills	Job
Nominal study time	Reflection	Communicative skills	Career
	Formal/informal learning	Learning to learn skills	Further study

Figure 2   From a learning system toward employability

Qualification structure: broad or narrow?

In the discussion of the relationship with vocational education, there is always the question of how broad vocational education should be. The answer to this question has immediate consequences for the contents of the curriculum, for the distribution of the subject matter across the study years, and for the choice of certain competences and groups of skills. The discussion among educational scientists regarding Bildung and Ausbildung – between general education and job-specific education – resembles a pendulum. The arguments vary over time, but eventually always return to the same principles (e.g. Nijhof, 1986; van Zolingen, 1995; Nijhof and Streumer, 1994).

The arguments are not new either. Many authors believe that education should not merely prepare for a (narrowly defined) job, while others think that a broad vocational education constitutes the best general education. The wider the definition, the more general the content (Nijhof, 1996). Thus Brown (1997) analysed effective characteristics of curricula in terms of learning to learn and transfer. An important starting point is the development of core or key skills, which can be used in a more general context by applying decontextualisation.

The relationship between curriculum characteristics and labour market perspectives

In the Sections above, labour market perspectives focused mainly on obtaining a job, on the transparency for suppliers of jobs with regard to the output of the qualification structure, and on the mobility and flexibility of the system and its participants. Regarding flexibility as output generated by participants of the education system, increases the chances of work, because polyvalence of learning routes or substitution creates new opportunities. The proposition is therefore that curriculum characteristics promote or help achieve these labour market perspectives. We have already pointed out that effects on the labour market cannot be attributed exclusively to curriculum characteristics, but that regional characteristics, economical and technological factors, and even individual characteristics of participants must also be taken into account.

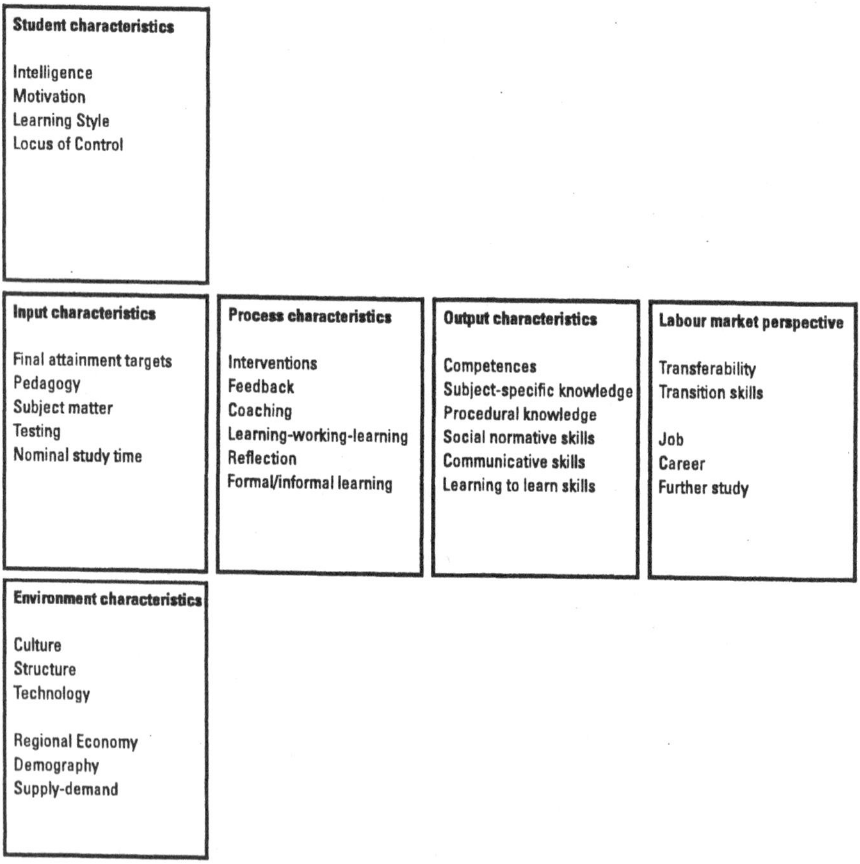

Student characteristics

Intelligence
Motivation
Learning Style
Locus of Control

Input characteristics

Final attainment targets
Pedagogy
Subject matter
Testing
Nominal study time

Process characteristics

Interventions
Feedback
Coaching
Learning-working-learning
Reflection
Formal/informal learning

Output characteristics

Competences
Subject-specific knowledge
Procedural knowledge
Social normative skills
Communicative skills
Learning to learn skills

Labour market perspective

Transferability
Transition skills

Job
Career
Further study

Environment characteristics

Culture
Structure
Technology

Regional Economy
Demography
Supply-demand

Figure 3   Research model for connecting curriculum characteristics and labour market perspectives

In the research concerning the transfer of training within companies, we find similar considerations. On the basis of a review, Baldwin and Ford (1988) created a model, the basic characteristics of which can be used for our purposes. (See Figure 3). The model attempts to show that three basic groups of characteristics are responsible for effects: characteristics of participants (often intelligence, motivation, preferences of interests, locus of control), characteristics of the curriculum (in this case dual, modular, traditional vs. non-traditional, individual vs. group), and environment characteristics (structure, culture, technology, economy).

Below, we wish to investigate on the basis of a relatively random selection of studies, whether – and if so, how – in particular the curriculum characteristics play a role in this model. With respect to the selection, we must add that we have not come across any systematic studies which illustrate in full the way in which the present qualification structure functions and which provide a comparative analysis. It would be too early to expect such. It is remarkable, however, that comparisons of national systems, such as those of Germany and the Netherlands (van Lieshout, 1994), or of England and Germany (Brown and Behrens, 1994), to name a few examples, often highlight the economic, legal and administrative aspects, but hardly ever study the effects of curriculum characteristics on labour market perspectives.

In the following Section, we will deal in greater detail with four recent studies that attempt to analyse the effects of learning routes. There are many studies regarding the returns and effects of vocational education. But studies in which the above-mentioned curriculum variables play or played an explicit role are difficult to find.

The choice is therefore selective and the conclusions are limited. Studies on the topics of mobility and flexibility will be discussed, because these effects can be attributed more or less directly to the curriculum.

Effects of modular vocational education I: internal mobility

Raffe (1994) has carried out a study on the effects of modular education in Scotland, which organised its vocational education in modules as early as 1984. The Scottish system was therefore regarded as a pioneer for the Dutch policy makers in those days. Raffe wondered whether the Scottish system promoted flexibility. He defined flexibility on the basis of four aspects: individual flexibility, curricular flexibility, flexibility of delivery and of learning routes. This emphasis on flexibility – which can also be observed in the Netherlands – was based on economic considerations, social pressure, and government decisions to transfer the responsibility for the learning process and the acquisition of the necessary skills to the students. Although Raffe does not say so explicitly, the supposition is that a flexible modular structure with individual responsibilities for students promotes the skill of what is called 'learning to learn'. This skill, in turn, would contribute to labour market mobility.

The Scottish flexibility model is based on:

- the diversity of the 'mixed model';
- modularisation;
- single qualifications; and
- flexibility between 'academic' and vocational education.

Modules are competence-oriented, have a size of 40 hours, are completed by means of criterion-oriented tests, evaluated by means of a national certificate (NC), and recognised by a national body: Scotvec.

The study covered representative groups of students. Many of the results were obtained from a year group which left the system in 1986, but the study ran for another three years until 1989. The students had taken different numbers of modules.

The main results were as follows:

> The types of young people who had taken modules, and their reasons for taking them were similarly varied. There was no 'typical' NC student; modules had been taken by males and females, by young people with all levels of attainment in academic qualifications, and by young people in all destinations at age 19. (Raffe, 1994, pp. 21-22).
> There were differences across the main sectors in the number of modules taken, in the main subjects followed, in the extent to which students could choose modules (average 13 modules), and in the kinds of students who took them. The picture that emerges from this study is of a national modular framework that has been flexible enough to be used with different types of students, for different purposes, and in different sectors of education and training. (Raffe, 1994, p. 22).
> (.......) the Scottish model of flexibility has also given various problems:
> - Academic drift, because of the low status of NC modules. Many school students attempt highers. The result is often an unsatisfactory curriculum and a high failure rate; attainments in the system are 'top heavy'.
> - Issues of choice and flexibility in a modular curriculum (flexibility is expensive and difficult to organise; the Scottish experience raises the question, of whether flexibility – of curriculum and delivery – is as important in initial as in continuing education).
> - Limited effects on participation (getting a vocational education is not a high priority because of the lack of status, the Scottish system may offer

some flexibility, but the ultimate incentive to participate is the exchange value of the qualification to which the flexible system leads).
- Coordination issues (is it realistic to rely so much on qualifications to coordinate flexible systems, or to pursue a 'hard currency economy'). (Raffe, 1994, p. 23).

The modular system has a low status and is not used as a selection tool for work. Only a few use the modules as a means of entry to higher education. Raffe wondered whether it was wise in this system to capitalise so heavily on qualifications (final attainment targets) to coordinate flexible systems (o.c. p. 29). This must be seen in the context of a qualification system which formulates in terms of fairly strict behaviourist-oriented competences and has little effect on the labour market. He doubted the transition to the labour market and to higher forms of education in this case study, which he only called an example to set up further research into themes.

Effects of modular education II: motivation and learning effects

Meesterberends-Harms (1994) studied the internal effects of modular vocational education in students as to motivation and effects. The main question concerned the effect of variants of modular education on study efforts and learning effects. By checking motivation, cognitive level and interest, she attempted to assess the above effects. Her main objective was to determine whether modular variants in terms of intended flexibility matter, a non-flexible modular variant, a flexible modular variant, a traditional modular variant (as control variable). The study covered three sectors (the construction, metal, and care sectors) in the daytime education/dual system and in Short IVE. The main objective of the study was to determine the internal effects of modular education at student level and yielded the following conclusions:

- a modular system may promote the effort made by students, although this effect is not dependent on conditions of the students themselves;
- the efforts made by students do not lead to enhanced effects; and
- modular systems as such do not create the effects in education, rather the opposite. In daytime education for workers, for example, a flexible system leads to lower learning effects.

The two above-mentioned studies regarding modules contain relatively little on labour market perspectives. We can see that the Scottish study looked at prestige and improvement of the level of students. After all, these have an indirect effect on the labour market. But modular systems as such have not increased prestige. As the modules are intimately related to so-called National Vocational

Qualifications (NVQs), which were derived directly from occupations, there was no opportunity for any transfer. This 'gap' in the system is now being repaired, initially by the introduction of so-called generic skills (GNVQs), but even now attempts are being made to generate a route from modular vocational education to higher education in order to enable a link with the so-called A-levels (Oates, 1997). Perhaps the Netherlands will soon also follow Scotland and England in this respect, restoring the connection between IVE-HVE and University, having also imported the modules in the mid-eighties.

The study by Harms shows that the relationship between motivation, effort, and learning effect does not necessarily follow from the use of modular systems. It looks as if the instructional quality of the modules can be increased by optimising time, varying pace, promoting feedback, and learning to master. In this sense, the characteristics of 'learning-to-learn skills' as mentioned by Brown and so prominently required or promoted in the labour market, may be more successfully developed within modular systems.

A study of transfer and transition skills

Moerkamp (1996) has carried out an interesting and intriguing study of the importance of transfer and transition skills for a professional career. Mobility and flexibility in professional careers are supposed to be conditioned by acquired knowledge and skills, and by transition skills. The latter are defined as (meta) cognitive skills and action orientations which enable workers to transfer their knowledge and skills, and to adequately respond to changing work situations. Use was made of the Enschede Cohort from 1964-1965. From this group, a subgroup whose educational level was Lower Vocational Education (LVE) or IVE (n=262) was selected for a survey. From this group, 57 respondents were interviewed concerning professional careers, transition moments, transition skills and supporting factors at transition moments. We will deal in greater detail with the findings relating to transfer and transition skills, as reported by the researcher.

> The transfer of *subject-specific knowledge and skills* is the most important aspect in these LVE and IVE students during their 15-20 year professional careers (o.c., p. 72).

This importance increases with later job changes. At the time of the first job change, i.e. going from the first job to the second, non-specific skills appear to be equally important as subject-specific knowledge and skills. First jobs are transition jobs, in which young employees learn a number of non-specific skills.

In 20% of all job changes, respondents replied that *not a single transfer* (italics added) of knowledge and skills had occurred, neither of specific, nor of non-specific skills. This percentage does not change much in the other job changes.

Confronted by such conclusions, one rubs one's eyes. Someone changes jobs, but there is no transfer of knowledge or skills whatsoever! In the researcher's own words:

> Apparently it is difficult in the case of a number of major changes to take any knowledge and skills with one and to reuse them. This is an important result.

I seriously doubt the validity of this conclusion. In my view, it is impossible to start a new job without having the minimum required competences and dispositions to successfully perform in this job. I do not know whether semantic problems have played a role in the interviews, because this conclusion defies any research of transfer or training. It must be presumed that the ability to recognise possibilities for transfer by respondents and in the language of the researcher may have played a role in this curious result. The researcher points at the relationship between IQ and 'no transfer of knowledge and skills'. Respondents with a lower IQ more often report an absence of transfer at job changes. The conclusion that no transfer of knowledge and skills at all takes place, seems unlikely to me. The respondent should have been fired the next day. Another problem may concern the ability on the part of the respondent to logically separate the learning results from school and experience at the workplace after a longer period of time. The accumulation of tacit knowledge (Nonaka, 1991) and the use of the latter by employees in companies has different stages of internalisation and socialisation, which can only be visualised by laborious explication. The study seems to suggest that the professional career appears to create a greater effect in the application of acquired knowledge and skills if there are few career changes, i.e. if the career follows a fairly homogeneous course.

> As differences between subsequent jobs increase, the chances of a transfer of *all* (italics added) knowledge and skills, as well as action orientations and personal skills, decrease (o.c. p. 73).

Of course it is important to find out what the effects of education were, in particular regarding the first job, because it may be assumed that the latter effect is the greatest. Moerkamp finds few direct effects of the education taken and differentiates for the different groups, technology, in-service, etc.. The imperfect recognition by respondents of transition skills in the case of major content differences between jobs apparently makes it impossible to draw any conclusions; not even as to the education taken.

However, in 80% of all cases (n=57) the majority of the respondents appear to have set great value on the original qualification package. This package probably looked quite different in the sixties than it does now, more than thirty years later.

It would have been interesting to determine exactly which factors of the curriculum (level, types of objectives, contents, learning and working experience) can in fact be made explicit and recognisable. This degree of making explicit by respondents and researchers appears problematic in the case of such a complex issue as transfer. Here, a metacognition is presupposed in the respondent: being able to recognise important learning moments in a career in terms of near and far transfer. Which is probably more than many traditional former LVE and IVE students are capable of.

With respect to the transition skills, the conclusion is drawn that these cannot be explicitly acquired during a course or education, but rather are the results of functioning in different contexts, which should differ neither too much nor too little from one another.

Here there is in fact a direct relationship with a curriculum characteristic: the learning route must be paved with *a variety of contexts* in order to allow informal and formal workplace experiences. It is therefore rather the variation of real contexts which appears to contribute to success. We believe that reflection on this experience may contribute to (meta) cognitive insights and action orientations which are necessary in order to be able to transfer in later situations.

It would be advisable to repeat this study with respect to groups whose educational level and intelligence are higher. It is expected that the latter groups may be better able to reflect on transfer and transition and may express such in a more dependable way.

Mobility in agricultural education

The Bureau of Labour Market Research (Arbeidsmarktonderzoek - BAO) of the Foundation for the Support of Agricultural Schools (Stichting ter Ondersteuning van Agrarische Scholen - STOAS) in Wageningen is carrying out research as to the effects of the new qualification structure in agricultural education. These effects are of course related to the movements in the labour market, mobility, flexibility, but also addresses the internal effects of the system, both old and new. In 1990, The Dutch Ministry of Agriculture, Conservation and Fisheries (LNV), which is responsible for agricultural education, introduced a new qualification structure on the basis of new final attainment targets. This introduction is progressing gradually, so as to allow a comparison of old and new. On the basis of a preliminary and partial analysis, it is possible to express some comments on external mobility.

We restrict ourselves to the views of respondents on the relevance of components of their education programmes for their current jobs. Views could be expressed on a needs scale. Respondents could give their opinion with respect to the need to give more attention to certain (areas of) competences (1= more; 2= the same; 3= less).

Table 1
Training needs after study (comparison of '87, '91, '94 cohorts)
(STOAS-BAO)

Course evaluation: the course should give more (=1), the same (=2) or less (=3) attention to the subjects concerned

	From cohort			Group Total
	'87 Mean	'91 Mean	'94 Mean	Mean
Level 2				
Subject matter theory	1.67	1.80	1.52	1.62
Information/computer science	1.50	1.85	1.64	1.70
Use of equipment or materials	1.75	1.73	1.60	1.65
Commercial and sales skills	1.92	2.17	1.72	1.89
Foreign languages	2.17	2.30	1.66	1.91
Written reporting	2.00	2.06	1.77	1.88
Oral communication skills	1.64	2.02	1.93	1.94
Practical orientation or traineeship	1.73	1.63	1.65	1.65
Career or study choice	1.75	1.72	1.60	1.65
Learning to apply for a job	1.83	1.57	1.58	1.59
Knowledge of company organisation	1.50	1.81	1.54	1.63
Knowledge of labour conditions	1.55	1.63	1.41	1.49
Working independently	1.36	1.52	1.64	1.58
Organisating and planning	1.50	1.85	1.54	1.64
Learning to study	1.92	1.94	1.84	1.88
Dealing with clients, patients, etc.	1.58	1.72	1.66	1.67
Level 3				
Subject matter theory	1.80	1.85	1.49	1.66
Information/computer science	1.76	1.81	1.46	1.63
Use of equipment or materials	1.81	1.82	1.55	1.69
Commercial and sales skills	2.00	1.99	1.77	1.89
Foreign languages	2.15	2.03	1.79	1.94
Written reporting	1.98	1.98	1.98	1.98
Oral communication skills	1.90	1.96	1.91	1.92
Practical orientation or traineeship	1.69	1.72	1.67	1.69
Career or study choice	1.95	1.88	1.63	1.78
Learning to apply for a job	1.87	1.86	1.71	1.79
Knowledge of company organisation	1.91	1.82	1.57	1.72
Knowledge of labour conditions	1.95	1.88	1.45	1.69
Working independently	1.90	1.79	1.69	1.76
Organisating and planning	1.85	1.80	1.53	1.68
Learning to study	1.97	1.95	2.00	1.98
Dealing with clients, patients, etc.	1.92	1.87	1.70	1.80

Table 1 (continued)
Training needs after study (comparison of '87, '91, '94 cohorts)
(STOAS-BAO)

	From cohort '87 Mean	'91 Mean	'94 Mean	Group Total Mean
Level 4				
Subject matter theory	1.75	1.79	1.61	1.70
Information/computer science	1.58	1.74	1.36	1.54
Use of equipment or materials	1.82	1.83	1.62	1.74
Commercial and sales skills	1.78	1.93	1.78	1.83
Foreign languages	1.96	1.96	1.75	1.87
Written reporting	1.85	1.92	1.83	1.87
Oral communication skills	1.77	1.91	1.76	1.82
Practical orientation or traineeship	1.72	1.76	1.83	1.78
Career or study choice	1.86	1.84	1.65	1.76
Learning to apply for a job	1.86	1.85	1.69	1.78
Knowledge of company organisation	1.76	1.87	1.65	1.75
Knowledge of labour conditions	1.84	1.90	1.47	1.70
Working independently	1.72	1.87	1.74	1.78
Organisating and planning	1.60	1.75	1.50	1.61
Learning to study	1.94	2.04	1.96	1.98
Dealing with clients, patients, etc.	1.73	1.85	1.77	1.79

In terms of the national qualification structure, three levels are distinguished:

Level 2: Short Intermediate Agricultural Education (Short IAE) or IAE-BW (beginning workers);

Level 3: Intermediate Agricultural School B or IAE-SE (self-employed);

Level 4: Intermediate Agricultural School A or IAE-M (management).

Differences between cohorts and between qualification structures will be traced. For the differences between the cohort levels 2, 3 and 4 ('87, '91 and '94 respectively), see Table 1.

The general conclusion is that the longer one works, the more there appears to be a tendency to consider the subjects offered as adequate. In general, we can observe that the need for additional education can be found in the most recently graduated cohort. This group apparently experiences the greatest gap between education and work, although the differences are marginal.

Within the areas of competence, a difference can be made between general competences and job-specific ones. General competences include, for example, the ability to work independently, learning to study, learning to apply for jobs, knowledge of labour conditions. Job-specific knowledge is subject knowledge, commercial knowledge, fluency in one or more foreign languages, knowledge of the use of equipment and materials. On average across all cohorts, the scores are between 1 and 2, and one cannot discern a clear pattern of more or less relevant areas of competence.

Table 2
Training needs after study per type of education 'old' and 'new' ('93-'94) (STOAS-BAO)

	Educational structure		Group Total
	Old Mean	New Mean	Mean
Level 2			
Subject matter theory	1.67	1.50	1.52
Information/computer science	1.64	1.64	1.64
Use of equipment or materials	1.67	1.59	1.60
Commercial and sales skills	1.67	1.73	1.72
Foreign languages	1.92	1.63	1.66
Written reporting	1.75	1.77	1.77
Oral communication skills	2.00	1.92	1.93
Practical orientation or traineeship	1.67	1.65	1.65
Career or study choice	2.00	1.54	1.60
Learning to apply for a job	1.50	1.59	1.58
Knowledge of company organisation	1.67	1.52	1.54
Knowledge of labour conditions	1.42	1.40	1.41
Working independently	1.58	1.64	1.64
Organisating and planning	1.58	1.53	1.54
Learning to study	1.83	1.84	1.84
Dealing with clients, patients, etc.	1.50	1.68	1.66
Level 3			
Subject matter theory	1.51	1.46	1.49
Information/computer science	1.44	1.48	1.46
Use of equipment or materials	1.51	1.60	1.55
Commercial and sales skills	1.80	1.74	1.77
Foreign languages	1.79	1.79	1.79
Written reporting	1.98	1.98	1.98
Oral communication skills	1.90	1.91	1.91
Practical orientation or traineeship	1.65	1.69	1.67
Career or study choice	1.62	1.65	1.63
Learning to apply for a job	1.79	1.59	1.71
Knowledge of company organisation	1.57	1.56	1.57
Knowledge of labour conditions	1.47	1.44	1.45
Working independently	1.69	1.70	1.69
Organisating and planning	1.51	1.56	1.53
Learning to study	2.05	1.94	2.00
Dealing with clients, patients, etc.	1.69	1.73	1.70

Table 2 (continued)
Training needs after study per type of education 'old' and 'new' ('93-'94) (STOAS-BAO)

	Educational structure		Group Total Mean
	Old Mean	New Mean	
Level 4			
Subject matter theory	1.61	1.59	1.61
Information/computer science	1.32	1.51	1.36
Use of equipment or materials	1.61	1.64	1.62
Commercial and sales skills	1.80	1.68	1.78
Foreign languages	1.73	1.83	1.74
Written reporting	1.79	1.99	1.83
Oral communication skills	1.75	1.83	1.76
Practical orientation or traineeship	1.84	1.77	1.83
Career or study choice	1.63	1.74	1.65
Learning to apply for a job	1.68	1.71	1.68
Knowledge of company organisation	1.66	1.65	1.66
Knowledge of labour conditions	1.43	1.59	1.46
Working independently	1.73	1.75	1.74
Organisating and planning	1.48	1.56	1.50
Learning to study	1.96	1.97	1.97
Dealing with clients, patients, etc.	1.78	1.74	1.77

The decreasing need, expressed in average scores across the different cohorts, may therefore indicate an evident learning function of the workplace or job, compensating for the need for any missing qualifications, either informally or formally by means of in-service training. As the qualification level rises, the need for additional training seems to decrease. But these differences are also marginal. The figures seem to indicate the need for procedural and declarative knowledge which must be regarded as necessary in a job. As the period covered is circa 7 years, in which time some graduates have had between 4 and 8 jobs, this fact may refer to a relatively stable need of 'occupational competences', as Bishop (1996) calls it.

If we compare the old and the new qualification structures (Table 2) in the same competence areas, we can ask ourselves the question whether different curricula also create different results in terms of required competences. This concerns the graduates of 1993-'94.

It seems as if the new qualification structure demands no greater competences than the old qualification structure. (The average scores between old and new are between 1.63 and 1.72, separated for levels 2, 3 and 4.) We must take into account, however, that the final attainment targets differ considerably from the old examination requirements (van Hooff, de Jong, Nijhof and Geerligs, 1995). The implementation of a new structure is still in its initial stage, also in terms of routine and professionalism of the implementers, and hence the figures in themselves can interpreted as positive. As a measure of the labour market they may possibly serve as input for further analysis at a more specific level.

The curriculum as a carrier of competences, old or new, can thus be qualified as one which can perhaps be better tuned to the demands of the labour market. In any case, there are no scores which indicate less attention for certain themes. An exception analysis might help to determine the origin of the evidently great need for further training and why it existed.

If we take a score of 1.55 or lower as an average measure for importance, we find the following groups of skills as relevant learning areas, which are considered important both in the old and in the new system: subject-specific knowledge (level 2), information science (levels 3 and 4), knowledge of the organisation of businesses (levels 2 and 3), knowledge of labour conditions (levels 2, 3 and 4), organising and planning (levels 3 and 4). The crucial areas are apparently business know-how and substantial subject-specific knowledge.

This first analysis leads to the preliminary conclusion that we cannot yet point at an evident relationship between curriculum characteristics and labour market perspectives. It is possible that (significant) differences can be found at the level of subaspects. This would require further analysis of the material and additional qualitative data in order to arrive at a better interpretation of the question relating to competences, also because the new qualification structure differs from the old one in two essential aspects: it has been modulated and provided with new final attainment targets (van Hooff, de Jong, Nijhof and Geerligs, 1995).

Conclusions

We have attempted to find a relationship in the form of a model between a number of characteristics of a learning route, individual and environment characteristics and effects (internal effects and external effects). On the basis of four studies, we wish to attempt – by way of as exercise – to formulate a number of conclusions with respect to the relationship between curriculum characteristics and labour market perspectives.

The primary supposition is that if a curriculum has been designed in a particular way and is a vehicle for competences, differences between learning routes will also yield differences between labour market perspectives after correction for personal and other characteristics.

On the basis of a study by Raffe (1994), we conclude that although students take a series of modules, they do not benefit from this in terms of moving on to a higher level, because the certificate prevents this. This is a political decision, however, rather than a curriculum characteristic. At the same time, Raffe (1994) asks the question whether it is wise to capitalise so heavily on qualifications as control instruments. But he does not provide an alternative. He does not consider modular systems – as they existed between 1984 and 1989 – as hard currency. Hence, in terms of curriculum characteristics we learn relatively little from this study with regard to labour market perspectives, also because politicians treat system development fairly dynamically.

The study by Meesterberends-Harms (1994) has shown us that although modular systems may help promote the efforts made by students, this does not immediately lead to a higher learning effect. Her comparison of two flexible modular variants and a traditional control variant for daytime education for workers/short IVE yields no differences as to learning effects. From this study we learn that the internal effects of education may be improved slightly by means of short-cycle learning processes for this group of students. Whether modular systems provide the solution for competence development also depends to a great extent on the optimisation of instruction components, such as feedback, learning to master, locus of control, etc.

Moerkamp's (1996) study shows that subject-specific knowledge is important for career development. This importance is dependent on later job changes. The professional career and the variation of contexts in which one may learn constitute the main conditions for transfer and transition. For an educational course this may mean that within certain margins, one can explicitly learn what transition may mean, allowing metacognitive experiences to be acquired.

The STOAS study (Lokman, van Woerkom and de Bruin, 1996), still in its initial stage, seems to support Moerkamp's conclusion that occupation-oriented competences are the most important ones for a first job. Otherwise, the study currently yields a number of general skills of a business-administrative nature, which may be of relevance to agricultural (entrepreneurial) occupations. We cannot at present discern any major differences between cohorts or between the old and new qualification structures in terms of the competences which are deemed necessary. A more thorough qualitative study would have to throw light on this question.

The conclusion is that there have been few substantial studies of the relationship between curriculum characteristics and labour market perspectives. The term substantial here means systematic, longitudinal, possibly experimental comparisons between learning routes (dual, traditional and project education) in the light of mobility, flexibility, transfer and transition.

Research aimed at the relationship between curriculum variants (in the qualification structure), acquired skills and mobility, seems a theme of great importance. In particular in order to gain insight in the effectiveness of intentional learning routes.

References

Baldwin, T.T., and Ford, J. K. (1988), 'Transfer of Training: A Review and Directions for future research', *Personnel Psychology*, 41, pp. 63-105.
Bishop, J. (1995), *Expertise en Excellence*, Working Paper 95-13, Centre on the Educational Quality of the Workforce, Cornell University: Ithaca, New York.
Block, A. de (1966), *Taxonomie van leerdoelen*, Standaard Wetenschappelijke Uitgeverij: Antwerpen.
Bloom, B.S. (1956), *Taxonomy of Educational Objectives. Handbook I: The cognitive domain*, McKay: New York.
Brandsma, T.F., Thuring-van der Linden, A.M.L., Schuit-van der Linden, C. (1996), *Invoering van de tweede generatie eindtermen in het MBO; voortgang en vernieuwing*, OCTO: Enschede.
Brown, A. (1997), 'Designing effective learning programmes for the development of a broad occupational competence', in: Nijhof, W.J., and Streumer, J.N. (eds.), *Key Qualifications in Work and Education* (forthcoming), Kluwer Academic Publishers: Dordrecht.
Brown, A., and Behrens, M. (1994), 'Comparative analysis of flexibility in vocational education and training: engineering and insurance in England and Germany', in : Nijhof, W.J., and Streumer, J.N. (eds.), *Flexibility in Training and Vocational Education*. Lemma: Utrecht.
Commissie Dualisering (1993), *Beroepsvorming langs vele wegen*, Distributie centrum DOP: Leiden.
Commission of the Skills of the American Workforce (1994), *High Skills and Low Wages*. Report of the Commission. Institute of Education and the economy: Washington.
Cronbach, L.J., and Snow, R. (1977), *Attitudes and Instructional Methods*, Handbook for Research on Interactions. Irvington Publishers: New York.
Droste, J.F.M., Grönloh, J.H.O., and Hövels, B. (1993), 'Startkwalificaties voor iedereen, maar hoe bereik je dat?', in: Droste, J.F.M., and Grönloh, J.H.O., *Startkwalificaties voor iedereen. Hoe bereik je dat?* (pp. 11-33), SLO/CIBB: Enschede/'s- Hertogenbosch.
Gagné, R.M., Briggs, L.J., and Wager, W.W. (1988), *Principles of Instructional Design*, Holt, Rinehart & Winston: New York.
Gielen, E.W.M. (1995), *Transfer of Training in a Corporate Setting*, Universiteit Twente: Enschede.
Goodlad, J.I. (1984), *A Place Called School,* Prospects for the Future, McGraw-Hill: New York.
Hooff, N.M. van, Jong, M.J. de, Nijhof, W.J., and Geerligs, J.W.G. (1995), *Eindtermen in het Middelbaar Landbouwonderwijs*. Een vergelijking van exameneisen en eindtermen, Universiteit Twente, Faculteit der Toegepaste Onderwijskunde, Vakgroep Curriculumtechnologie: Enschede.

Ingen, D.C. van (1996), *Rendement van beroepsonderwijs*, Max Goote Kennis centrum: Amsterdam.

Jong, J. de (1995), 'Opleiden op de werkplek: een review', *Pedagogische Studiën*, 72 (1), pp. 9-23.

Klink, M. van der (1997), 'Leren en opleiden op de werkplek', in: Nijhof, W.J. (ed.), *Ontwikkelingen in het beroepsonderwijs en de volwasseneneducatie, Beroepsonderwijs in ontwikkeling*, Samsom: Alphen aan den Rijn.

Lieshout, H. van (1994), *Beroepsonderwijs in Duitsland vanuit Nederlands Perspectief*, Onderzoeks-school Arbeid, Welzijn & Sociaal Economisch Bestuur, Universiteit Utrecht: Utrecht.

LNV (1991), *Overzicht van Diploma's en Certificaten* (ODC), Ministerie van Landbouw, Natuur & Visserij: 's Gravenhage.

Lokman, I, Woerkom, M. van, m.m.v. Bruin, C. de (1996), *Rendement in de BVE sector, Een vooronderzoek naar de haalbaarheid van nieuwe rendementsindicatoren*, Bureau Arbeidsmarktonderzoek STOAS: Wageningen.

Meesterberends-Harms, T. (1994), 'Modular Instruction, student investment and school output', in: Nijhof, W.J., and Streumer, J.N. (eds.), *Flexibility in Training and Vocational Education*, (pp. 151-171), Lemma: Utrecht.

Ministerie van Onderwijs en Wetenschappen (1993), *Format voor kwalificatie structuren December 1993*, LOB: Zoetermeer.

Moerkamp, T. (1996), *Transitievaardigheden en transfer in de beroepsloopbaan*, werkdocument W 140, OSA: Den Haag.

Nijhof, W.J. (1983), *Over het ontwerpen van Curricula*, Oratie, Universiteit Twente: Enschede.

Nijhof, W.J. (1993), 'Het ontwerpen van onderwijsleerpakketten', in: Nijhof, W.J., Franssen, H.A.M., Hoeben, W.Th.J.G., and Wolbert, R.G.M. (eds.), *Handboek Curriculum. Theorieën, Modellen en Technologieën*, Swets en Zeitlinger: Amsterdam/Lisse.

Nijhof, W.J. (1993), 'Inleiding en Rationale', in: Nijhof, W.J., Franssen, H.A.M., Hoeben, W.Th.G.J., and Wolbert, R.G.M. (eds.), *Handboek Curriculum. Modellen, Theorieën en Technologieën*, Swets & Zeitlinger: Amsterdam/Lisse.

Nijhof, W.J., and Remmers (1989), *Basisvaardigheden nader bekeken*, Faculteit der Toegepaste Onderwijskunde, Universiteit Twente: Enschede.

Nijhof, W.J., and Remmers (1990), 'Basisvaardigheden in het Beroepsonderwijs', *Pedagogische Studiën*, 67 (9), pp. 389-399.

Nijhof, W.J., and Streumer, J.N. (1994), *Verbreed Beroepsonderwijs*, Academisch BoekenCentrum: de Lier.

Nijhof, W.J. (1966), 'Verbreding en verdieping van het beroepsonderwijs', in: Dijck, L. van, Hövels, B., Nijhof, W.J., Wieringen, A. van (eds.), *Jaarboek 1995, Max Goote Kenniscentrum*, Vuga: Amsterdam.

Nonaka, I. (1991), *The Knowledge Creating Company*, Harvard Business Review, Nov.-Dec., pp. 96-104.

Novak, J., and Gowan, L. (1990), *Learning how to learn*, Cornell University, Ithaca: New York.
Oates, T. (1997), 'A Converging System? Explaining difference in the Academic and Vocational Tracks in England and Wales', in: Nijhof, W.J., and Streumer, J.N. (eds.), *Key Qualifications in Work and Education* (forthcoming), Kluwer Academic Publishers: Dordrecht.
Olbrich, G., and Pfeiffer, V. (1980), *Lernzielstufen*, BIBB: Berlijn.
Ouden, M.D. den (1995), 'Gedragsverandering na een opleiding', *Pedagogische Studiën*, 72 (1), pp. 23-36.
Raffe, D. (1994), 'The New Flexibility in Vocational Education'. in: Nijhof, W.J., and Streumer, J.N. (eds.), *Flexibility in Training and Vocational Education*, pp. 13-33, Lemma: Utrecht.
Romiszowski, A.J. (1981), *Designing Instructional Systems*, Decision making in course planning and curriculum design, Kogan Page: New York.
Thijssen, J. (1996), *Leren, Leeftijd en Loopbaanperspectief* (dissertation), Katholieke Universiteit Brabant: Tilburg.
WEB (1995), Wet van 31 oktober 1995, houdende bepalingen met betrekking tot de educatie en het beroepsonderwijs (Wet educatie en beroepsonderwijs), Staatsblad van het Koninkrijk der Nederlanden, 501.
Wolf, A. (1997), Competence Based Assessment: does it shift the Demarcation Line, in: Nijhof, W.J., and Streumer, J.N (eds.), *Key Qualifications in Work and Education* (forthcoming), Kluwer Academic Publishers: Dordrecht.
Zolingen, van (1995), *Gevraagd: Sleutelkwalificaties* (dissertation), Katholieke Universiteit Nijmegen: Nijmegen.

Acknowledgement

I thank Dr. Ineke Lokman, of the Bureau for Labour Market Research, for supplying the data and the analyses.

9 Does Curriculum Matter? A Theoretical Clue to an Empirical Puzzle

Arie Glebbeek and Sietske Waslander

Introduction

In 1995, a book was published in the United Kingdom which developed the trenchant argument that blames Britain's comparatively low productivity on British education: its content, the way it is organised, and the educational practices applied. Even more remarkable than this conclusion is this book's unusual attempt based on many years of research in different countries, to explicate and connect the different links in the chain of *Productivity, Education and Training*.

> To understand how countries differ, and what policies are appropriate (...) today, we shall have to ask not simply how many years are spent by a pupil in school or in training, but rather what is the subject-matter that has been taught and learnt, and what proportions of pupils reach various levels of competence (Prais, 1995, p. 2).

This Chapter deals with the same little-understood topic: the impact of curriculum organisation on human productivity and consequently on the labour market position of workers with different kinds of education. The main bodies of research in this field, embedded in the traditions of Sociology's stratification paradigm and Economics' human capital paradigm, concentrate heavily on the impact of level of education on occupational status and earnings (cf. Hartog's contribution to this book). More specific attention to types of education can be found in studies looking at mismatches in the labour market, but the limited scope (regions, cases) and the narrowly defined outcome criteria (usually only the chances of employment) of such research often inhibit a systematic analysis of schooling effects. In a way, the large-scale research conducted by the Dutch Research Centre for Education and the Labour Market (ROA) reaches furthest, but here too the journey ends at the school gate before the signpost naming the type of education (e.g. ROA, 1995). How labour market outcomes are related to what happens within schools has not yet been systematically investigated. The present Chapter, together with the contributions by Nijhof (Chapter 8) and Heijke, Koeslag and van der Velden (Chapter 10) can therefore be seen as an attempt to open up a black box.

There are probably several black boxes. The basic link between education and earnings suggests that both within schools and in the labour market something happens that converts educational content into job levels and income (OECD, 1996, p.88, 10n). When, in addition, we consider the pupil as the ultimate carrier of this conversion, the connection can be broken down into three black boxes (see Figure 1).

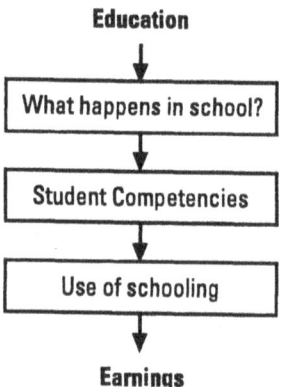

Figure 1   The three black boxes in the school-to-work transition

The first link, hidden from everyday view, consists of what actually occurs behind the school walls. The mainstream human capital interpretation of the connection between education and earnings assumes a rational and effective instruction process. However, it has proven difficult to establish to what extent this is indeed the case and, moreover, what instruction practices achieve better or worse results. Secondly, instruction is supposed to turn into competencies of students. Yet, neither the level of competencies nor the variations between students are measured in any direct way in research dealing with the school-to-work transition. The third and final link in the chain consists of the recognition and valuation of different competencies by employers and the subsequent utilisation of these in the labour process. This transformation is also largely hidden in the shadows in the background.

Each of these black boxes, and the connections between them, are topics of much discussion and uncertainty in the literature. The distinctions made by curriculum sociologists between the *intended, implemented* and *achieved* curriculum already indicate that what happens in school and how this affects the competencies of students is anything but a clear and standardised process (Jackson, 1992, p. 9). The endless discussion about the explanation of 'human capital', 'screening' and 'credentials' for the use of education in the labour market is ample evidence that the subsequent links in the chain are ambiguous too (Weiss, 1995; Wielers and Glebbeek,

1995). Groping in the dark like this regarding the intermediate processes need not be a problem. No science is without its black boxes, and it may be wise to leave them closed, especially when the relations at stake do not spur confusion or misunderstanding. As we shall see in this Chapter, however, the basic link between education and the labour market turns out to be highly problematic as soon as features of the curriculum are taken into account.

The empirical basis is small. As indicated above, theoretical murkiness regarding the impact of curriculum on student competencies and earnings is accompanied by a lack of research directly connecting curriculum and the labour market. This is the case in the Netherlands but also holds true for the international scene. An international literature search conducted for the purpose of this Chapter revealed a remarkable lack of relevant references. Despite its capacious 1,043 pages (!), the *Handbook of Research on Curriculum* (Jackson, 1992), published under the auspices of the American Educational Research Association, gives no systematic attention to the impact of curriculum in the labour market. A recent publication claiming 'to provide the first systematic study of the effects of secondary school curriculum on ... success in the labor market' observes that 'there is little hard evidence on the relationship between courses taken in high school and labor market outcomes' (Altonji, 1995, pp. 409-410).

What, then, are the issues if we want to investigate the impact of a school's curriculum on the labour market position of its graduates? In the educational literature we find many definitions of the term curriculum, ranging from 'narrow' to 'broad' (Zais, 1976; Jackson, 1992). Most educationalists agree that there is no need to restrict the concept of curriculum to courses or course content alone; operating conditions and the ways in which students are exposed to the subject matter must be taken into account as well (see also Nijhof's Chapter in this book). Curriculum content and the related organisation of the educational process together determine the *intended learning experiences* that make up the core of the curriculum as a policy document. Adding to this, educational sociologists have stressed the fact that, in the wake of daily routines, the school curriculum also accounts for many *unintended learning experiences* (e.g. Young, 1971; Reinert and Zinnecker, 1978; Gamoran, 1995). All these influences together direct towards a maximum definition of the curriculum, fanning out in three layers as shown in Figure 2. Various authors suggest different distinctions, some of which appear to lie somewhere in between or to run across the demarcation lines of this definition (see Zais, 1976, pp. 6-13).

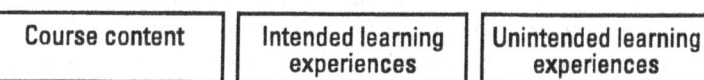

Figure 2 **Defining the curriculum**

In this Chapter, the demarcation problem is 'solved' by the limitations of our own empirical research. Our data only allow for the analysis of the relationship between course content (or field of study) and labour market position. Be that as it may, the discussion above sufficiently indicates that, considering the impact of curriculum, the *organisation of the learning process* is equally – or maybe even more – important for the development of competencies that are relevant in the labour market. Although there is even less empirical apprehension about these effects than about the impact of courses, the next Section will show that distinct opinions and heated controversies exist on this subject (e.g. OECD, 1994; de Weert, 1994; Prais, 1995). For future research, here is a challenging invitation to also open up the 'black box' in the school-to-work transition from the viewpoint of the learning process.

The remainder of this Chapter is as follows. In the next Section, we elaborate on major claims and high expectations of current curricula, especially with regard to labour market outcomes. In the following Section, the empirical basis for these claims is shown to be strikingly weak, presenting educational sociologists with a puzzle. The final Section develops a conceptual framework that may be helpful in solving the puzzle.

Claims on the curriculum

The curriculum has been the subject of dispute for at least twenty-four centuries. Plato considered the understanding of generally valid principles to be the aim of education, mainly to be achieved by learning mathematics. Isocrates, on the other hand, considered good judgement and rhetoric to be the basic objectives, and he therefore stressed the importance of language and literacy in education (Held, 1995). Today, both views on the *content* of the curriculum can still be found, for example in the debate about the pedagogical task of the school (cf. van der Ploeg, 1995). With respect to the *organisation of learning*, Bowles and Gintis (1976) and Bernstein (1977) made notable contributions by disclosing the connection between the stratified organisation of learning and the also stratified organisation of work. Still, 'the curriculum' is largely untrodden terrain for sociologists (Glebbeek and Jonker, 1986; Gamoran, 1995).

Many disputes about the curriculum can be traced back to a role conflict of education. On the one hand, education is meant to provide people with the opportunity to develop themselves to the fullest and prepare them for real life as a full-fledged member of society. On the other hand, education is meant to produce potential employees and prepare people for the world of work.

In this Chapter we only consider education in this second role, i.e. as the supplier of human capital to employers. Yet, even in this restricted role, the way in which schools can best perform this task is fiercely debated. The customers of the school system regularly complain, and many of them decide to carry out tasks that should have been dealt with by the supplier. Although the nature of the complaints varies with time and spokesperson, 'insufficient' is invariably the keyword. Partly driven by these complaints, the debate continues as to *what* it is the supplier should deliver, *how* the production process should be shaped, and what *criteria to apply* to the final product. In other words, the disputes are about – in this order – the intended, the implemented and the achieved curriculum, or – alternatively – the aims, the processes and the outcomes of education. Now that technological changes are widely interpreted as announcing the era of a *knowledge economy*, opponents in the curriculum debate build their diametrically opposed cases on the very same announcement.

What is to be produced?

An important issue in the debate on intended curriculum is the question how broad or specific education should be. On the one side, a plea is made for the production of general skills (Husén, 1968; OECD, 1994, 1995b), on the other side a need for more specific and vocational skills is proclaimed (Prais, 1995; Booth and Snower, 1996).

The plea for *general skills* is based on the decreasing relevance of specific skills. Mobile workers in a flexible labour market continually change jobs, companies and even occupations. Global market competition and rapid technological change make for a short life span of products before they are improved, renewed or replaced. Innovation becomes pivotal for companies and countries to take part in the global economy.

As is the case with products, knowledge and skills also get out of date fast, and an ongoing production of new competencies is crucial for the ever-necessary innovation. As education becomes never ending, educational systems are being redesigned to get them in tune with the concept of 'life-long learning' (OECD, 1994). For these reasons, teaching specific skills in compulsory education is deemed inefficient. Students would be better off mastering skills applicable across contexts – *transferable skills* – in combination with so-called meta- or *transferring* skills (see also de Weert, 1994). The latter skills enable one to solve unfamiliar problems, while 'learning to learn' is a meta-skill as well.

Canadian research showed that, according to employers, the ideal employee is somebody with a wide range of meta-skills: this person has 'learned to learn' and 'is flexible, adaptable and capable of adjusting to change' (Business Roundtable, 1995). A recent OECD-study in twelve countries also pointed to the importance attributed, by both employers and the general public, to competencies such as self-confidence and 'learning to learn' (OECD, 1995b).

At the same time, other authors argue equally urgently for the inclusion of more *vocational skills* in the curriculum. On the basis of a series of international case studies in four industries, Prais (1995) concluded that low productivity in the United

Kingdom could in part be attributed to the low participation rates in vocational education, especially at the intermediate level. In contrast, Germany's 'dual' educational system – with its strong emphasis on vocational skills – is said to stimulate the use of more advanced technologies, higher productivity and less job division within firms, while innovations are more rapidly implemented and the quality of products is higher. As Western economies cannot compete in the world market on the basis of labour costs, the mainstay of these economies are high-quality, technologically advanced products. In manufacturing and the service sectors alike, according to Prais, high-quality production can best be achieved by an extended system of vocational education.

Educational philosophers also put forward arguments in support of specific skills in the curriculum. In their view, knowledge and competencies are always connected with context and substance. Doubts are raised whether, for example, problem solving can be learned independently of a concrete and specific educational content (see also de Weert, 1995). The Dutch experience of the subject of 'general technical skills' introduced in lower vocational education during the seventies – which turned out a dramatic failure – is a case in point.

Claims for general skills as well as claims in support of vocational skills are justified by developments on the markets for products and labour, creating new demands on curriculum content. Given the prevailing structure of curricula as a 'collection' of separate subjects (Bernstein, 1971), the educational answer is not seldom to introduce a new subject, for example 'information technology'. According to some experts (e.g. Goodson, 1995), this division into subjects – portrayed as a remnant from a Calvinistic past – stands in the way of real change. Adaptations of the intended curriculum are said to be insufficient; what is required is a transformation of the implemented curriculum. It is believed that in order to achieve the new aims, fields of study need to be integrated, as is done for example in project-education and problem-oriented education. This takes us to the issue of educational technology.

What production techniques should be applied?

What factors determine the effectiveness of educational production? This question is the central theme of what is by now a long tradition of school effectiveness research. As yet, various determinants have been identified but the effects seem small and not always consistent (Scheerens, 1992; Reynolds, 1994; van der Velden, 1996). In the absence of decisive results, the debate about the technology of education can flourish unrestrictedly. Again, the two main opposing sides in this debate both look ahead to the future knowledge economy. For one thing, a plea is made for new practices in education such as projects and learning-by-doing (Brady, 1996), for another it is argued that uniform class-based instruction is a better safeguard for quality (Aldcroft, 1992; Prais, 1995).

The idea that the organisation of learning should mirror the organisation of work in order to facilitate the preparation for work, serves as the starting point for those who advocate more group work and project-based learning. In the post-Fordist era, it is claimed, labour relations are becoming less hierarchical, employees are being given more responsibilities, be it individually or as a group, and mutual communication and co-operation are to become important components of the production process itself. Moreover, demarcations between professions and disciplines are withering away. Increasing flexibility, globalisation and innovation require employees to be able to handle uncertainty and to be motivated for continuous learning.

A similar production process in education will better prepare students for the demands placed on them in the labour market. This means that separate subjects should be replaced by interdisciplinary problem-based learning, and that individual learning should make way for group work, teaching students to co-operate on tasks for which there are no *a priori* right or wrong answers. Moreover, passive instruction (such as lecturing) should be replaced by active practice with the student in charge of his or her own learning. The 'study house', soon to be introduced in Dutch secondary education, is geared to similar aims.

Student motivation should be further enhanced by tasks that carry substantive meaning for them. Therefore, education should be based on each student's interests and be attuned to individual capacities. While each student works at his or her own level, the final product of education is accomplished by combined co-operative efforts.

Prais (1995) is very critical about activity-based learning and puts forward a fervent plea in support of whole-class teaching with classes composed of students with roughly the same level of competence. The problem of education is not a lack of highly educated, but rather the trouble is to be found in the tail of the achievement distribution. Economic progress can only be made if all citizens achieve a basic level of competence. The considerable differences in achieved levels of competence block the way for further economic development.

Prais argues further that it needs to become clearer what exactly is behind qualifications in terms of knowledge and skills. The present variation in competencies of students holding exactly the same qualification, such as the British GCSEs, considerably reduces the information value of these qualifications. Reliable information regarding competencies of potential employees enhances the workings of the labour market (see also OECD, 1996).

The best guarantee for all students to achieve a minimum level of competence is whole-class instruction, Prais claims. This educational technology hardly tolerates varying levels of knowledge among students and allows teachers to set (minimum) standards. In contrast to students in charge of their own learning process, lack of motivation does not inhibit adherence to standards in this case (see also Yair, 1995). Prais asserts most of all that activity-based learning is very time-consuming; precious time that can be used more adequately and efficiently. Aldcroft (1992) comes to the similar conclusion that a minimum level for all can best be achieved by a technology built around class-based instruction combined with a highly standardised curriculum and regular testing. Realising that these proposals risk being too easily discarded as conservative, he raises the pertinent question of whose interests should prevail:

> If this would seem to some a reactionary note against the liberal and progressive educational principles of recent decades, one might spare a thought and a measure of sympathy for many of the pupils who have failed to acquire core skills and have therefore found difficulty in proceeding further with their education and training (Aldcroft, 1992, p. 149).

What requirements should the final product meet?

Given the debates about the what and how of the educational process, no one will be surprised by now to find that controversy also exists about the criteria to be applied in evaluating the product of education. While output criteria require clarity as to what is produced, process criteria presume an understanding of the production process. The issue of competencies needed by school-leavers in the labour market refers to the achieved curriculum. Yet, considerations about the achieved curriculum only make sense in conjunction with the intended and implemented curriculum.

Nevertheless, as policy implementation is being decentralised, the need for central monitoring generally increases, and this also holds for the field of education. As finance systems change from input-based to budget-based, and organisations are given greater autonomy regarding their production process, the need to monitor and control the output becomes more urgent. In the case of education, this requires the development of measures for student competencies that can constitute valid indicators.

A large-scale international project to develop educational indicators was started by the OECD in the 1980s. Using data of the International Association for the Evaluation of Educational Achievement, IEA, indicators have so far been developed for Mathematics, Science and Literacy (OECD, 1992, 1993, 1995a). A currently debated issue in OECD ranks is whether these indicators do sufficient justice to relevant educational outcomes, that is, up-to-date student competencies (Philips et al, 1995). Considering that only a selection of the current educational goals is evaluated, while other goals are gaining weight in the burgeoning knowledge economy, initiatives are presently taken to develop indicators for Cross-Curricular Competencies (Trier and Peschar, 1995). The goal of a pilot study in nine countries was to develop indicators for four new domains: Politics, Democracy and Civics; Problem-solving; Self-concept/Self-perception; Communication. Peschar and Waslander (OECD, 1997) report on the results of this pilot study.

All in all, appealing to the same economic trends, contradictory claims are being laid on the curriculum. This holds for *what* should be produced, for *how* this should be done, and for *which criteria* should be applied to the final product. When so much is expected from curriculum reform, we feel there is sufficient reason to examine the impact of existing differences in curricula on the labour market position of their graduates.

Curriculum effects

The impact of curriculum differences can be assessed most accurately if the level of education can be controlled for in research. Otherwise, curriculum differences very easily get mixed up with differences in the abilities of graduates (Weiss, 1995). The finest basis for comparison can be found in academia: as a result of educational selection the student population is relatively homogeneous, while curricula differ substantially.

During the summer of 1995, the University of Groningen initiated a survey amongst a large sample of its graduates. The research was conducted by Wilko Karrenbeld and Jaap Kramer under our supervision. A questionnaire was sent to over 7,700 graduates and the total response was 47% (Karrenbeld and Kramer, 1995). Here we only focus on a sub-sample of recent graduates (1993 and 1994) in order to assess curriculum effects most accurately. Table 1 gives an overview of the labour market situation of these graduates.

Table 1
Labour market status (summer 1995) of graduates (1993/1994) of the University of Groningen

	Men %	Women %
Self-employed	3.8	2.6
Employed, full time	64.4	57.8
Employed, part time	3.8	12.9
Postgraduate (PhD student)	10.4	6.7
Temporary worker	2.1	4.0
Unemployed	14.8	14.5
Not looking for work	0.7	1.5
Total	100 (N=940)	100 (N=877)

Source: Karrenbeld and Kramer, 1995, p. 46

To classify the labour market position more succinctly, we used five indicators:

1 *Job search (A)*, time until first job.
2 *Job search (B)*, subjective rating on a scale from 'easy' to 'difficult'.
3 *Income*, gross annual income.
4 *Job level (A)*, according to official classification (CBS, 1993).
5 *Job level (B)*, subjective rating.

A recurring theme in the school-to-work literature is whether labour market positions of graduates can be expressed in a single dimension. Many studies use more than one dimension to indicate this position, in particular employment chances and job level (van der Velden and Wieling, 1994). Lining up to the hypothesis – prevalent in the preceding Section – that curriculum effects may be addressed in a univocal way, we aimed to reduce the five indicators to just one. The standard problem now is what to do with the unemployed who, for that very reason, have no job level. In this case we solved the problem by classifying the unemployed (including those not looking for work) at the lowest job level. This makes sense, since labour market positions of the unemployed do not exceed those of graduates having a low-status job. Moreover, these unemployed graduates entered the labour market at most two years earlier, and are therefore just at the beginning of their careers. Hence, it is out of the question that a substantial work history should be taken into account. Our ranking therefore does justice to the common notion that labour market entrants first have to combat for a place in the arena (see Karrenbeld and Kramer, 1995, pp. 53-54).

Each of the five variables mentioned above was reduced to five categories and then included in a scale analysis. The reliability of the scale (Cronbach's alpha) was 0.87, which is satisfactory in all respects. As a check, a factor analysis was done including the variables in their original form, revealing one factor explaining 67% of total variance. These findings support a unidimensional interpretation of the concept of labour market position. We therefore added the scores on the five variables to construct a new variable ranging from 5 to 25. The distribution appears to be centred to the right, indicating that most graduates have a favourable labour market position. However, over one-fourth of the graduates is located at the bottom half of the scale, demonstrating considerable variation in labour market positions (see Figure 3).

We can now return to our central question: does Labour Market Position vary with curriculum, that is, with fields of study? Table 2 gives the mean scores of 24 disciplines, in a similar fashion as the way in which ROA classifies types of education on the basis of their means (ROA, 1995). It is clear at once that the picture closely fits our expectations based on labour market reputations of the different fields of study. Only Theology is a bit of an anomaly, we only have a small number of observations there, and Sociology ranks surprisingly high, presumably caused by a local effect (a special course attracting large numbers of students from schools for

Business Administration and Economics). The general picture allows for the familiar ranking of four clusters:

1 Science, Medical and Mathematics.
2 Science, Physics, Law and Economics.
3 Social Sciences.
4 Humanities.

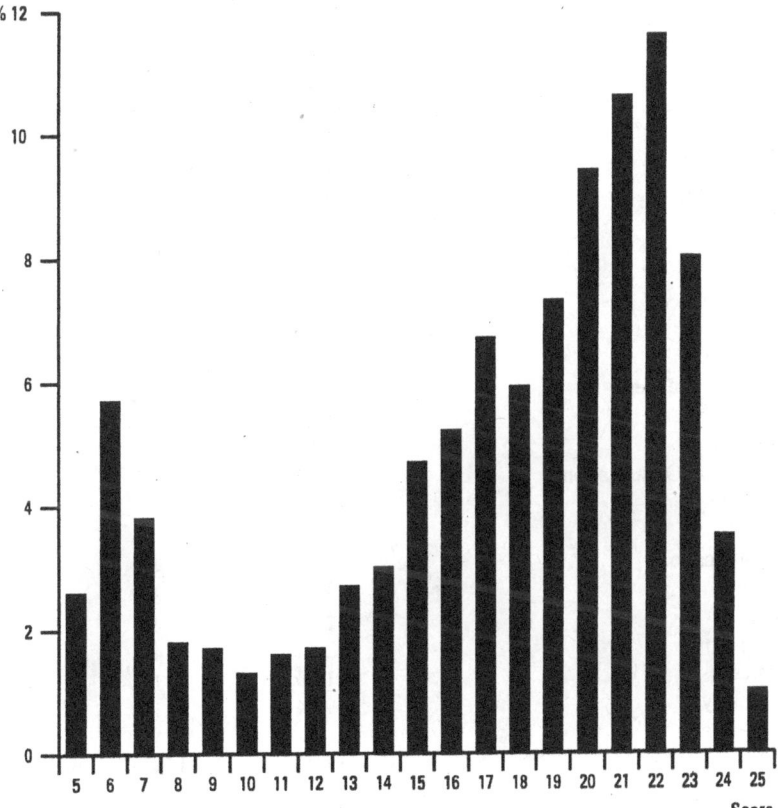

Figure 3 Distribution on the scale for labour market position
Source: Karrenbeld and Kramer, 1995

However, closer inspection casts doubts on the relevance of these differences in means. To what extent is the labour market position of graduates really affected by the curriculum? A second look at the data uncovers a massive amount of variance around the means. Putting this under closer scrutiny, we performed an OLS regres-

Table 2
**Average Labour Market Position (scale 5-25) by field of study in 1995
(N>10; 1993 and 1994 graduates of the University of Groningen)**

	%	N
Medical Science	22.47	118
Pharmacy	21.63	19
Mathematics	19.92	13
Information Science	19.68	19
Theology	19.18	11
Law	18.70	264
Econometrics	18.19	42
Management	17.89	162
Sociology	17.42	36
Economics	17.18	304
Chemistry	16.53	75
Natural Science	16.00	33
Psychology	15.91	82
Modern Languages	15.72	25
Biology	15.45	55
Education	15.38	115
International Organisations	14.63	41
Geography	14.38	50
Communication	13.45	40
History	13.26	38
Dutch	12.85	20
Liberal Arts	12.54	41
Classics	11.00	16
Art History	9.74	19
Total	17.06	1641

Source: Karrenbeld and Kramer, 1995

sion analysis including the fields of study as a chain of 24 dummy variables (Economics left out as reference category), thereby representing a maximum curriculum effect. In a next step, the respondent's sex was included as control variable (after all, the gender composition of the disciplines differs notably) and a third step included whether the graduate still lives in the northern part of the country (a weak economic region). The results are given in Table 3. Although the differences

Table 3
Effects of field of study on Labour Market Position
(standardised regression coefficients)

	Model 1	Model 2	Model 3
Medical Science	0.25***	0.25***	0.27***
Pharmacy	0.09***	0.09***	0.09***
Mathematics	0.04	0.04	0.05*
Information Science	0.05*	0.05*	0.06*
Theology	0.03	0.03	0.04
Law	0.10***	0.10***	0.12***
Econometrics	0.03	0.03	0.02
Management	0.04	0.04	0.02
Sociology	0.01	0.01	0.02
Philosophy (N<10)	0.01	0.01	0.00
Chemistry	-0.02	-0.02	-0.01
Natural Science	-0.03	-0.03	-0.02
Psychology	-0.05*	-0.05*	-0.03
Modern Languages	-0.03	-0.03	-0.02
Biology	-0.06*	-0.06*	-0.04
Education	-0.08**	-0.09**	-0.05*
International Organisations	-0.07**	-0.07**	-0.07**
Geography	-0.09***	-0.09***	-0.07**
Communication	-0.10***	-0.11***	-0.09***
History	-0.11***	-0.11***	-0.09***
Dutch	-0.09***	-0.09***	-0.07***
Liberal Arts	-0.13***	-0.13***	-0.12***
Classics	-0.11***	-0.11***	-0.10***
Art History	-0.14***	-0.15***	-0.13***
Female		0.01	0.00
Northern Region			-0.16***
Multiple R	0.45	0.45	0.47
R^2	0.20	0.20	0.22
Adj. R^2	0.19	0.19	0.21
Standard error	4.99	4.99	4.93
F-value	17.0***	16.3***	17.9***
Constant	17.18	17.16	17.81
N	1641	1641	1641

* $p<0.05$; ** $p<0.01$; *** $p<0.001$
Source: Karrenbeld and Kramer, 1995

indicated by the means in most cases show up as significant effects, the findings are especially telling in another respect: No more than 20% of the variation in labour market positions can be accounted for by different fields of study. These findings are hardly the result of our choice to use a composite measure of labour market position. When we repeat the analysis with just the most commonly used measure by economists – income – this only raises the explained variances to 23% in Model 1 and 25% in Model 3 (results not shown). These percentages are likely to be overestimated because of the dummy strategy (see below) and also because we were unable to control for differences in ability of the students. In the Netherlands, as much as elsewhere, the more able students tend to choose science more often than other subjects (CBS, 1987), thereby creating a selection bias in favourable returns to these fields of study. In sum, the conclusion is justified that the aforementioned 20% of explained variance by the curriculum must be considered as an upper limit. The remainder is individual variation.

Although using dummy variables for the different disciplines, as we did above, is a common procedure, we think it has some serious flaws. In analyses using this strategy, dummies sometimes represent the entire effect of education, and sometimes they are used in addition to an estimate for the educational level (Griffin and Alexander, 1978; Bakker, 1987). In both cases, however, every random effect in the data is treated as if it were a systematic connection between education and jobs, in other words, 'noise' is mistaken for 'message'. In this way, dummies do indicate the maximum impact fields of study may have but, without theoretical foundation, this practice soon invites some form of capitalisation on chance. If the aim is to establish whether an impact of fields of study is more than just a coincidental and unstable phenomenon, we reject this strategy for analysis as inappropriate.

Several years ago we therefore started to search for a measure allowing for a curriculum effect to be established that is both theoretically relevant and stable over time (Waslander and Glebbeek, 1996). Starting point for this endeavour was that it had to result in an ordinal variable, in which fields of study are ranked a priori by a clearly specified criterion. Relevant dimensions can be derived from both the human capital theory and the screening and credentials theory.

Why would any lasting differences in returns between different fields of study exist? We think three main arguments can be advanced:

1 *Some fields of study are more demanding than others.* The formal stratification by educational levels is incomplete and allows for a certain informal stratification by fields within the levels. Graduates of the more difficult fields are more scarce and therefore receive higher rewards.
2 *Some fields of study are less appealing than others.* Types of education differ in the activities to be conducted during the course and the kind of work they prepare for. A sweeping statement may be that most people prefer dealing with culture and human beings to dealing with technology and matter. When choosing a field of

study, students weigh this preference against the prevailing labour market signals, and accept a smaller material gain because of immaterial rewards.
3 *Some fields of study are favoured by professional market control.* Certain professions are capable of keeping rewards above the market level by means of collective bargaining or by law, or succeed in maintaining an artificial scarcity of supply as a result of restrictions on educational inflow. This strategy has always been typical of the learned professions, such as Medicine and Pharmacy, which, perhaps not coincidentally, head the list of Table 2.

The first two factors may result in compensating differentials between fields of study while the third is an indication of monopoly rent (see Rosen, 1986; Collins, 1979).

All these explanations refer to supply and demand ratios in the labour market as the medium through which differences occur. This is in line with the founding principles of neo-classical economics, the basis of the human capital theory. According to this theory, only skills the market can use will prove to be worth the investment. The implication is that financial rewards can differ substantially between fields of study, corresponding with a relative demand for specific skills acquired in school. Thus, the ratio between supply and demand is a relevant dimension for ranking different fields of study. Building on the assumption that varying ratios become apparent in varying unemployment figures, Glebbeek and Mensen (1986) constructed a measure for *Supply and Demand Ratio*.

The labour queue variant of the *screening theory* considers the labour market to be a training market (Thurow, 1975). Any new employee has to learn new or additional skills and needs to be (further) socialised – requiring the employer to make investments – before she/he reaches the required level of productivity. To estimate training costs, candidates are screened with regard to educational qualifications (among other things). These qualifications are used as a cheap device to obtain information about ability and other personal characteristics that are relevant for the learning pace. Whether valid or not, some fields of study have the reputation of being highly selective, demand greater perseverance, and require more from the abilities of students (they are 'more demanding') which increases their value as a screening device in the labour market. Following this perspective, we subdivided the traditional educational levels using characteristics of students entering specific courses. To rank courses at the level of Lower Vocational Education, we used standardised achievement test scores (CITO), at the levels of Intermediate and Higher Vocational Education we made use of the entry qualifications of the students, while ranking academic fields of study was possible on the basis of students' average grades achieved during secondary school. The result was a measure for the *Selectivity* of fields of study.

To these two indicators, both based on 'objective' figures, a more subjective measure was added: the *Reputation* of a field of study with regard to the labour market. The idea behind this was that objective measures might not sufficiently appreciate certain factors so that an overall assessment might result in a more comprehensive classification of courses. We assumed that experts were most able to make such an overall assessment. Hence 168 career guidance officers were asked and found willing to rank 26 fields of study. This allowed us to develop a Reputation Scale following Thurstone's method of pair-wise comparisons (see Waslander and Glebbeek, 1996, for further details). In effect, this third measure comes down to professional judgements of the labour market perspectives of various courses.

Thus, we could use three measures in which fields of study were ranked according to a theoretically relevant criterion. As we cannot know from the outset which theory is 'correct' nor which operationalisation is 'best', we subjected all three measures to an empirical test. Note that these measures are not limited to the university level, as was the case with the research findings above, but address the whole range of the educational system.

Table 4
Explained variances (adjusted R^2) of regression models with varying educational variables.

			Education variables		
	Years	Dummies	Selectivity	S/D-Ratio	Reputation
OSA (N=515)					
Job level	0.24	0.26	0.24	0.13	0.17
Income	0.29	0.31	0.28	0.26	0.26
NPAO (N=463)					
Job level	0.24	0.38	0.22	0.15	0.16
Income	0.28	0.29	0.29	0.29	0.29

Note: Job level was measured on a scale from 1 to 7. Income is the log of net hourly wages. Social background variables were included in all models. Job level was included in the models explaining income

Source: Waslander and Glebbeek, 1996

We compared the effects displayed by the three new variables with the usual measure for educational level (*Years*) and the maximum effect of curriculum as displayed by dummy variables (*Dummies*). We used data from two surveys representative of the Dutch labour force (NPAO Survey 1982 and OSA Labour Supply Panel 1985-1988) whose times of collection were close to the data and statistics on which our new variables were based (oldest data refer to 1983, most recent data to 1991). Table 4 shows the results of both surveys for the whole group of respondents. The existence of a systematic effect of curriculum should manifest itself in particular in the explained variances we find with the new variables. It is therefore sufficient to show the R^2-values for the different analyses with alternating measures. In order to control for class-based subject choices biasing the estimates, three background characteristics were included in each analysis: educational level of both the father and the mother and job level of the father. The respondent's job level and income were the outcome variables.

The findings with *Dummies* for fields of study indicate that level of education may underestimate the total effect of education. Although the explained variances increase only modestly, this increase is consistent for both outcomes and both data sets. However, strongly contrasting our expectations and theory, the explanatory power of the three new measures of curriculum is consistently – and in some cases quite considerably – lower than that of the educational level. This holds true if we focus our analyses on a more homogeneous age group or specify a more complex path model (Waslander and Glebbeek, 1996). Clearly, there is no theoretically interpretable, systematic effect of curriculum.

So far, we have drawn on Dutch data. This raises the question whether our lack of results is consistent with findings from abroad. Below, we summarise the five most important studies emerging from our literature search. As is so often the case in social science, these are all American studies due to the superior quality of the data. Possibly this partly accounts for the similarity between the conclusions.

As early as 1982, Kerckhoff and Jackson investigated the impact of different types of education on the labour market position of young men. In their view, the impact of education is grossly misread in sociological stratification models that depend solely on the usual indicator for educational level: years of schooling. Important aspects of the curriculum would thus remain neglected, they argue.

> Both non-regular educational experiences and being in the college preparatory curriculum were therefore expected to increase our ability to explain the individual's occupational attainments, over and above the explanatory power due to social origins and years of schooling (1982, p. 27).

The 'experiences' referred to here are mainly vocational training courses outside the school, of which a positive impact might obviously be expected in addition to years of schooling. Participation in the college preparatory curriculum is also likely to be beneficial, even for those not moving on to college. Kerckhoff and Jackson analyse the impact of these new education variables on four different aspects of the labour market position of former high school students at ages 25 and 33. Although the authors are quite pleased with their results, for whites (three quarters of their sample) the effects are actually very small (1982, p. 41). Substantial effects are only found for blacks and the authors devote their conclusions mainly to these differences, which give them at least something to tell.

A by now almost classic study deals with labour market effects of academic as opposed to vocational courses during high school (Rumberger and Daymont, 1984). In contrast to the previous authors, Rumberger and Daymont are sceptical from the outset about the impact of different curricula (1984, pp. 158-159). Whether indeed more relevant skills for the labour market are acquired in vocational training than in academic curricula, is for them not clear cut. In a carefully conducted analysis the researchers examine effects for several groups and with several outcome variables.

> Our results compare quite closely with those of other recent studies. Like these studies, ours did *not* find systematic advantages to any single type of high school curriculum, particular vocational. (...) The results of this research suggest that policies designed to improve the secondary school curriculum may improve the educational outcomes of high school, *but do little to improve the economic outcomes*. (...) Vocational and academic course work may simply be substitutes for each other, with each developing general as opposed to specific skills (Rumberger and Daymont, 1984, pp. 184-185, our emphasis).

Hotchkiss and Dorsten (1987) report an analysis of 'curriculum effects on early post-high school outcomes'. They are surprised by the fact that 'despite the clear implication in the literature that curriculum effects extend beyond high school, most empirical studies focus on outcomes measured while respondents remain in high school and/or on college entrance' (p. 193). Aiming to change this situation, they take 'initial steps' to illuminate effects of the curriculum in the labour market. Two curriculum variables are introduced – the first being an index of the status of various courses and the second a typology of the vocational emphasis in the courses taken – and brought to bear on nine indicators of the students' positions two years after completion of high school. These indicators comprise college attendance, income and job level of current or most recent job (for those not in college), and expectations of further educational and occupational career. Although the authors claim that their findings clearly confirm the idea that curriculum 'does something' in later life, close reading reveals that effects appear mainly with regard to further education and career *expectations* of the respondents, but hardly manifest themselves in the 'real' labour market outcomes such as income and job level (p. 210). While a few of these last effects are significant in statistical terms (a rather idle result with over 10,000 cases), they turn out to be trivial in absolute terms (see Hotchkiss and Dorsten, pp. 202-203, 205).

In a 1990 article, Bishop endorses the popular concerns expressed in *A Nation at Risk* about the consequences of unsatisfactory science achievements of high school students for the productive powers of America's economy. He acknowledges the reason behind these concerns: 'Clearly, there is a large gap between the science and mathematics competence of young Americans and their counterparts elsewhere' (Bishop, 1990, p. 101). This gap is partly due to the comparatively small proportion of young Americans taking these subjects during high school:

> The apparent cause of these low enrolment figures is the perception of most high school students that there is little connection between how much they learn in mathematics and science courses and their future success in the labour market. (...) The analysis of the NLS Youth data (...) shows that this perception is correct. (...) The tendency of so many American high school students to avoid rigorous mathematics and science courses and their poor performance on international science and mathematics tests, may, therefore, well be a rational response to the lack of labour market rewards (Bishop, 1990, pp. 122-123).

As we already alluded to, Altonji published his large-scale study in 1995 which he promotes as '... the first systematic attempt to measure the effects of specific high school courses on wage rates and years of college' (1995, p. 434). This research, adopting sophisticated econometric methods, uses a meticulous index of the number of hours spent on the different subjects and enables the inclusion of separate subjects as well as combinations of subjects in the analyses. Several models are estimated, with varying (combinations of) background variables as controls. Dependent variables are hourly wages, the increase in hourly wages, and the number of years spent in higher education. Results and discussions are given for each of the subjects.

> Without such information, there is little basis for policy discussions about the effects of changes in high school requirements on labor market success. Evidence relating what a student actually does while in high school or college to labor market success is also a key to understanding why years spent in school have economic value (1995, p. 434).

In spite of this starting point and his rigorous approach, Altonji is unable to demonstrate important curriculum effects. As far as effects go, the results are comparable with the research mentioned above and can be summarised by the author's lamenting comment in the last paragraph: 'For those like myself who believe that curriculum matters, the puzzle is 'why are the estimates so small...?'

The curriculum puzzle

When considering solutions for this puzzle, we think two propositions must be kept in mind (Glebbeek, 1988; Glebbeek and van der Velden, 1994). These propositions break away from the 'naive model' of the school-to-work transition, in particular from the assumptions about uniformity and homogeneity.

1. Education does not produce a homogeneous product. A crucial distinction between most industrial products and 'products' of the educational system is that in the latter case there exists a substantial variation of quality behind identical certificates. Both the extent of the variation and the susceptibility of jobs to this variation determine the labour market value of these certificates. This is an important source of variation and uncertainty with regard to effects of specific courses in the labour market.
2. The link between education and job is not the same for all jobs in the labour market. Jobs differ in the way and extent to which necessary skills can be acquired in school. As a result, education plays different roles for different jobs. A well-known attempt to get a conceptual hold on this is Lutz and Sengenberger's typology of labour market segments (1974). These authors distinguish segments by the extent to which job performance is dependent upon occupational skills, firm-specific skills, or general skills.

These two propositions carry the notions of the crucial elements of the role of education role in the labour market: productivity and information. In the literature these two elements are usually contrasted in the already mentioned human capital and screening hypotheses (Weiss, 1995). While the first considers education as enhancing productive skills, the latter looks upon education as providing information about desired personality traits such as perseverance, adaptability and trainability.

Productivity and information are not rival goods, however, and the two hypotheses do not preclude one another. Rather, they emphasise that the one or the other effect will be dominant depending on different conditions of the labour market. Pursuing this argument, we would like to arrive at a theoretical model integrating the two elements. One such model has been proposed (Glebbeek, 1988; Glebbeek et al., 1989) which can be described as the Training Costs Model.

Training costs are the sum of all money, time and effort that must be invested in an employee before s/he is able to perform as required (Thurow, 1975). Employers assess courses on the basis of indicators of the training costs of their graduates. Thurow's labour queue theory does not elaborate which factors determine these training costs. We seek to expand his theory by specifying these factors, combining elements of the human capital and the screening theory. This leads to a model in which the expected training costs for graduates from a particular course for a particular job are determined by three interacting components:

1. The extent to which the required skills are covered by the curriculum of the course (Preparation component).

2   The risk that an individual graduate possesses the skills being taught in the course to an insufficient degree (Homogeneity component).
3   The course-related indicators of the effort necessary to bridge the gap between the skills supplied and those demanded (Trainability component).

The expected training costs of graduates will be lower, and their position in a particular labour queue more up front, (1) the more a course is specifically geared to a particular job, (2) the better the quality of graduates is controlled, and (3) the more favourable the estimates of graduates' trainability are.

Table 5
Dimensions of choice in curriculum design

COURSE CONTENT
vocational	-	academic
specific skills	-	general skills
subject based	-	problem oriented
optional	-	compulsory
technical/exact	-	verbal/social
limited qualification structure	-	unlimited qualification structure

ORGANISATION OF THE LEARNING PROCESS
class-based instruction	-	'active learning'
homogeneous groups	-	heterogeneous groups
class teacher	-	subject teacher
year groups	-	individual routes
cumulative learning	-	separate modules
combination school/work	-	school learning only

EVALUATION
vague objectives	-	specified objectives
national standards	-	local standards
external accrediting	-	internal accrediting
fixed standards	-	relative achievement
all at minimum levels	-	all at individual levels

Assuming these three components determine training costs, and therefore the graduates' labour market position, the pertinent issue is: how are indivdual (or in case of statistical discrimination: average) training costs of graduates affected by the various aspects of the curriculum? It is useful here to recall the broad interpretation of curriculum mentioned in the first Section. Improved vocational preparation, achieved at the level of course content, can be completely reversed if other conditions of the learning process do not support this preparation or if it has an unfavourable impact on the other two components of training costs. We strongly believe that this theoretically derived understanding is the clue to solving the curriculum puzzle. In order to elaborate on this, we need to assert not only the different components of training costs, but also the different components of the curriculum. A common distinction made in the literature on curriculum design specifies three main components: course content, organisation and evaluation (see Zais, 1976, p. 97).

The fundamental choices each curriculum designer faces are outlined in Table 5. Although we do not in any way claim to provide an exhaustive overview of the various aspects in which curricula differ, we do think that the dimensions we have identified are the most important ones. The reality of curricula who differ in innumerable aspects is also the experience of other curriculum researchers: 'Clearly, though we have sought to limit the meaning of curriculum construction, *its parameters remain immense*' (Zais, 1976, p. 17, our emphasis).

With so many different parameters, chances are great that some of the many curriculum parts are out of tune and have unintended and uncontrollable bearings on the training costs of graduates. To be more precise, two sources of dissonance between curriculum components can be distinguished:

1 Trade-offs.
2 Inconsistencies.

	Course Content	Organisation	Evaluation
Preparation	1	2 3	
Homogeneity		2 3	3 4
Trainability	1	3	4

Figure 4 Effects of curriculum on components of training costs: a framework (numbers refer to examples given in the text)

Trade-offs refer to inevitable contradictions. Inconsistencies can be avoided, but are difficult to eliminate in organisations characterised by what sociologists call 'loose coupling' of the comprising elements (Meyer, Scott and Deal, 1983). If we combine the three main components of the curriculum with the three components of the

Training Costs Model, we create a framework to identify the various areas for trade-offs and inconsistencies to occur (Figure 4). This framework immediately suggests that it is far from obvious that course content alone would be sufficient to minimise training costs for all students in a predictable way.

The reader can probably fill in this diagram from his/her own experiences with school. To illustrate, we give four examples of trade-offs and inconsistencies using the design parameters of Table 5. The numbers of the examples are added to Figure 4, indicating between which components of training costs trade-offs and inconsistencies are likely to occur.

1 Broad preparation - trainability. Here we have one of the most debated curriculum issues of our time. Increasing variability and flexibility of the labour market calls for people who are prepared for a variety of jobs and who are capable of dealing with change. General skills, transferable between contexts and promoting the mastering of specific skills in new contexts, may become more important than ever before. Frequently mentioned in this respect are: analytical skills, problem solving capability, social and communication skills, knowing how to find and handle information, and 'learning to learn'. There is, however, no plain connection between these broad competencies and a broad curriculum. There are narrow vocational courses with a strict learning regime where one acquires more of these general skills than in a broadly oriented, incoherent hodgepodge of modules. Curriculum designers sometimes tend to confuse 'broad' with 'a bit of everything' and the resulting wastelands of superficiality provide fewer transferring and transferable skills when compared with a solid, thorough vocational course. '(De)-pending on the nature of the learning experiences, any subject can be reduced to *learning about* or become the means for the *how* of disciplined thinking', as the well-known curriculum expert Hilda Taba once remarked (Taba, 1962, p. 266). The same wisdom can in our days help understand why a seemingly irrelevant school type such as the Gymnasium, where one learns languages nobody speaks, nevertheless has a good reputation in the labour market (see *Box*).

   In some cases, the inconsistency can take the shape of a downright trade-off:
   - broad preparation → superficiality → less trainability → narrow range of employability
   - narrow preparation → thoroughness → more trainability → broad range of employability.

   A broadly oriented curriculum seeks to optimise the average preparation for different kinds of jobs, but this may be at the expense of another component of training costs: developing trainability.

2 Individual routes - homogeneity. The average preparation for work is, by definition, maximised when each student is educated to *his* maximum ability. This pleads for differentiation of the educational process and, where possible,

individual routes within courses. Educational sociologists have provided an elaborate account of the widespread practice of this kind of formal and informal differentiation within schools (Clark, 1978; Kingston and Lewis, 1990). Moreover, achieving one's potential is a highly valued educational goal. It appears hardly, if at all, possible in practice to justify slowing down some student's development for the sake of realising more equality of outcomes. It is abundantly clear, however, that such individual differentiation comes at the expense of

> During the Summer of 1996, a Latin teacher in Belgium made a case for the economic value of the Classics, succinctly putting the principle referred to above:
>
> The study of Greek, Latin or both:
> 1 provides a general intellectual education; it teaches young people to think, to distinguish between the essential and the negligible, and it practices memory; (...)
> 5 enables them, by thorough knowledge of structure, logic and vocabulary of the Classics, to learn modern languages very quickly. (...) With regard to the first aspect mention must be made that mathematics also practices thinking, but in a different and more restricted way: to solve a mathematical problem, there is usually only one way and there is only one right answer. To translate a Latin text involves different ways and different right solutions, one has to deliberate for and against and creativity is required. (...) In short, the translation of a Greek or Latin sentence requires a high level of attention (concentration), a well-trained memory (grammar and vocabulary need to be known) and a critical mind (common sense or judgement). When acquiring and practising these qualities for as long as six years, the problems of everyday life, which as we know are innumerable, will be solved more quickly and, most of all, better. (Robert van Puyvelde (Koninklijk Atheneum Hoboken) in *De Standaard*, 22 June 1996)

homogeneity of output. The training costs of graduates will show considerable variation and the signals emanating from the educational system become less reliable in the labour market (OECD, 1996). The value of certificates as warrants decreases and employers will utilise other signals in their selection process.

3 Active learning - homogeneity. The fundamental issue for any curriculum is: how are students invited to 'learn'? The organisation of the learning process is therefore crucial for every impact a course may have.

The point – namely, that if we want students to learn something, we ought to engage them in activities likely to lead to it – is so obvious that it seems hardly worth making. We mention it here, however, only because public school curriculum practice has so consistently violated the principle (Zais, 1976, p. 356).

In the second Section of this Chapter we saw that many modern educationalists believe that 'active learning' (e.g. projects) will yield better results than traditional class-based instruction. If by means of active engagement students learn more, the preparation for working life will improve and trainability can also be enhanced. The not uncommon opposition to this principle (e.g. Prais, 1995, pp. 95-96) is that not all students cope equally well with this practice, causing individual differences to exacerbate as compared with uniform class-based instruction. Additionally, more heterogeneous and less controllable learning activities can inhibit quality control.

4 Quality control - trainability. 'No one turns out a high-quality product unless someone sets quality standards', Thurow (1992) says in his critique of the American educational system. 'The world's best school systems operate under a strong centralized ministry of education that sets tough standards that everyone must meet' (Thurow, 1992, p. 262). Output financing without external quality control, as operating in Dutch universities today, is one of the striking inconsistencies of many educational systems, inflating the homogeneity component of training costs. Yet, a strict regime of quality control may also come at an educational price. A learning process ruled by 'exam drills' does not provide the kind of intellectual climate to fully develop trainability. The shadow cast by 'The Exam' invites an instrumental attitude in teachers and students, with comprehension, understanding and the exploration of boundaries making way for 'petty facts' and 'empty tricks'. If the balance tips, students rather than having 'learned to learn' will have learned that learning is no fun at all and needs to be avoided whenever possible.

Only in the exceptional case where all curriculum aspects minimise all three components of training costs, a strong effect of curriculum in the labour market is to be expected. However, this situation is far removed from the reality of public education. In a report on behalf of the OECD, Miller recently described the product and the production process of public education as being wrapped in clouds of mystery (OECD, 1996). Not only are we ignorant about which competencies lead to productivity, or which competencies the future economy will need, but we also do not know how different competencies are enhanced by education. In spite of politicians, school boards and educational leaders vehemently discussing which courses tomorrow's society needs, there is still a yawning gap between this official curriculum and the implemented and achieved curriculum, a gap of which even the magnitude is unclear.

This interpretation finds support in the results of school-effectiveness research which aims to discover the features of curriculum and school organisation that contribute most to student success. The results of this research are generally disappointing and indicate that even the link between curriculum and student competencies, as outlined in Figure 1, is very much unclear. Dutch school-effectiveness research has yielded very few convincing results (Creemers, 1991; Scheerens, 1992; van der Velden, 1996). Dreeben comes to a similar conclusion when reviewing American sociology of education and gives an interpretation based on the ideas of organisation theorists about ritual aspects of the educational organisation. Observers like Weick (1976) and Meyer, Scott and Deal (1983) found that

> ...schools operated on the basis of a weak, uncodified, and nonrational technology. (...) Schools, they said, 'do not control their work processes very well, particularly those most closely related to their central educational purpose – instruction'. (...) This argument was consistent with the results of research on school effects: an organization with a weak and loose-jointed technology should not be expected to produce great results (Dreeben, 1994, p. 36).

If even the impact of curriculum on student competencies is so obscure, we should not be surprised about the results concerning curriculum effects in the labour market. What the school curriculum produces in the labour market is probably first and foremost: variation.

Conclusion

The available research strongly indicates that claims about the curriculum are often 'overclaims'. Despite heated controversies about the organisation and content of the curriculum, it is unrealistic to expect much of curriculum effects as long as educational institutions are unable to guarantee a more compelling technology to produce their output. That they are unable to do so, and are characterised by heterogeneity and variation instead, may not be irrational and is possibly endemic to the institutions' nature. 'Loose coupling, which permits the simultaneous operation of inconsistent programs, permits schools to be responsive to contradictory environmental pressures' (Meyer, Scott and Deal 1983, p. 59). In this Chapter, we used the Training Costs Model to trace the meaning of these inconsistencies for the effects of curriculum in the labour market. It was not difficult to demonstrate how different aspects of the curriculum may produce opposing effects on training costs. The most profound curriculum aspect which, on second thoughts, is most consistently related to all three components of training costs, is educational *level* – which would explain the recurrent findings in research.

This conclusion also bears policy implications. For research institutes engaged in monitoring the school-to-work transition, such as ROA, it seems appropriate not only to report on averages but also to give information on the dispersion of labour market outcomes. For we feel that these are directly relevant to future students having to decide on a field of study. Substantial variance in outcomes implies that individuals may exercise considerable control over what returns their education will have. In this case, a sensible choice is a highly individual matter, since chances to capitalise on education depend primarily on personal capacities and motivation. And with respect to these, individuals themselves are the best judges.

References

Aldcroft, D.H. (1992), *Education, training and economic performance 1944 to 1990*, Manchester University Press: Manchester.
Altonji, J.G. (1995), 'The effects of high school curriculum on education and labor market outcomes', *Journal of Human Resources*, 30 (3), pp. 409-438.
Bakker, B.F.M. (1987), *Onderwijs en de kans op werkloosheid*, CBS: Heerlen.
Bernstein, B. (1971), 'On the classification and framing of educational knowledge', in: Young, M.F.D. (ed.), *Knowledge and control*, Collier-Macmillan: London.
Bernstein, B. (1977). *Class, codes and control, Towards a theory of educational transmissions* (revised edition), vol. 3, Routledge: London.
Bishop, J.H. (1990), 'The productivity consequences of what is learned in high school', *Journal of Curriculum Studies*, 22 (2), pp. 101-126.
Booth, A.L., and Snower, D.J. (eds.) (1996), *Acquiring skills. Market failures, their symptoms and policy responses*, Cambridge University Press: Cambridge.
Bowles, S., and Gintis, H. (1976), *Schooling in capitalist America*, Routledge & Kegan Paul: London.
Brady, M. (1996), 'Educating for life as it is lived', *The Educational Forum*, 60, pp. 249-255.
Business Roundtable (1995), *Essential components of a successful education system*, Business Council of British Columbia: Vancouver.
CBS (1987), 'Eindexamengegevens vwo van eerstejaarsstudenten bij het wetenschappelijk onderwijs in het studiejaar 1983/84', *CBS Mededelingen*, nr.7868, Central Bureau of Statistics: The Hague.
CBS (1993), *Standaard Beroepenclassificatie 1992*, Central Bureau of Statistics: The Hague.

Clark, B.R. (1978), 'Academic differentiation in national systems of higher education', *Comparative Education Review*, 22, pp. 242-258.
Collins, R. (1979), *The credential society*, Academic Press: New York.
Creemers, B.P.M. (1991), *Effectieve instructie, Een empirische bijdrage aan de verbetering van het onderwijs in de klas*, SVO: The Hague.
Dreeben, R. (1994), 'The sociology of education. Its development in the United States', *Research in Sociology of Education and Socialization*, vol. 10, pp. 7-52, JAI Press: Greenwich.
Froomkin, J.T., Jamison, D.T., and Radner, R. (1976), *Education as an industry*, Ballinger: Cambridge.
Gamoran, A. (1995), Curriculum: the sociological agenda, Paper presented at the ISA-conference RC04, Jerusalem, 27-29 December.
Glebbeek, A.C., and Jonker, A. (eds.) (1986), *Het omstreden leerplan, Sociologische beschouwingen rond de inhoud van het onderwijs*, van Gorcum: Assen.
Glebbeek, A.C., and Mensen, Th. (1986), Waar ligt de sleutelmacht van de school? Paper presented at the congress of the Dutch Sociological and Anthropological Association, Amsterdam, 3-4 April.
Glebbeek, A.C., (1988). 'De arbeidsmarktpositie van opleidingen. Ontwikkeling en illustratie van een theoretisch model', *Tijdschrift voor Arbeidsvraagstukken*, 4 (3), pp. 75-89.
Glebbeek, A.C., Nieuwenhuysen, W., and Schakelaar, R. (1989), 'The labour market position of Dutch sociologists. An investigation guided by a theoretical model', *The Netherlands' Journal of Social Sciences*, 25 (2), pp. 57-74.
Glebbeek, A.C., and Velden, R.K.W. van der (1994), 'De regionale arbeidsmarktwaarde van opleidingen', in: Laan, L. van der, and Vermeulen, M. (eds.), *Onderwijs en arbeidsmarkt in de regio*, pp. 39-54, Eburon: Delft.
Goodson, I.F. (1995). The context of cultural interventions. Learning and curriculum, Paper presented at the ISA-conference RC04, Jerusalem, 27-29 December.
Griffin, L.J., and Alexander, K.L. (1978), 'Schooling and socio-economic attainments: high school and college influences', *American Journal of Sociology*, 84, pp. 319-347.
Held, K. (1995), *Trefpunt Plato, Een filosofische reisgids door de antieke wereld*, Ambo: Baarn.
Hotchkiss, L., and L.E. Dorsten (1987), 'Curriculum effects on early post-high school outcomes', *Research in the Sociology of Education and Socialization*, vol.7, pp. 191-219, JAI Press: Greenwich.
Husén, T. (1968), 'Lifelong learning in the 'educative society'', *International Review of Applied Psychology*, 17 (2), pp. 87-99.
Jackson, P.W. (1992), *Handbook of research on curriculum*, Macmillan: New York.
Johnes, G. (1993). *The economics of education*, St. Martin's Press: New York.
Karrenbeld, W., and Kramer, J. (1995), *Academici en het MKB*. Doctoral Thesis in Sociology, University of Groningen: Groningen.

Kerckhoff, A.C., and Jackson, R.A. (1982). 'Types of education and the occupational attainments of young men', *Social Forces,* 61 (1), pp. 24-45.

Kingston, P.W., and Lewis, L.S. (eds) (1990). *The high-status track. Studies of elite schools and stratification,* State University of New York Press: Albany.

Lutz, B., and Sengenberger, W. (1974). *Arbeitsmarktstrukturen und öffentliche Arbeitsmarktpolitik,* Otto Schwartz & Co: Göttingen.

Meyer, J.W., Scott, W.R., and Deal, T.E. (1983). 'Institutional and technical sources of organizational structure: explaining the structure of educational organizations', in: Meyer, J.W., and Scott, W.R. (eds.), *Organizational environments,* Sage: Beverly Hills.

OECD (1992), *Education at a Glance,* OECD: Paris.

OECD (1993), *Education at a Glance,* OECD: Paris.

OECD (1994), *The curriculum redefined: schooling for the 21st century,* OECD: Paris.

OECD (1995a), *Education at a Glance,* OECD: Paris.

OECD (1995b), *Public expectations of the final stage of compulsory education,* OECD: Paris.

OECD (1996), *Measuring what people know,* Human capital accounting for the knowledge economy, OECD: Paris.

OECD (1997), *Prepared for Life?* How to measure cross-curricular competencies. Results of a pilot-study in nine OECD-countries, OECD: Paris.

Philips, G., Grisay, A., Peschar, J.L., and Granheim, M. (eds) (1995), *Measuring what students learn,* OECD: Paris.

Ploeg, P. van der (1995), *Opvoeding en politiek in de overleg-democratie,* Democratische verdeling en normering van pedagogische autoriteit, PhD Thesis, University of Utrecht: Utrecht.

Prais, S.J. (1995), *Productivity, education and training.* An international perspective. Cambridge University Press: Cambridge.

Reinert, G.B., and Zinnecker, J. (1978), *Schüler im Schulbetrieb,* Rowohlt: Reinbek.

Reynolds, D. (ed.) (1994), *Advances in school effectiveness research and practice,* Elsevier: Oxford.

ROA (1995), *De arbeidsmarkt naar opleiding en beroep tot 2000,* Research Centre for Education and the Labour Market: Maastricht.

Rosen, S. (1986), 'The theory of equalizing differences', in: Ashenfelter, O.C., and Layard, R. (eds), *Handbook of labor economics,* Part 1. North-Holland: Amsterdam.

Rumberger, R.W., and Daymont, Th.N. (1984), 'The economic value of academic and vocational training acquired in high school', in: Borus, M.E. (ed.), *Youth and the labor market.* Upjohn Institute: Kalamazoo.

Scheerens, J. (1992), *Effective schooling: research, theory and practice,* Cassell: London.

Taba, H. (1962), *Curriculum development: theory and practice.* Harcourt Brace Jovanovich: New York.

Thurow, L.C. (1975), *Generating inequality*, Mechanisms of distribution in the US economy, Basic Books: New York.

Thurow, L.C. (1992), *Head to head.* The coming economic battle among Japan, Europe and America, William Morrow: New York.

Trier, U.P., and Peschar, J.L. (1995). 'Cross-curricular competencies: rationale and strategy for developing a new indicator', in: Philips, G., et al. (eds) *Measuring what students learn,* OECD: Paris.

Velden, L.F.J. van der (1996), *Context, visie, aanpak en effectiviteit,* De bestrijding van achterstanden van Nederlandse leerlingen in het basisonderwijs, PhD Thesis, University of Groningen: Groningen.

Velden, R.K.W. van der, and Wieling, M.H. (1994), 'De arbeidsmarktkansen per opleiding'. In: H. Scholten and Groot, S.C. de (eds), *Arbeidsmarkt en sociale zekerheid: beleid in beweging,* pp. 106-114, Eburon: Delft.

Waslander, S., and Glebbeek, A.C. (1996). 'Maakt het uit 'wat' je leert? Over de vraag of het effect van onderwijs in een loopbaanmodel wordt onderschat door geen rekening te houden met de opleidingsrichting', *Mens en Maatschappij,* 71 (4), pp. 308-328.

Weert, E. de (1994), 'Translating employment needs into curriculum strategies', *Higher Education Management,* 6 (3), pp. 305-320.

Weick, K. (1976), 'Educational organizations as loosely coupled systems', *Administrative Science Quarterly,* 21 (1), pp. 1-19.

Weiss, A. (1995), 'Human capital vs. signalling explanations of wages', *Journal of Economic Perspectives,* 9 (4), pp. 133-154.

Wielers, R., and Glebbeek, A.C. (1995), 'Graduates and the labour market in the Netherlands: three hypotheses and some data', *European Journal of Education,* 30 (1), pp. 11-30.

Yair, G. (1995), Moody Minds. The quality of learning experiences of American adolescents in schools, Paper presented at the ISA-conference RC04, Jerusalem, 27-29 December.

Young, M.F.D. (1971), *Knowledge and control,* New directions for the sociology of education, Collier-Macmillan: London.

Zais, R.S. (1976), *Curriculum: principles and foundations,* Harper & Row: New York.

10 Education, Skills and Wages

Hans Heijke, Mieke Koeslag and Rolf van der Velden

Introduction

To optimise the match between education and the labour market, course curriculums must be evaluated continually in the light of new developments in the labour market. Technological changes taking place in the labour market not only have far-reaching consequences for the structure of jobs, but also for the content and organisation of work and the skills required for professional practice (see Alfthan, 1985; Spenner, 1985; Bailey, 1990). To enable employees to adapt to these constant changes in the labour market, some argue in favour of giving initial education the task of teaching long-lasting skills with a high transferable value (Nijhof and Streumer, 1994; Brandsma et al., 1990). In their view, the emphasis in preparing for occupations should be on developing the generally applicable skills of students, rather than on developing occupation-specific skills (see also OECD, 1989).

This creates a dilemma for those responsible for designing educational courses. Greater emphasis on generic skills means that students are prepared for a wider range of occupations in the labour market. This increases their flexibility in the labour market and makes graduates less vulnerable to changes of employment levels in a specific segment of the labour market (ROA, 1995). At the same time, however, such graduates are less easily employable in particular jobs, because they possess relatively few occupation-specific skills. This means that these graduates are less productive than those who have been specifically trained for a particular occupation. On the other hand, if the emphasis in education is placed on providing students with occupation-specific skills, graduates may be immediately employable in a limited number of occupations, but as a result may be less flexible in the labour market.

This Chapter explores to what extent experienced deficiencies in the preparation for occupations with respect to both the more generic and the more occupation-specific skills affect the earnings level in the labour market. In this context, we examine both the general educational characteristics such as level and subject, and the specific nature of the skills acquired through education. Using the job-matching theory and the human capital theory, we can model the relationship between educational characteristics and skills on the one hand, and wages in jobs on the other. The basic principle underlying the job-matching theory is that the available labour force has certain skills that may or may not have been acquired through education, and that jobs set certain skill demands. The match between the skills available and those required determines the level of earnings (Tinbergen, 1956; Hartog, 1985). First, we will investigate the match between the attained and required education, in terms of educational level, educational subject and types of skills. Second, we will examine to what extent deficiencies and surpluses relating to the education taken and the skills acquired in this way affect wages.

In the next Section, we will model the relationship between educational characteristics, skills and wages in greater detail. The effects of educational discrepancies on wages will be introduced in the model in two steps. First, we will consider any discrepancies with regard to the match between the subject of education required and followed and the level of education required and attained. Then we will consider discrepancies with regard to the match between the required and available skills in terms of the experienced deficiencies in specific knowledge and skills in the performance of a job. In the third Section, we will discuss the data source used for estimating the models and the way in which clusters of skills were formed. The fourth Section contains descriptive statistical data of the research population and the experienced discrepancies in the three distinct areas of the occupational domain of a type of education. This Section describes firstly whether there are any discrepancies with respect to the subject of education and the level of education. Next, the discrepancies are described in terms of deficiencies of specific skills in the distinct areas of the occupational domain of a course. The fifth Section presents and discusses the empirical findings of the estimates of the wage models. The final Section rounds off with the conclusions of the study carried out.

Theoretical model

In this Section, we develop the model to be used for the mapping of the effects on wages of experienced deficiencies in the preparation for occupations. The model is based on two theoretical principles: the human capital theory and the job-matching theory. Both theories have their roots in the neoclassical theory which presupposes a labour market which functions perfectly, using wages as an allocation mechanism. The earnings of individuals in their jobs here are equal to their marginal productivity. The higher the productivity in jobs, the higher the wages paid.

The human capital theory and the job-matching theory differ with regard to the explanation given for productivity differences. According to the human capital theory, job productivity is determined exclusively by the amount of human capital acquired by the individual holding the job (Becker, 1964; Mincer, 1974). This theory therefore focuses primarily on the investment in relevant skills for the labour market which can be acquired in initial education or on the job (Schultz, 1961; Becker, 1964). Without these skills, individuals will be less productive in jobs in the labour market. The job-matching theory adds to this that the productivity of individuals with a particular amount of human capital will not be equal in every job, but also depends on the job itself, and is therefore the result of the interaction between education and job characteristics (Tinbergen, 1956; Hartog, 1992; Sattinger, 1993).

During the first step of the analysis, we will investigate to what extent discrepancies relating to the educational level and subject affect the wages paid. The wages paid in a job can be formalised as a function of both the individual investment in human capital and the quality of the match between educational and occupational characteristics as indicated by level and subject.

$$W_{ij} = f\left(HC_i, DL_{ij}, DSu_{ij}\right) \qquad (1)$$

where:
W_{ij} = the wage of individual i in job j;
HC_i = the amount of human capital acquired by individual i;
DL_{ij} = the discrepancy between the required educational level in job j and the acquired educational level of individual i; and
DSu_{ij} = the discrepancy between the required educational subject in job j and the acquired educational subject of individual i.

The above-mentioned earnings function will be investigated by estimating two empirical models. The first model (1a) includes only human capital factors. The analysis focuses on the extent to which individual investments in human capital affect wages. Following the human capital theory, we expect that such investments will lead to higher wages. The second model (1b) includes not only human capital factors, but also indicators representing the discrepancy between the qualifications acquired and the qualifications required for the job. The match between the required subject of education and the acquired subject and between the required level of education and the acquired level constitute the two indicators for the discrepancy in this model. On the basis of the job-matching theory, we expect that being employed in a job below one's educational level, or being employed in a job which does not match one's subject of education, yields lower wages than being employed in a job which matches the educational level and subject. On the other hand, we expect that working in a job above one's educational level will yield higher wages than being employed in a job which matches the acquired educational level. We do expect, however, that the absolute level of the effect of a less adequate match on the wage level in the first case (i.e. overeducation) is greater than in the second case (undereducation). This means therefore that, on the basis of the educational level attained by an individual, working in a job below this level results in a greater wage loss than the potential gain of working in a job above one's educational level.

In this study the match with respect to the educational subject will be based on a division of the range of jobs in which graduates of a course find employment into three areas. These are jobs for which the course provides:

1. exclusive preparation, the *exclusive own domain;*
2. non-exclusive preparation, the *non-exclusive own domain;* and
3. no preparation, the *alternative domain.*

The first area of the occupational domain of a course – the jobs for which the course prepares exclusively – consists of jobs in which the course concerned is an exclusive requirement. In jobs for which the course does not prepare exclusively, other courses with related subjects also have access. The third area of the occupational domain of a course concerns jobs for which the subject of the course involved is not required.

During the second step of our analysis, we will investigate to what extent experienced deficiencies regarding the utilisation of specific skills in a job, affect wages. This research step concerns experienced deficiencies or surpluses with respect to a variety of skills, including professional competence, organisational and institutional knowledge, intellectual and social skills, etc. To a certain extent, these deficiencies and surpluses can be regarded as a particularisation of the more overall match with respect to the educational subject rather then the match with respect to the educational level. We will therefore investigate the wage model which includes the specific skills discrepancies in greater detail, omitting the indicator for the discrepancies as to educational subject. The model to be studied in this research step is therefore:

$$W_{ij} = f\left(HC_i, DL_{ij}, DSk_{ij}\right) \qquad (2)$$

where:
W_{ij} = the wages of individual i in job j;
HC_i = the amount of human capital acquired by individual i;
DL_{ij} = the discrepancy between the educational level required in job j and the educational level acquired by individual i;
DSk_{ij} = the discrepancy between the required skills in job j and the skills of individual i.

In equation 2 we estimate an earnings function which includes both human capital factors and indicators for discrepancies in terms of required versus acquired educational level and in terms of specific skills deficiencies and surpluses experienced in the job. Thus we control for the quality of the match with regard to the acquired and required educational level. If no deficiencies or surpluses are experienced relating to the educational level attained, there may still be specific skill discrepancies that influence the performance in one's job. It is expected that specific skill discrepancies will have a negative effect on wages. Any experienced skill surpluses, however, will probably have no effect, or a minor positive one.

Data source and skills clusters

The data for the analysis in this Chapter derive from the Higher Vocational Education Monitor, an annual survey of graduates from Higher Vocational Education. The survey registers the process of entry in the labour market, collecting data concerning the job search process, unemployment spells, the social status and the characteristics of current jobs.

Data were taken from the survey carried out in the Autumn of 1994 (van de Loo et al., 1995; Pagrach et al., 1995) and relates to graduates from the 1992/93 school year from 170 different types of Higher Vocational Education. These types of education can be divided into 7 educational sectors: agriculture, education, technology, economics, health care, social and community work and fine arts. From these data, we have selected respondents who had completed a full-time course in Higher Vocational Education, had paid employment at the time of the survey, and were not older than 36 years. This yielded a population of 7,325 cases.

The survey devotes considerable attention to determining how important particular skills are for the respondents in order to perform properly in their jobs. Each respondent was also asked to indicate whether he or she believed that more attention should be given to the skill concerned during the educational course ('experienced deficiency'), that the emphasis was more or less right, or that less attention should be given to this aspect ('experienced surplus'). The list of skills was taken from previous literature on the classification of jobs (Algera, 1991), supplemented by the views of experts in the relevant sectors of Higher Vocational Education. The skill requirements were formulated so as to be independent of occupational or sectoral specificities.

The graduates were presented with a list of 38 skills classified under three headings: Knowledge, Competences and Personal Traits. 'Knowledge' comprises skills with some relation to knowledge or understanding of the occupational field. 'Competences' comprises a classification of skills relating to applying and analysing this occupation-specific knowledge and understanding, complemented by manual skills, presentation techniques, leadership and communication skills, and the ability to collect and document information. 'Personal traits' covers skills such as originality, creativity, independence, empathy, adaptability, ability to cope with stress, self-discipline, systematic evaluation and physical fitness.

The respondents were asked to rate the importance of each of these skills in relation to proper performance in their current jobs. They were presented with a 4-point scale on which to indicate their answers. The scale ranged from unimportant (category 1), through fairly unimportant (category 2) and fairly important (category 3), to very important (category 4). Respondents were also asked to indicate whether the attention paid to the skills involved during the course should be greater, equal, or less.

To reduce the number of skills in the analysis to manageable proportions, we combined the 38 skills distinguished in the data into a number of groups of interrelated skills using a cluster analysis. This analysis was based on a matrix in which the rows represent the skills and the columns represent the graduates. Each row shows the score profile of the graduates for one skill. Cluster analysis is used to combine those skills for which the score profiles show a given degree of similarity, using the squared Euclidean distance between two items as a criterion (Aldenderfer and Blashfield, 1984). Using this measure, the distance between two skills is determined by squaring the difference between the scores for those two skills for each graduate, and adding the resulting differences for all of the graduates.

Having determined the squared Euclidean distance between each pair of skills in the matrix, the skills are then clustered as follows: The two skills with the most similar score profiles are combined in the matrix as one new element (cluster). Then the squared Euclidean distances for all skills (one of which is now a cluster) are recalculated for the new matrix, and the two skills (or the skill and the cluster) whose score profiles exhibit the greatest similarity are again combined to form a cluster. This method ensures that the intra-variance of the clusters is as low as possible, whereas the inter-variance is as high as possible (Aldenderfer and Blashfield, 1984).

The clustering process could in principle have been repeated until all skills had been combined in one cluster, but this would only be sensible if the skills concerned were sufficiently homogenous. The endpoint of the clustering process is determined in the light of two types of criteria, a statistical and a qualitative one. The statistical criterion is that the clustering process should stop at the point at which the Ward coefficient rises relatively sharply. Since this criterion does not always provide a sufficiently definite endpoint, the similarities between the skills (clusters) are also considered. The clustering process comes to an end when the two skills to be combined next are considered as having too little in common.[1]

Eventually, seven skill clusters were formed, combining 23 of the skill items. Table 1 presents an overview of these clusters and the items included in each cluster. The largest cluster combines items which relate to attitudinal characteristics. There also seems to be a particularly strong interrelationship between skills which refer to the knowledge and skills that are specific to an occupation. In addition to these two large clusters, a number of smaller clusters were created, leaving 15 items not clustered. It was then decided to make a more limited selection of the remaining clusters and items. All clusters created were selected, along with three of the remaining skill items. These were the items 'communicative skills', 'IT skills' and 'leadership'. For each of the selected clusters, we have calculated the average score for each of the respondents' answers on the underlying items. The question of

Table 1
The skill clusters used in the study

Cluster 1: **attitudinal characteristics:**
 - Collaboration with colleagues; teamwork
 - Independence and initiative
 - Accuracy, precision, meticulousness
 - Adaptability, flexibility and ability to improvise
 - Ability to cope with stress and uncertainty
 - Self-discipline, perseverance

Cluster 2: **intellectual skills:**
 - Originality, creativity, conceptual and innovative abilities
 - Empathy
 - Systematic evaluation, establishing and using feedback

Cluster 3: **occupation-specific knowledge:**
 - General theoretical knowledge of the discipline
 - Specialised professional knowledge
 - Occupation-specific methods and techniques
 - Keeping up with recent developments in the professional field
 - Application of (theoretical) knowledge and techniques in practice

Cluster 4: **organisational knowledge:**
 - Understanding of the processes and organisation of the business
 - Understanding of financial management of the organisation
 - Understanding of administration and other managerial matters

Cluster 5: **presentation skills:**
 - Written presentations (letters, reports, articles)
 - Verbal presentation (telephone, public presentations)

Cluster 6: **planning skills:**
 - Planning, co-ordinating and organising activities
 - Gathering relevant information for activities

Cluster 7: **institutional knowledge:**
 - Understanding of legislation and regulations relevant to the professional field
 - Understanding of labour laws, employment conditions and requirements, and work safety

Item 8: **communication skills:**
 - Making and maintaining contacts with customers, patients, students etc.

Item 9: **IT skills:**
 - Knowledge of computer programs and information technology

Item 10: **leadership:**
 - Leadership

whether a particular aspect should be given more, the same amount of, or less attention during the course is recoded as two dummy variables: more attention ('deficiency') or less attention ('surplus'). For each skills item in a cluster, two dummy variables were made: one indicating the deficiency of the skills item and another indicating the surplus of the skills item. Within each cluster, the dummies were calculated and divided by the number of skills items in the cluster.

Descriptive statistics, skill requirements and deficiencies

Appendix A presents data on a number of statistical aspects of the variables used in the analysis. In addition to a number of control variables such as gender, age and the characteristics of the firm in which the respondent works, there are three groups of variables. The first group comprises a number of variables which indicate the human capital which individuals have accumulated, such as previous education, educational sector within Higher Vocational Education, board experience and work experience. The second group of variables are indicative of the quality of the job match with respect to both the level and the subject of education. The variables in the third group relate to the importance of the skills required to perform properly in one's job as discussed in the last Section, and to any deficiencies and surpluses which may have been experienced as regards these skills.

A total of 27% of the respondents said that for their current job their employers attempted to recruit only people whose educational background was in the field which the respondent had in fact studied. These are said to be working in the 'exclusive own occupational domain' of that type of education. More than half of the respondents said that either their own education or education in a related subject was required. These school-leavers are said to be working in the 'non-exclusive own occupational domain'. Finally, 19% of the respondents held a job for which no specific subject of study was required, or the requirement was education in a subject completely different to that which the respondent had in fact studied. These are said to be working in the 'alternative domain' of that type of education.

The graduates were also asked to indicate the minimum educational level demanded by their employers for the jobs they had. A total of 57% had jobs for which Higher Vocational Education was the minimum level required, 22% had jobs for which a lower educational level was required and another 22% had jobs for which a higher level (at least the second phase of Higher Vocational Education or University Education) was required.

Table 2 shows the average scores and standard deviations for the importance of each of the defined skills within each of the three domains. A variance analysis was used to assess the extent to which these scores varied systematically according to the domains in which the respondents worked. Any such differences would be expected to be especially evident with respect to the occupation-specific skills, which would be important primarily in the domain which is specific to that type of education. The generic skills were not expected to show systematic differences between the domains.

Table 2
The importance of the skill clusters, by occupational domain
(1=unimportant, ..., 4=very important)

Importance	exclusive own domain		non-exclusive own domain		alternative domain		'explained' variance(%)
	mean	s.d.	mean	s.d.	mean	s.d.	
Attitudinal characteristics	3.63	0.37	3.61	0.39	3.44	0.59	2.6
Intellectual skills	3.49	0.51	3.37	0.54	3.10	0.78	4.8
Occupation-specific skills	3.48	0.42	3.27	0.51	2.71	0.90	17.5
Organisational knowledge	2.49	0.80	2.69	0.80	2.56	0.90	1.2
Presentation skills	3.19	0.70	3.30	0.71	3.09	0.93	1.2
Planning skills	3.24	0.64	3.29	0.63	2.98	0.89	2.9
Institutional knowledge	2.83	0.77	2.75	0.79	2.48	0.93	2.3
Communication skills	3.46	0.82	3.37	0.85	3.16	1.03	1.4
IT skills	2.86	0.85	2.91	0.89	2.74	1.02	0.5
Leadership	2.78	0.98	2.64	0.98	2.38	1.10	1.8

In general, attitudinal characteristics, intellectual skills, occupation-specific skills, communication skills and presentation skills were considered to be the most important ones. This was true regardless of the domain in which the respondent worked, except for the case of occupation-specific skills, the importance of which was, as expected, much lower in the alternative domain than in the own domain. In fact, the domain in which respondents were employed explained 18% of the variance in the scores for this skill cluster. The systematic differences between the three domains for the other skills were very low.

Table 3 shows the average scores of the deficiencies experienced in relation to each of the skill clusters. The scores range from 0 to 1, where 0 means that the respondents considered it unnecessary to give any of the underlying skills more attention in education, while the score 1 means that the respondents considered it necessary to give each underlying skill more attention in education. A score between 0 and 1 means that the respondents think that more attention would be desirable for some of the underlying skills.

On average, more than a quarter of the respondents considered it necessary that particular skills should be given more attention. The scores for the 'deficiency' variables are considerably higher than those for the 'surplus' variables (cf. Appendix A). The differences between the skill clusters are small. For those clusters which relate to occupation-specific knowledge and skills, institutional knowledge, communicative skills, IT skills, and presentation skills, more than 30% of the respondents is in favour of giving more attention to these skills in the educational courses. Less than 25% of the respondents thought that more attention should have been given to organisational knowledge and intellectual skills. For the other skill clusters, between 25% and 30% of the respondents experienced deficiencies.

Table 3
Deficiencies experienced with regard to the skill clusters, by occupational domain

Deficiency experienced	exclusive own domain		non-exclusive own domain		alternative domain		'explained' variance (%)
	mean	s.d.	mean	s.d.	mean	s.d.	
Attitudinal characteristics	0.27	0.28	0.28	0.28	0.29	0.31	0.03
Intellectual skills	0.24	0.27	0.24	0.30	0.26	0.32	0.05
Occupation-specific skills	0.33	0.26	0.32	0.25	0.27	0.26	0.80
Organisational knowledge	0.20	0.33	0.24	0.33	0.26	0.35	0.44
Presentation skills	0.36	0.40	0.38	0.41	0.38	0.42	0.04
Planning skills	0.29	0.34	0.30	0.36	0.29	0.35	0.03
Institutional knowledge	0.37	0.41	0.30	0.37	0.31	0.38	0.69
Communication skills	0.36	0.48	0.35	0.48	0.37	0.48	-*
IT skills	0.29	0.45	0.31	0.46	0.33	0.47	-*
Leadership	0.25	0.43	0.30	0.46	0.33	0.47	-*

* Because the dependent variable in this case is a dummy rather than a cluster of skills, no variance analysis could be applied. From an inspection of the proportions it is clear that the differences between the domains are negligible

The differences between the domains are also small. The main difference concerns the occupation-specific knowledge and skills, which are important in particular in the (exclusive) own domain of a course, and less so in the alternative domain of the course (cf. Table 2). Table 3 shows that deficiencies in these skills are experienced primarily in the own domain of a course. Although in the alternative domain of a course there is no greater importance attached to presentation skills, organisational skills, IT skills, attitude characteristics, leadership, intellectual skills, and communicative skills, the deficiencies experienced in these skills are nevertheless greater than in the own domain of the course. Evidently, in education generic skills are acquired which can be used adequately in the alternative domain.

Wages

In this Section, we will first investigate to what extent discrepancies relating to the educational level and subject of education effect wages. Subsequently, we will investigate to what extent the discrepancies relating to the utilisation of specific skills in the jobs have an effect on wages.

To be able to estimate the effects on wages resulting from discrepancies relating to the subject and level of education, a model with two variants was developed in the second Section. This model includes those variables which refer to the individual's human capital: the educational sector within Higher Vocational Education in which the respondent studied, the level of any previous education, the length of the study, board experience, paid and relevant work experience acquired in the course of the study, and work experience in the respondent's current job. The other variables in the model – gender, ethnicity, age, profit sector and location of the firm – are included for control purposes. In accordance with the human capital theory, we expect all of the experience variables to have a positive effect on earnings.

The first variant of the model (model 1a) is restricted to above-mentioned human capital and control variables. In the second variant (model 1b) indicators for discrepancies relating to the level and subject of education were added to the first variant. From the job-matching theory one may deduce that being employed in a job below one's educational level, or in a job which does not match one's subject of education, as indicated by the degree of exclusivity of the occupational domain, yields lower wages than being employed in a job which matches the educational level and subject. On the other hand, working in a job above one's educational level, should yield slightly higher wages than being employed in a job which matches the acquired educational level.

To assess the effects on wages of discrepancies relating to the utilisation of skills in a job, a second model was developed in the second Section (model 2). The latter model includes the above-mentioned control variables, the variables indicating the human capital of individuals, variables to control for the quality of the match between the acquired and required educational level, and variables representing the specific skills deficiencies and surpluses experienced in a job. It is expected that experienced skills deficiencies will have a negative effect on wages, while experienced surpluses will have hardly any effect on wages, or a minor positive effect. In this model the variables representing the match between the educational subject and the occupational domain are left out of the model, because the experienced skills deficiencies and surpluses may be highly correlated with the quality of the match between the acquired educational subject on the one hand, and the required educational subject on the other hand.

Table 4 shows the results of the analyses carried out. The logarithm of the gross hourly wage was used as dependent variable. Model 1a, containing the education and experience variables only, explains 10% of the variance of gross hourly wages in graduates. This seems very little, but one must remember that the research population consists of newly graduated students from Higher Vocational Education. As a result of the very similar starting wages for this category, there is only little variance to be explained.

Table 4
Wage equation (OLS of the logarithm of the gross hourly wage)

Variable	Model 1a parameter	Model 1a standard deviation	Model 1b parameter	Model 1b standard deviation	Model 2 parameter	Model 2 standard deviation
Intercept	2.255*	0.056	2.271*	0.010	2.312*	0.057
Age	0.021*	0.002	0.021*	0.002	0.021*	0.002
Male	0.023*	0.007	0.016*	0.007	0.013	0.007
Ethnic minority	0.020	0.031	0.034	0.030	0.028	0.031
Profit sector	-0.009	0.008	-0.008	0.008	-0.013	0.008
Firm size (≥ 50 empl.)	0.017*	0.007	0.011	0.006	0.013	0.007
Location of firm:						
North	-0.032*	0.013	-0.028*	0.012	-0.034*	0.013
East	-0.049*	0.008	-0.044*	0.008	-0.040*	0.008
West	ref.	ref.	ref.	ref.	ref.	ref.
South	-0.034*	0.008	-0.035*	0.007	-0.028*	0.008
Foreign	0.064*	0.016	0.061*	0.016	0.064*	0.017
Previous education:						
Senior General Sec. Educ.	ref.	ref.	ref.	ref.	ref.	ref.
Pre-university Education	0.011	0.008	0.011	0.008	0.010	0.008
Senior Voc. Sec. Educ.	-0.007	0.008	-0.007	0.008	-0.001	0.008
Higher Vocational Educ.	0.041	0.023	0.015	0.022	0.038	0.023
University Education	-0.011	0.044	-0.003	0.043	0.002	0.043
Other	-0.020	0.024	-0.016	0.023	-0.005	0.024
Educational sector:						
Agriculture	ref.	ref.	ref.	ref.	ref.	ref.
Education	0.053*	0.017	0.009	0.017	0.024	0.017
Technology	0.039*	0.012	0.026*	0.012	0.015	0.012
Economics	0.010	0.012	0.009	0.011	-0.005	0.012
Health care	0.130*	0.014	0.106*	0.014	0.106*	0.015
Social and community work	0.075*	0.015	0.074*	0.014	0.065*	0.015
Fine Arts	-0.124*	0.024	-0.094*	0.023	-0.088*	0.025
Length of study	0.0005	0.0003	0.0002	0.0003	0.0004	0.0003
Experience:						
Board experience	0.009	0.007	0.009	0.006	0.005	0.007
Paid work experience during study	0.004	0.008	0.005	0.008	0.004	0.008
Relevant work experience	0.021*	0.007	0.017*	0.006	0.014*	0.006
Work exp. in current job (in months)	0.005*	0.0005	0.004*	0.0005	0.004*	0.0005

Table 4 (continued)
Wage equation (OLS of the logarithm of the gross hourly wage)

Variable	Model 1a parameter	Model 1a standard deviation	Model 1b parameter	Model 1b standard deviation	Model 2 parameter	Model 2 standard deviation
Job match:						
Exclusive own domain			0.054*	0.010		
Non-exclusive own domain			0.034*	0.008		
Alternative domain			ref.	ref.		
Overeducation			-0.106*	0.008	-0.112*	0.008
Undereducation			0.010	0.008	0.014	0.008
Matching level			ref.	ref.	ref.	ref.
Experienced deficiencies in:						
Attitudinal characteristics					0.012	0.014
Intellectual skills					0.003	0.013
Occupation-specific skills					-0.036*	0.013
Organisational knowledge					0.002	0.010
Presentation skills					0.012	0.008
Planning skills					-0.005	0.010
Institutional knowledge					0.013	0.008
Communication skills					-0.014*	0.007
IT skills					-0.002	0.007
Leadership					0.005	0.007
Experienced surpluses in:						
Attitudinal characteristics					-0.050	0.042
Intellectual skills					-0.031	0.031
Occupation-specific skills					-0.013	0.028
Organisational knowledge					-0.036*	0.014
Presentation skills					0.011	0.024
Planning skills					0.014	0.023
Institutional knowledge					0.018	0.014
Communication skills					0.003	0.018
IT skills					0.013	0.013
Leadership					0.004	0.015
Adj. R^2	0.103		0.158		0.145	
Df	5853		5696		5080	
N	5869		5725		5128	

* = significant at a confidence level of 95%

The model shows that graduates with an educational background in the fields of 'Health care' or 'Social and community work' are significantly better paid than those with an educational background in 'Agriculture' (the reference category), as are those with 'Technical' and 'Education' training, while those having studied 'Fine Arts' are paid significantly less. The other variables for training and experience, such as previous education or board experience, have no significant effect on earnings, with the exception of the number of months that the respondent has worked in his or her current job and any relevant work experience during or prior to the course in Higher Vocational Education, which have a significantly positive effect on earnings.

Model 1b gives a considerably better fit than model 1a. Discrepancies relating to the subject and level of education taken seem to significantly determine the respondent's wages in the job. The partial effect of working below the level of Higher Vocational Education ('overeducation') results in wages which are 11% lower. As expected, the partial effect of undereducation is small and not significant. Graduates working in the occupational domain which is specific exclusively to their own education earn 5.4% more than those working in the alternative domain, while graduates working in the domain which is specific to their type of education, but not exclusively so, still earn 3.4% more than those in the alternative domain. From the results of model 1b, we can deduce that flexibility (i.e. accepting jobs for which the subject of education obtained is not a requirement) has a negative effect on wages. Such shifts lead to 3-5% lower gross hourly wages.

Model 2 provides nearly the same fit as model 1b. But the model including human capital variables and indicators for discrepancies relating to the educational level and subject (model 1b), explains the earnings differences between graduates far more parsimonious than does the model which includes human capital variables, discrepancies relating to the educational level, and indicators for discrepancies relating to the utilisation of specific skills in the performance of jobs (model 2). The results of model 2 with respect to the individual categories of skills are fairly limited. We only found a significant negative effect on wages of experienced deficiencies in occupation-specific skills and communication skills and a – difficult to explain – significant negative effect of a surplus of organisational knowledge. The results of models 1b and 2 seem to indicate that employers hardly reflect the individual skill discrepancies in the wages, but on the contrary focus mainly on the observed discrepancies relating to the educational level and subject acquired and required. The course taken, rather than job performance is an important determinant for wages during the first years after entry in the labour market. A notable exception may be an insufficient preparation in occupation-specific skills which are highly related to the educational subject. Experienced deficiencies in this area do have a negative effect on wages. This effect is 3.6% which is nearly of the same magnitude as the effect of the match between the educational subject and the domain of the job. An insufficient preparation in communication skills yields 1.4% lower wages.

Conclusion

Educational courses in Higher Vocational Education have always been strongly oriented towards vocational preparation. In this respect, Higher Vocational Education is quite unlike University Education, where less emphasis is given to specific preparation for an occupation. Nevertheless, the importance of generic skills has also been increasingly emphasised within Higher Vocational Education (cf. Nijhof and Streumer, 1994; WRR, 1995). It has been said that, as a result of technological and organisational changes, more attention should be devoted to skills which can be transferred from one job to another (OECD, 1989).

A greater emphasis on generic skills gives students access to a wider range of occupations. The price to be paid for this is fewer occupation-specific skills, rendering students less easily employable in jobs which rely heavily on occupation-specific skills than students who do possess such skills.

In this Chapter we have examined to what extent deficiencies in the preparation of occupations have an effect on the earnings of graduates of Higher Vocational Education in the labour market. We have also described the effects on earnings in jobs created by accepting employment which is less in line with one's level of education. Two models have been estimated, of which the first explores the effects on earnings of discrepancies relating to the educational subject and level of education, while the second investigates the effects on earnings of discrepancies relating to the utilisation of generic and specific skills in the performance of jobs.

The results of these estimates show that discrepancies relating to the educational subject and level of education – in particular accepting employment below one's level of education and working in jobs requiring a different subject of education as preparation – have a negative effect on earnings. Of the discrepancies relating to the skills deficiencies experienced in jobs, on the other hand, only the experienced deficiencies in occupation-specific skills and communication skills affect the wages negatively. The negative effect of the occupation-specific skills matches the negative effect we found of a poor match between the educational subject and the job, because the presence of this skill category is determined by the type of education taken.

It may be concluded that earnings in jobs of graduates, shortly after their entry in the labour market, are determined largely by the subject and the level of their education. As graduates have little or no work experience, employers may have difficulties in assessing the actual productivity of school-leavers, and hence their earnings. The educational characteristics of graduates – their subject and level of education– constitute the primary sources of information for employers to establish the appropriate level of their earnings while the skills deficiencies that may be present have not yet manifested themselves and are therefore hardly reflected in the earnings. Presumably, the wages reflect primarily the skills attributed to the level and subject of education. On the other hand, it is remarkable here that out of the knowledge and skill deficiencies, it is the occupation-specific skills deficiencies which are closely related to the educational subject taken that have a significant effect on wages, while the same is not or hardly true for general skills, such as attitudinal characteristics and intellectual skills, with the exception of communication skills. This suggests that employers may not have a direct interest in observing any deficiencies or surpluses of general skills in individuals, and in reflecting these in the wage levels, because the presence of such skills fails to provide any special distinction from their competitors. Such may, however, be the case when it comes to filling any gaps created by deficiencies in occupation-specific knowledge and skills that are scarce in the labour market.

The results of this study emphasise the dilemma outlined in the introduction to this Chapter, which is related to the acquisition of generic skills versus occupation-specific skills. The results suggest that, at least for graduates of higher education, the greater flexibility in the labour market that may result from a relatively large availability of generic skills is paid for by a relatively lower wage level in those occupational domains where a relatively large appeal is made to the availability of occupation-specific skills.

Note

1   This concerned the skill clusters 'attitudinal characteristics' and 'intellectual skills'.

References

Aldenderfer, M.S., Blashfield, R.K. (1984), *Cluster analysis*, Sage University paper 44, Sage Publication: California.

Alfthan, T. (1985), 'Developing skills for technological change: some policy issues', *International Labour Review*, 124 (5), pp. 517-529.

Algera, J.A. (1991), *Analyse van arbeid vanuit verschillende perspectieven*, Swets & Zeitlinger: Amsterdam/Lisse.

Bailey T. (1990), 'Jobs of the future and the skills they will require. New thinking on a debate', *American Educator*, 14 (1), pp. 10-15; pp. 40-44.

Becker G.S. (1964), *Human Capital; A Theoretical and Empirical Analysis with Special Reference to Education*, National Bureau of Economic Research: New York.

Brandsma T.F., Nijhof, W.J., Kamphorst, J.C. (1990), *Kwalificatie en Curriculum. Een internationaal vergelijkende studie naar methoden voor de bepaling van kwalificaties*, Forum 7, Swets & Zeitlinger: Amsterdam/Lisse.

Hartog J. (1985), 'Earnings Functions; Testing for the Demand Side', *Economic Letters*, 19 (3), pp. 281-285.

Hartog J. (1992), *Capabilities, Allocation and Earnings*, Kluwer Academic Publishers: Boston, Dordrecht, London.

Knuver, J.W.M. (1993), *De relatie tussen klas- en schoolkenmerken en het affectief functioneren van leerlingen*, RION: Groningen.

Loo, P.J.E. van de, Hoevenberg, J., Velden, R.K.W. van der (1995), *De arbeidsmarktpositie van afgestudeerden van het hoger beroepsonderwijs. HBO-Monitor 1994*, HBO-Raad: Den Haag.

Mincer, J. (1974), *Schooling, Experience and Earnings*, National Bureau of Economic Research: New York.

Nijhof, W.J., Streumer, J.N. (1994), *Verbreed Beroepsonderwijs*, Faculteit der Toegepaste Onderwijskunde, Vakgroep Curriculumtechnologie, Technische Universiteit Twente: Enschede.

Organisation for Economic Co-operation and Development (1989), *Education and the Economy in a Changing Society*, OECD: Paris.

Pagrach K.J., Loo, P.J.E. van de, Pisters, J. (1995), *De arbeidsmarktpositie van afgestudeerden van het hoger beroepsonderwijs. HBO-Monitor 1994, Statistisch supplement*, HBO-Raad: Den Haag.

Researchcentrum voor Onderwijs en Arbeidsmarkt (1995), *De arbeidsmarkt naar opleiding en beroep tot 2000*, ROA-R-1995/3E, Universiteit Maastricht: Maastricht.

Sattinger, M. (1993), 'Assignment Models of the Distribution of Earnings', *Journal of Economic Literature*, 31 (2), pp. 831-880.

Schultz, T.W. (1961), 'Investment in human capital', *The American Economic Review*, 51 (1), pp. 1-17.

Spenner, K.I. (1985), 'The upgrading and downgrading of occupations: issues, evidence and implications for education', *Review of Educational Research*, 55 (2), pp. 125-154.

Tinbergen, J. (1956), 'On the Theory of Income Distribution', *Weltschaftliches Archiv*, 77 (2), pp. 155-175.

Wetenschappelijke Raad voor het Regeringsbeleid (1995), *Hoger onderwijs in fasen*, rapporten aan de regering no. 47, SDU: Den Haag.

Appendix A: Descriptive statistics (unweighed set) of graduates from Higher Vocational Education, 1994

Variable	Percentage	Average	Standard deviation
Gross hourly wage (in DFL)		18.99	4.48
Age		24.85	1.82
Male	48		
Ethnic minority	1		
Profit sector	64		
Firm size (>= 50 employees)	65		
Location of firm:			
North	6		
East	21		
West	45		
South	24		
Foreign	4		
Previous education:			
Senior General Secondary Education	34		
Pre-university Education	31		
Senior Vocational Secondary Education	31		
Higher Vocational Education	2		
University Education	1		
Other	2		
Educational sector:			
Agriculture	9		
Education	7		
Technology	22		
Economics	38		
Health care	13		
Social and community work	10		
Fine Arts	2		
Length of study (months)		49.13	10.47
Experience:			
Board experience	31		
Paid work experience during study	16		
Relevant work experience	35		
Work experience in current job (months)		9.70	6.34
Job match:			
Exclusive own domain	27		
Non-exclusive own domain	54		
Alternative domain (education in other fields is required)	19		
Job level < educational level	22		

Appendix A: Descriptive statistics (unweighed set) of graduates from Higher Vocational Education, 1994 (continued)

Variable	Percentage	Average	Standard deviation
Job level = educational level	57		
Job level > educational level	22		
Importance of:			
(1=unimportant, ..., 4=very important)			
Attitudinal characteristics		3.59	0.42
Intellectual skills		3.35	0.58
Occupation-specific skills		3.23	0.61
Organisational knowledge		2.63	0.81
Presentation skills		3.25	0.73
Planning skills and gathering info.		3.24	0.67
Institutional knowledge		2.72	0.82
Communication skills		3.35	0.88
IT skills		2.90	0.89
Leadership		2.63	1.00
Experienced deficiencies in:			
Attitudinal characteristics		0.27	0.28
Intellectual skills		0.24	0.30
Occupation-specific skills		0.31	0.25
Organisational knowledge		0.23	0.33
Presentation skills		0.37	0.41
Planning skills and gathering info.		0.29	0.35
Institutional knowledge		0.31	0.38
Communication skills		0.35	0.48
IT skills		0.31	0.46
Leadership		0.29	0.45
Experienced surpluses in:			
Attitudinal characteristics		0.02	0.09
Intellectual skills		0.03	0.12
Occupation-specific skills		0.04	0.12
Organisational knowledge		0.09	0.24
Presentation skills		0.03	0.14
Planning skills		0.04	0.15
Institutional knowledge		0.09	0.24
Communication skills		0.03	0.18
IT skills		0.07	0.25
Leadership		0.05	0.23

Appendix

The Dutch Education System

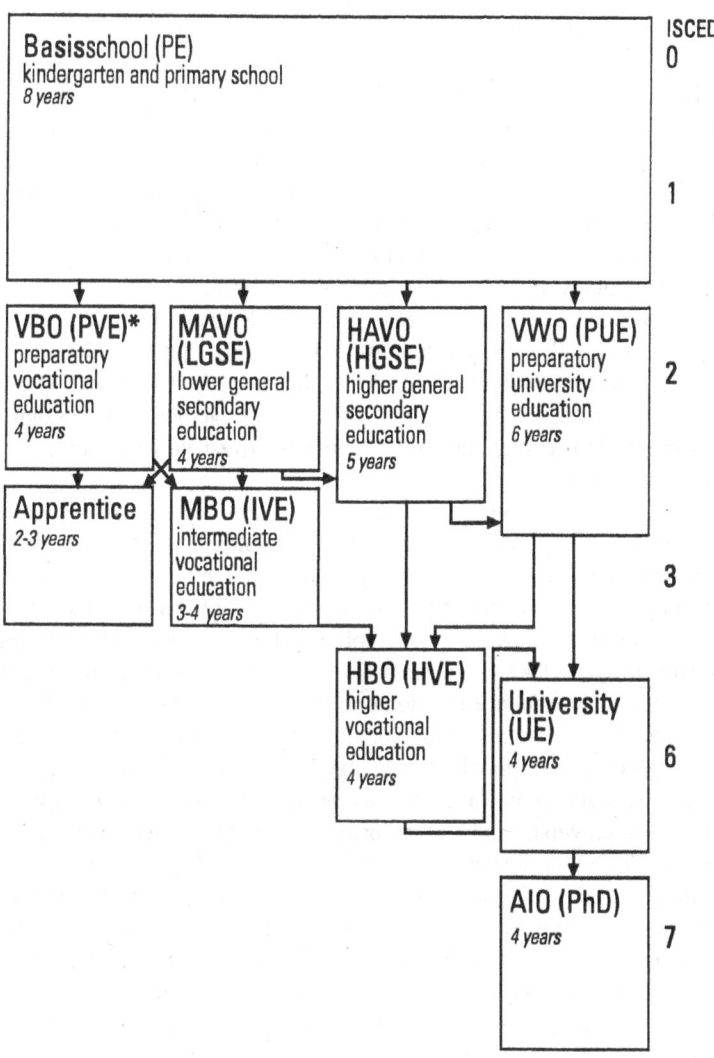

English abbreviation between brackets
* Formerly, 'lower vocational education' (LVE)

In the Dutch educational system, kindergarten and primary school were combined ten years ago into one primary school (basisschool) for children aged 4 to 12. After primary school, children choose between three levels of general education and preparatory vocational education (VBO). The highest level of general education (VWO) takes 6 years and prepares children for university. In practice, however, almost half of those in VWO go to higher vocational education (HBO). HAVO provides general education at a lower level, and therefore gives no access to university, but only to higher vocational education. For this type of education, which takes 5 years, many school-leavers continue their education at a lower level than formally intended, namely intermediate vocational education (MBO). MAVO is the lowest level of general education. It takes 4 years and provides entrance to intermediate vocational education. Recently, the Ministry of Education introduced a skills structure ('kwalificatiestructuur') for intermediate vocational education. This structure specifies four different qualification levels within the MBO, and sets down the qualifications that are allowed, together with the skills and knowledge required to obtain the degree. VBO, the vocational track, used to be the lowest vocational education, as it was generally recognised that this level no longer sufficed as an adequate entrance level for the labour market in the Netherlands. Students are therefore encouraged to continue their education in intermediate vocational education or in the apprenticeship system.

At the third level, there is higher vocational education and university education. Both take 4 years, with university education being oriented more towards academic skills, while higher vocational education prepares students directly for a certain occupation. In principle, access to both university and higher vocational education is open to everyone who has a VWO diploma (for both university and higher vocational education), a HAVO degree (only for higher vocational education) or a MBO degree (higher vocational education only). Rationing of places is rare. Only in a few cases capacity constraints or labour market problems may lead to rationing, based on a weighted lottery, in which the weight depends on the points obtained in VWO, HAVO or MBO. Only for medicine does this *numerus clausus* appear to be permanent. Both at university and higher vocational education, there is only one level of qualification. The only university level qualification is called 'doctorandus', which is equivalent to a Masters degree. The qualification at HVE level is called a HBO diploma. After graduating from university, students may continue their academic development by writing a Ph.D. thesis. They are however, in that case, not considered students, but employees. These specific jobs are indicated by the term AIO. For that reason, the Ph.D. degree is not separately classified in the educational classification.